Signed for his good

Gilbert Davis

by Donald Cowie

Montreux 1972.

Gilbert Davis
well known Art Collector

SWITZERLAND
The Land and the People

Mr. Cowie was the founder of the
International Antiques Yearbook and the author of
Antiques: How to Identify and Collect Them.

SWITZERLAND
The Land and the People

Donald Cowie

SOUTH BRUNSWICK AND NEW YORK:
A. S. BARNES AND COMPANY
LONDON: THOMAS YOSELOFF LTD

A. S. Barnes and Co., Inc.
Cranbury, New Jersey 08512

Thomas Yoseloff Ltd
108 New Bond Street
London W1Y OQX, England

ISBN 0-498-07738-1
Printed in the United States of America

for my son
Peter Duff Cowie
who suggested it

CONTENTS

ACKNOWLEDGMENT

The author and publisher are grateful to the Swiss National Tourist Office for the illustrations that appear in this book.

SWITZERLAND
The Land and the People

1

MENTAL

THE SWISS TRAIN ARRIVED AT THE DEPOT EXACTLY ON TIME. EVERY-
one checked that with reliable Swiss watches. Like the woman travel
editor of an English Sunday paper who wrote: "Switzerland is an
irritating place. The trains are always on time." Also she wrote something about cleanliness and efficiency and how it spoiled the scenery
for those who travelled in search of "romance." Evidently "romance"
for her meant peeling paint, ruined cities and starving cats.

In the clean train quite a few complete strangers were soon talking
to each other. They talked because they were, in spite of themselves,
quite excited. To be in a clean Swiss train on a sunny morning with
a blue lake on one side and a white mountain on the other is to experience a kind of euphoria.

A person from Pittsburgh, Pennsylvania, said: "I guess these Swiss
have about the most perfect country. It's a manageable size. It's beautiful, civilized, and they don't have politics."

"We *do* have politics," said a quiet man opposite, "but you don't
hear so much about them. Maybe we prefer not to wash our dirty
linens in public."

"Like some of us do," said the Pittsburgh man. "For example, we've
just had a presidential election. For the last two years it's terrible.
Whereas your president, sir, I believe he's elected only for a year,
everyone in the government taking a turn like a rotary club. So far
no one's told me the name of the man who's your president this year.
Does anyone know?"

Cathedral and old town of Basle on the river Rhine.

The train was silent save for the whisper of the wheels over the rail divisions, and for our scratching of heads.

No one knew the name of the current Swiss president except the quiet man in the corner. He wore a dark suit with a light tie, and his face was sallow as if he worked too hard at nights or was suffering from some wasting disease. But he had a kind mouth and wary eyes.

He gave us a name. German.

"Gee!" exclaimed the Pittsburgh man. "How do *you* know?"

"Well," said the quiet Swiss, "I should know, because it's me."

That is a true story, and its significance is the stepping-off place for a book which is being written partly as a poet writes, to share pleasure, but also to pluck from knowledge and experience of Switzerland those facts and ideas that have made that country important.

We need such facts and ideas as never before. If we have continual trouble amid plenty it is because we are running our world wrong and just don't have the answer to our problems. We know we have come to a decisive turn in history, and if we continue to go ahead as now then we shall probably destroy our civilization.

By aerial ropeway above the starry Alps.

This book is being written because maybe little Switzerland can teach us something.

It is one of the smallest countries of the world. Its area of only 15,944 square miles is well under half that of Pennsylvania itself, and Pennsylvania is by no means a large American state. Switzerland's population of some five million is less than that of many a city elsewhere. Then, too, a great part of its land is uninhabitable mountainside, and the tiny population is itself divided rigidly into three self-contained language and ethnic compartments (five, if the English and Romansh speaking communities are included).

Thus it has all the disadvantages that make ultimately for advantages in a tough cosmos.

Little ancient Greece was the same, and the original city of Rome, and maybe modern Scotland could be the same if she had the courage to break away from England. It is necessary to have mountains and a tricky climate and lack of natural resources and a small population brought up the hard way.

Imagine a competition to decide what was the best country in the world. The judges would have to give points for certain attributes, such as standards of living, financial reserves, achievements in the arts, science and industry, also relative success in avoiding maladies of the body and mind ranging from malnutrition to sex troubles, wars and strikes. Beauty, cleanliness and efficiency of cities, towns and villages would be taken into account. Taxation, particularly of income and inheritances. Amount per head of population contributed to world charities. Quality of clothes, bathroom fittings, building materials. Longevity and infantile mortality. Hospitality. Courtesy.

In such a test Switzerland would probably come out at the top. She has those mountains that make her one of the most beautiful countries, and that also force her to work and play hard. The scenery is so bright on the eyes that it provides raw material for a lucrative tourist industry. Tourism as such was invented by the Swiss, including most of the comforts and tricks of the modern hotel. There is no other country in the world where it is equally possible to stop and drink a cup of coffee or spend the night cheaply anywhere without fear of dirt or disappointment. The standard frays a little at the edges with increasing shortage of good, trained staff, but remains far ahead of other countries. The air *smells* cleaner when the traveller enters Switzerland by road from neighboring countries, or by air from America or England; and the signs on the roads are newly washed, and there is solidity everywhere, and price systems for everything that make even native swindlers hesitate before they bite.

It is a very old country, going back to prehistoric times. Traces have been found of lake dwellings, built in the water on piles, also of cave habitations in the high mountains, that were used by the original Swiss thousands of years before Nero got married in woman's clothes.

Yet today Switzerland is one of the most modern countries of the

A typical early Swiss print of the "vedute" type as engraved by T. Hurlimann after G. Lory. No other country has produced such beautiful prints, but this one also shows the unique charm of the landscape (specifically the Lake of Lowerz, near the heart of the country, Schwyz).

world, if that means new buildings, the latest gadgets, and up-to-date standards of lettering and decoration. Coming from New York, London or Paris to a quiet small Swiss town is like looking at a ten-year-old magazine and then an up-to-date copy of the same journal. Often the buildings might be old and quaint in general outline, but in detail they are frequently as mint new as the crusty loaves in the bakeries. This is because the Swiss know it pays to keep property in good repair.

Sometimes it can be inconvenient to live with this. There can be a lot of dust and noise from continual rebuilding, and often it can be distressing to see a loved landmark disappear. But progress must be paid for, and means a minimum in Switzerland of ruins, disease-infected old walls and furniture, the leprous beauty of peeling paint, and of traffic jams. There is no reason why the poorest should live in squalor; and road arrangements are constantly changed and modernized so that often long journeys can be undertaken through semi-urban areas without more than a few brief stops.

Most of these statements will be elaborated later in this book. The

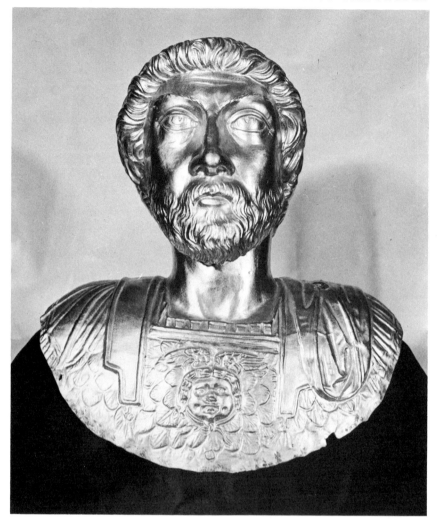

Gold bust of the Roman Emperor Marcus Aurelius, excavated at Avenches.

purpose of the present chapter is to give an astronaut's view in order to establish a thesis for development.

Thus a few sentences will suffice immediate to demonstrate how Switzerland also heads the league politically. All countries have what the political scientists call constitutions. The Swiss have worked out one that really operates efficiently and keeps bad men at bay. It will be analyzed in due course. But meanwhile it must be pointed out that this constitution has helped the Swiss not only to keep out of damaging wars for a long, long time, but also to avoid such social evils as strikes, devaluation of the currency, and conflicts between classes.

World civilization today faces disaster because the major powers and quite a few of the minor ones have wasted their substance and spirit in unsuccessful wars. If those wars had succeeded it might have been different, but so much has been destroyed in the modern wars that once-proud and mighty nations have been brought down into the rubble, and even the giants such as America and Russia have lost more than they can afford and show it by their distress.

Once upon a time, as will be shown later, Switzerland was one of the most feared countries in Europe; and she won nearly every war that she fought. To this day the Swiss are individually a pugnacious people. They drive fiercely on the roads. They spend their weekends at violent sports; outstanding among them is marksmanship, which makes the mountains often resound like the sound track of a Western film. When Charlie Chaplin wisely brought his millions to Switzerland he bought a lovely property, resembling an English country house, at Corsier above Vevey on shining Lake Léman, and at once found his meditations disturbed by the cracking of rifles on a shooting range nearby.

In spite of this, or maybe because of it, the Swiss have successfully kept out of all the wars that have operated like a cancer to destroy the modern world. They have suffered a lot during those wars, both from lack of food, raw materials and trade, and from pangs of conscience and the awareness of isolation. But, unlike the other countries, they have not wasted their innermost spirit in those wars. They have kept alive many of their ideals. Their clever children do not want to sit down with doped cigarettes in their mouths and daisy-chains around their necks and seek the ineffable, Oriental peace of no-thought and non-commitment.

A young Swiss couple were drinking Neuchâtel wine in a Zurich café. That wine is thin and cold, the distillation of a winter's morning. The café overlooked the river waters of the Limmat. Swans indited their question marks there.

The question to the young couple was: "Do you manage to save any money?"

The girl answered eagerly: "But of course." And the boy with his square jaw and soldier eyes said portentously: "Each month we contrive to put something in reserve. It is necessary."

The same question almost anywhere in America would have elicited the answer: "You're kidding! Of course we have to save, to pay for last year's vacation." And almost anywhere in Britain save parts of

Scotland it would have evoked: "Good heavens, no! We haven't a chance." Followed by an amused expression which meant: "What a damned cheek you have! As if we would tell you anyway."

Values are all.

Americans do save money, if chiefly in reverse the days. They must, or the national inventory would not grow as it does each year. But the national outlook, wisely or not, is that if you can have it now and pay later then maybe you will come out ahead on the deal, especially if there is another war or round of price increases.

Britons also mount up a stockpile. The figures of national savings show it. But, as indicated above, they dislike talking about their financial affairs, the inheritance of an aristocratic past. Their secret ideal is

One of Switzerland's loveliest regions, near Appenzell.

the man who never touches money but leaves his steward to dispense it to the mob. They want to pretend they have no bother about money at all. You don't talk about it, anymore than you do about God or your piles. Unavoidable evils.

Values might be defined as the speedometer readings of human existence. Life is led according to those readings. And if you despise money, or seek to outwit it by credit schemes, then eventually you will not have so much as the man who likes it, is not ashamed of it, and carefully looks after it.

So we have come to another of the Swiss faults. They have a yen about their franc. They love to make a profit and put part of it aside for tomorrow and the children. And so today they probably have as much real money per head of population as any people in the world— and probably more. They certainly retain enormous reserves in gold and foreign exchange, and their currency is covered many times by those reserves. When the dollar or the pound or the French franc or the German mark falls on the exchanges because the Americans, the British, the French or the Germans are misbehaving themselves, the Swiss franc always goes to the top of the table. It has long been the hardest currency there ever has been.

It may not remain so. That depends entirely on whether the Swiss continue to run their country as described in this book.

And if the rest of the world run their countries the same way as the Swiss there might be little fear for the future.

A strange 19th-century book was written called *The Swiss Family Robinson.* It was as different from Defoe's *Robinson Crusoe,* on which it was based, as an airline timetable is from the thoughts of St. Augustine. Whereas Defoe's castaway was a worried man with metaphysics always at the back of his mind, the Swiss family just got on with making the island habitable. To this end they improvised madly with makeshift tools.

And that is still essentially the attitude of many Swiss, not all but most, to the problems of human existence. One new gadget is worth a whole library of philosophical speculation. Pragmatism.

It comes again from the mountains, where, to keep alive, it is necessary to have good clothing and boots and plenty of devices for scaling precipices, making paths and otherwise defeating the ravening wild animal that is nature in the raw. In the old days they had to make their water pipes up there out of hollowed logs. They had to devise a social organization that quickly brought aid to anyone caught in a storm. They did not help each other because they wanted to but because they had to. Ingenuity was constantly necessary to counter the gigantic horrors of the Alps.

To this day when they want to get cattle down from the high mountain pastures quickly in the face of a storm they will still hang them to a wire and slide them down.

Talking of wire brings back the memory of that storm above Grindelwald. One minute it had been a bright world of green cow pastures and toy chalets and picture postcard mountains with cute sugarloaf tops. Five minutes later there was only the driving rain and snow. The shooting party was riding down a rough track in a jeep-like vehicle when something broke. The vehicle came to a halt, bogged-down, and the man who knew about engines, an Englishman, said it would be necessary to fetch a spare part from a garage, in the town, many miles and a whole blizzard away.

A Swiss in the party went up in the trees and found a wire fence. He twisted off a piece of wire, came down, and made a substitute part out of the piece. The engine started and took the party home, where the Swiss at once made inquiries so that he could send the farmer some compensation for his broken fence. A member of the party exclaimed: "Your standards of honesty are certainly higher than ours!"

The Swiss replied: "I don't think it is honesty. But we have a law about these things. A good law. After all, it might have been my fence up there that had the wire cut."

Perhaps the ethnic composition of Switzerland has something to do with it. The original inhabitants of the country were very tough troglodytes who were eventually submerged by long-headed Celts of the kind who also started France and Britain. Those Celts were given commonsense by fair, round-headed German people, and given a good legal civilization and some of the humane arts and crafts by the Romans. Today the mixture is about 72 percent German, 20 percent French, 6 percent Italian, and 2 percent other languages. Accordingly about 56 percent state their religion as Protestant, 42 percent Catholic, and 2 percent other religions. Perhaps this mixture is just about right for balance.

Germany, France and Italy are all countries of extremes, their undoing. Put them together with a hard core of Celtic mountaineers at the helm and you get Switzerland before the British, the Jews and the Americans came.

The British invented winter sports for Switzerland and brought their social civilization to the mountain villages and certain resort towns such as Montreux and Lausanne. Numerous Jewish refugees from Russian and German pogroms, accepted by a country that has always placed hospitality high among its values, brought financial expertise and artistic culture. Latterly the Americans have greatly assisted the modern industrialization of Switzerland, and, from Geneva especially, have donated—their word—certain freedoms of personal self-expression as well as valuable notions of organizational efficiency.

Thus Switzerland is still a young and growing country. To cope with hand-labor demands it has imported a large number of Italian and Spanish workers from the poorer parts of Italy and Spain. This immigration has so proliferated that already the Swiss, with characteristic efficiency and lack of sentimentality, have started to back-peddle and many of the least desirable among the workers have been sent home lest their fecundity change the whole ethnic picture of the country. Also to avoid the race-riots and pogroms that afflict softer lands who invite strangers in warmly and then hate them when there are too many strange faces about.

The Swiss have reacted with similar, characteristic wisdom to property-buying by foreigners in modern times. The Germans in particular started to buy so much land and build so many rich villas in certain parts of the Tessin and around Lake Lucerne that prices of property soared unnaturally and there were jokes about "little Germanies" everywhere. So more laws were passed and the invasion was defeated just in the nick of time. The effect of the typical Swiss laws was that foreigners could no longer buy property in Switzerland in their own names. They had to pay for the formation of a Swiss company with a majority of Swiss on the board and that company could own the property.

There are many reasons why Switzerland does not suffer much from the industrial unrest that is ruining the economies of other western lands, and those will be discussed later. But one reason today is that if the large number of imported workers in Switzerland want to strike or otherwise make a nuisance of themselves they are liable to lose their precious working permits and be sent home quickly and without appeal.

And the laws about foreigners and property in Switzerland ensure that in an emergency such real estate would still at least nominally be Swiss-owned.

It all sounds very efficient and off-putting.

In a modern novel dealing with fashionable drug-takers in California a character suggests a trip to Switzerland, and another character looks up dreamily from hashish to say: "Oh, no, nothing ever happens there."

It might have been thought that would have been a recommendation to youngsters intent on avoiding responsibility and the worries of their parents' lives.

But of course it was not true. Live in the smallest village of Switzerland and there will be sufficient happenings each week to provide a great novelist with all the plots he needs. Live in a large tourist town such as Lucerne or Lausanne and sometimes be quite horrified by the goings-on there, especially among the retired, international people.

Just because Switzerland does not have wars or strikes and has a small population superficially governed by strict laws it has by no means escaped from the dramas that are daily staged by human nature. It does seem that no matter how hard you work or legislate you cannot conquer the old Adam. A young girl in Switzerland who wanted to be a writer departed from the country because it was "so dull," and settled in South Kensington, London. There she occupied a solitary bed-sitting room and came back eventually with the complaint that if little had been happening in her Swiss home town then London by comparison had been completely uneventful. During six months of bed-sitting room life she had found only a few people who would talk to her and the newspapers and radio had been devoted mainly to politics. Even the queers had lacked the color she associated with the breed in Zurich and Geneva.

Then she picked up a local Swiss newspaper and pointed to the innumerable crisp paragraphs about sex crimes and accidents and frauds and diamond weddings and strange happenings in the quiet streets by night.

If she stays at home now and uses that material she will probably become a good and readable novelist.

The same applies to the frequent criticism of Switzerland that, although it might be clean and good for mountains and cuckoo-clocks, it has had no great men or great moments. It has, say the jealous sneerers, paid for its material success and efficiency by lacking a Shakespeare and a Hitler and knowing only the smug summits of mediocrity.

That is not true. Per head of population Switzerland has produced as many great people as any country, possibly more. Some of them will be mentioned in due course. Its great moments range from battles in which it completely destroyed invaders so that they never came again to the recent building of an autoroute along a slender viaduct on stilts right round a mountain over a lake. And a few other events, as shall be seen.

2

PHYSICAL

SWITZERLAND IS THE BACKBONE OF EUROPE, AND WHEN IT BEGINS to suffer from slipped discs the whole continent will need pain-killing drugs.

The so-called Swiss Alps comprise some 115 peaks, under which nestle about 50 fine lakes. The climate ranges from perpetual snow on the top to sub-tropical at the lowest place (Ascona). Roughly the Alps tend to run in parallel lines east-west. Between the ranges are fertile valleys. A final northwestern wall is provided by the Jura mountains; and the high hills and even mountains to the south of Lake Constance partly fill the otherwise dangerous gap there. The Germans have throughout history poured in that way, the ancient Alemanni, the Habsburgs, and more latterly the tourists and depositors of gold.

Arrival in Switzerland by any route is nice but the most spectacular entries are by road, best of all across the interminable farmlands of France and then the worn-out, woody mountains of the Vosges. Eventually there is a pass, the Col de Bussang, that to the Alpine passes is like an old cheese biscuit before a *cordon bleu* meal. Once over the top a traveller experiences the first hairpins, then swift flatness to Basle.

The shabby French customs waves the motorist through, after which he meets the Swiss—smartly uniformed and physically what every mother wants her son to be, while the city unfolding is to the absolute newcomer like a fairy dream after the mess which is so much of France.

Basle does not necessarily remain a fairy dream. Its architectural

At the top of the Simplon Pass—the Hospice, the cars and the cows, where in winter there is only icy desolation.

outlines may already resemble illustrations from a child's Germanic story book, rounded towers narrowing up to points, protruding and roofed balconies for Rapunzel's hair, gateways over which the heads of talking horses could conceivably hang. The city will never cease to be cleaner and newer and fresher than all others which bestraddle the Rhine in spite of its great age and medieval frame. But with closer acquaintance Basel will soon exchange magic for tough contemporary expertise in all kinds of industry but especially banking and the fabrication of chemical drugs for medicinal purposes. The people, often German and French mixed, are among the shrewdest and hardest-working in the world, so must not be expected to exude charm or dance through the evenings with Tyrolean abandon.

Therefore the Lucerne signs should be followed.

The road will take some time to shake off the discreet and smoke-less if undeniable factories. But very soon the pastures and the trees and the half-timbered farmhouses are everywhere around.

These pasturelands of Switzerland, whether in the midland valleys or *tals* now being traversed, or inaccessibly high up against the snow, have the quality of a shaven lawn, and so they have been shaven, frequently by hand. The grass cut off will often be heaped neatly on a piece of sackcloth, which, twisted, will be humped on the back and taken down for the wintertime. Then in spring the excessive lushness and the green will be encouraged by odoriferous applications of liquid manure that, through the hard months, has been similarly cherished.

The contrast between grasslands of the New World and those of Switzerland is symbolic. Whereas the prodigal owners of prairies eventually turn their heritage into a dust bowl the Swiss create with their own hands fertility where formerly there was none.

That was yesterday? Not altogether. At the time of writing four-fifths of the Swiss still live outside the five large cities, Zurich, Basel, Geneva, Berne and Lausanne.

It remains a pastoral country predominantly; and this journey to Lake Lucerne is a fitting introduction to the rural beauty of it, matched only by similar scenes in the shires of England.

Each village is a collection of large farmhouses and a hotel distinguished from the others by its golden sign. Half-timbers support immense roofs with overhanging eaves, functionally designed to support the yard-high snow of winter and to stop it from dripping down coat-collars in spring. The roofs and façades of this midlands region are constructed heavily with curving eaves often yellow-painted against the white of the walls and the brown timber of the lateral rows of balconies, which most of the year present the dangle green and scarlet of that geranium which should be the Swiss national flower.

The style is a mixture of the heavy Bernese and the more timbered, less overhanging Zurich peasant architecture, and should not be confused with that of the chalet as such, which was originally developed in the French-minded Vaud. The real chalet is to be found in the Alps above Montreux, roughly the same in design as that used for the cuckoo clock.

Switzerland has churches, cathedrals, castles and country houses of all periods, and some of them are interesting. None of them are equal to the best of other lands. The true architecture of the country is a peasant art and as such is often unequalled elsewhere, from the huge, shallow-roofed farmhouses of Neuchâtel to the tall, white and pink blocks with heavy, slated, overhanging roofs of the Grisons. The style of the Tessin is naturally Italianate, all-colored, almost flat-roofed with the Roman tiles; and in Berne the loveliness comes from great terrace houses with colonnades to the pavements, houses of farmers turned bur-

Why Swiss chalets have wide, overhanging roofs.

The old covered bridge at Lucerne.

ghers often with entrances for the hay and dung still. The colored statues of knights standing in fountains and the great clocks with faces of blue, green or red and hands of gold vie with the geraniums to provide prettiness but also to recall the jackboot past of Burgundian and Austrian overlords.

The niceness of buildings in Switzerland primarily stems from their peasant origin; and here on the road from Basle to Olten with its covered bridge and busy industry, and from Olten to Lucerne via Sursee near the first of the lakes, the Sempachersee, will be observed villages that, particularly, if it is Saturday afternoon, seem to consist principally of those flowered old farmhouses like clean, shaggy dogs, and people of all ages at the side of the road sweeping. If so much as a leaf is left at their porticoes on Sunday morning there will be scope for the neighbors to talk, and that in Switzerland, as occasionally but not so frequently elsewhere these degraded days, is the unforgivable shame.

This revelatory penetration into Switzerland may be halted by Lucerne itself, the first of the great holiday towns, a product not so much of the Swiss as of the English between about 1850 and 1939. It is a very old town with well-kept relics of the past such as the Kapellbrucke (1333) and the Spreuerbrucke (1407), roofed-over timber bridges decorated with 17th-century paintings; and the octagonal, 14th-century water tower. But the atmosphere does not differ notably from that of similar old holiday towns across the world (save that there is no trace at all of the vulgarity that has ruined much of the coastline of the United States, the Mediterranean and the English Channel north and south).

There is no need to worry because no one who arrives in Lucerne looks at architecture or probes deeply into the atmosphere engendered by tourists like him or herself. The eyes mount as upwards on the façade of a Gothic cathedral to heaven and the white tips of the high mountains. Then down again to the blue water of the perfect lake (whereon little steamers ply like mechanical swans).

It is the true Switzerland of the mountains at last; and if the new arrival wisely continues round the lake to spend his night at Brunnen he may have a memorable experience.

It is an attractive little town, the lakeside suburb of Schwyz—and Schwyz is a place of lovely old houses that might be regarded as the heart of Switzerland because the name of the country was originally derived from it.

Until recently Brunnen was at once spoiled and made rich by the St. Gotthard traffic that had to thunder through it. A lucrative toll was taken from travellers. Nowadays a bypass road with spectacular tunnel diverts a lot of trade away from Brunnen—and the town has been transformed into a charming resort of comparative quietness again.

There was no intention to spend the night in Brunnen, especially when an elderly Italian porter stood outside a hotel beckoning. But there was also a middle-aged woman, with the severely-bunned hair and tight face that are often typical of the Swiss hotelkeepers' wives who get that way because it is tidier and they do so much of the work. She smiled also, so the car was stopped and the bait taken.

No doubt the fish proved to be a good catch, but they will always consider themselves to have been privileged by the experience.

The hall and dining room were modern but the bedrooms creaked

Many remarkable road tunnels now pierce the Alps. This is the entrance to the San Bernardino.

with pitchpine and exuded an aroma of clean linen and resin mixed.

There were the inevitable balcony and the evening lake below.

Great shapes across the lake were mountains. They retreated into darkness save at the high tops where they presented the rosy embarrassment of a touch of the sun still.

Dinner was like a military parade. The attractive German waitresses could not have been more efficient, save when they sliced the good steak into thin pieces before placing it on the plate. The Fendant proved itself again one of the best of the Swiss white wines, as good with red meat as with fish or poultry, provided it was remembered that the slightly effervescent quality of it could sometimes quickly mount the alcohol to the head and enlarge a mood from happiness to transports of delight, from unhappiness to deep depression, or, indeed, from mild irritability to strong rage.

On this occasion it was the well-known euphoria of the holidaymaker at his first night's stand who finds everything to be excessively good. It is a law like Newton's and so often it is assisted by shrewd hoteliers who give of their best on the first night. If the guest stays in the hotel for any length of time he is less satisfied the second day and on the third day he begins to grumble. He is back to earth. Not only guests and fish but also hosts and hostesses tend to afflict the nostrils after three days.

Sleep was deep but broken at 7 A.M. by pneumatic drills at work

The Italian Swiss live thus. No wonder they have a sunny temperament.

on some rock face not far away. People from lazier countries find the early-rising proclivity of the Swiss to be a grave fault.

But when the balcony was gropingly reached and the eyes rubbed there could only be thankfulness for such a tocsin on such a morning.

The lake was a blue mirror that perfectly reflected mountains like those in the pictures of primitive painters—high, lowering and with mist-wreathed, menacing shapes. It was a landscape by Hieronymous Bosch but also by Turner (who indeed, had painted it often).

The great peak was the Urirotstock, towering.

Down over there, across the immaculate water, under the shocking pile of dark- and white-tipped stone, was the little *Tellskapelle* on the site where traditionally the Swiss mythological hero sprang ashore from the bailiff Gessler's boat.

More historically certain, the representatives of the three forest cantons, Uri, Schwyz and Unterwalden, did meet nearby on August 1, 1291, and sign a document that is still to be found in the Bundesbriefarchiv of little Schwyz, a document that may be regarded either as in the same class as Magna Carta and the Declaration of Independence, or indeed as the true stuff of which the great and enduring myths are made. All that document really established was the determination of the local people to stand together on certain points of law.

Nevertheless modern Switzerland began thus, out of those fearsome mountains, in this clear, sun-filtered air, above this deep and temporarily still lake.

So at Brunnen the heart of the matter can be seen. But, of course, it is by no means all.

The Swiss Alps owe much of their beauty to their youth. They were created by convulsions of the earth's interior a long time after other ranges such as the Jura, whose limestone peaks have often been worn almost entirely away by the touch of the years.

The Alps are clearcut, high, and pristine new, which consequently gives an essential character to much of Switzerland. The Swiss must always be up-to-date. It is an occupational disease with them. And, because new mountains do not yield old mineral deposits, the Swiss must be ingenious, hardworking, and importers of raw materials. Then they must become skilled at publicity and hotel keeping, so as to make money from those strangers who come to stare at or risk their lives on those massive lumps of uselessness.

And as mountaineers they must be independent. It is their birthright, simply derived from the days when they could sit on peaks and roll down stones on foolish invaders.

Even today a people who wanted to remain aloof from the follies of a nuclear age could be 50 percent certain of survival if they literally remained aloft in the high Alpine valleys.

This is because of the peculiar mountain climate, another strong moulding influence on the character of Switzerland. At any time lower wind currents are diverted into the valleys and in calm winter weather the cold air sinks under its very weight to make the lower regions comparatively unhealthy and the upper regions crystal clear. Should a nuclear miasma spread across Europe most of the poison will accumulate among and kill the plainsmen. So the future of humanity in the high Alps may be assured; and meanwhile the country can continue to make its fortune from the innumerable tourists who take the second or third holiday of their increasingly opulent years at a snow resort of the uplands, in late December, January, February or March.

Brunnen was the beginning, and there were even better Brunnens in German Switzerland, little resorts around the Vierwaldstattersee (short for Lake Lucerne, meaning the lake of the four forest cantons) such as Weggis of the orchards and modern German villas, looking across at the strange Burgenstock (a mountain promontory whose hotels with their smart shops are nicely in steps and stairs of financial class) and at Lucerne's guardian peak Pilatus. Then Vitznau and Gersau are almost sub-tropical resorts in miniature, while Küssnacht, lacking some of the prettier attractions of the others, has vied with them successfully thanks to the maintenance of two shrines, another William Tell chapel on the alleged spot where the hero actually shot Gessler, and a similar more modern edifice with suitable car-parking facilities to mark the spot where a beautiful Belgian queen was killed in a horrible motor accident.

Such resorts are not, however, so important and representative of the true Switzerland as those of the high mountains that look down disdainfully upon and pour their drainage into the lakes. These are found in two main regions with subdivisions, first the part of eastern Switzerland known as the Grisons, and second the central and southwestern area comprising the Bernese Oberland and the Valais.

The road from the Schwyz heartland ran back northeast via Zug to Zurich. Zug has fiscal rather than scenic significance, as will be explained in a later chapter, although its lake is actually fresher and cleaner than many of the others.

Zurich is a beautiful city, especially on a fine day when the lake is white-peppered with sailing boats. Every ancient building has been restored, often over-restored. The banks are impressive and the hotels can be good. It has nearly half a million of population at the time of writing. One in ten of all Swiss live there. The capital, Berne, has less than half as many inhabitants. Yet somehow there is no desire to linger in Zurich as in Berne. It is felt instinctively that the essential Switzerland is no more here than the essential America is in New York. With complete temporal success something very important is inevitably lost. The road is best followed out towards the Grisons via the Walensee and Chur signs.

The Walensee is one of the most spectacular lakes in Switzerland. From the Chur road it is an immensely deep pit with water of an extraordinary green color and the north side is a precipitous cliff that rises a sheer 3300 feet from the water to the lambent sky.

Then Chur (or Coire in French) is a medieval town on pronounced Roman foundations that is clean and efficient in the Swiss way, just the right size for decent communal living, and possessed of an extraordinary climate amid these mountains that permit fruit and the vine to flourish and sweet chestnuts and fig-trees to soften the scene.

The strange car was parked between brand-new blue lines and a white-coated pharmacist instantly darted out of his shop to present the owners with a parking disc for the free parking that was then wisely common all over Switzerland. It was a characteristic gesture, even if the disc forever afterwards advertised the trader's wares.

From Chur exploratory forays were made to Liechtenstein's semi-independent principality on the Austrian frontier, where the castle of Vaduz contains its millionaire collection of pictures and looks down benignantly, as well as it might, on the town which is chiefly a place where they sell souvenir gifts and stamps. And, more rewardingly, the cantons of nearby Appenzell and St. Gall comprised a largely unspoilt region of the kind of small towns and villages that are pictured in Germanic tales for children. St. Gall itself is an industrial city, once opulent as an exporter of machine-made embroidery based on a former linen trade.

But industry has been unable to obscure the beauty of old buildings here, starting with the former Benedictine abbey that was actually founded by an Irishman (St. Gall or Caillech). The Abbey Church is perfect 18th-century baroque, and, for those who like the apotheosis of the ornate, is a welcome holiday from Munich. Even more interesting is the library of some 40,000 volumes and 1800 manuscripts, one of the few remaining in the world that teaches us how learning was kept alive in the dark ages and how the Renaissance was in due course made possible.

Oriel windows peep from old houses throughout St. Gall. The

narrow valley in which the city is situated pokes its finger up into the Forealps, a region rent by valleys, most of which have villages that have remained relatively unchanged in outward form for hundreds of years.

Then the search for the true Switzerland continued south up the St. Moritz road. Parpan was a few houses and an excellent hotel whose bedroom windows provided frames for pictures of snowcapped mountains. During an evening walk it was noticed that thin tendrils of a leathery substance were hanging under the wooden eaves of barns. Closer up they were not so thin. They were like ruddy palings of weatherbeaten timber, the dried meat of the Grisons that yields one of the most favored of Swiss delicacies, although the poor peasants who once had to live on it would probably prefer something out of a foreign can now.

Lenzerheide farther up the road does big business as a snow resort. The searchers after Switzerland continued onwards and eventually turned left and mounted to Davos.

Here is something that once was the essential Switzerland for many people but is so no longer, thanks perhaps to modern drugs, or thanks just to those periodic strange migrations that characterize the history of diseases as well as those of men. Davos is very high (5118–5358 feet), and has a sheltered, almost perfect mountain climate thanks to the wooded slopes that protect it from cold northerly and easterly winds. In 1867 Alexander Spengler opened the first sanatorium there for the treatment of tuberculosis or pulmonary consumption. *The Magic Mountain* of Thomas Mann is not only one of the few great novels of the 20th century; it is also a perfect picture of the exquisite unhappiness that was formerly Davos (and Leysin in the Alpes Vaudoises).

A truly sensitive soul cannot feel at ease in Davos today although pulmonary consumption has long since ceased to make the last years of life a horror for the many and a source of considerable profit for the few. He or she must still see the emaciated figures under blankets on the balconies there, hear the coughs, attend at the weekly examinations: and the graveyard of the English church at Davos-Platz should not be visited.

Far better to note how the wise Swiss have built a plenitude of aerial ropeways so that the modern visitors can rise high above it all on skis. It is possible easily to attain the summit of the Weissfluh, 9344 feet, by funicular and a walk, and of course there is a modern restaurant there waiting, with the kind of view that the guide books can only describe as superb. Thence the skiers will gracefully twist and

The daring railway past a typical village of the Grisons.

turn down infinite pistes to St. Wolfgang, Klosters, Kublis and Fideris, skiers who have even been seen with the cigarettes in their mouths that, at home, may introduce them to the even worse scourge of the lungs that has neatly replaced consumption.

Arosa on another road from Chur is even higher than Davos and has become increasingly fashionable, which means that there is more gloss on the paintwork and it can charge good prices. The climate is outstanding among the ski resorts, and there are few better slopes and average snow conditions.

But St. Moritz is all. The main road from Chur eventually reaches the easy Julier Pass, or another road can be taken from Davos. And St. Moritz is not just a winter sports resort. It is one of those unique creations of man whose name is a household word the world over and whose larger hotelkeepers can charge more or less what they like for undeniably splendid accommodation. And it all started, as did most of these historic resorts, with a daring English climber who knocked at a farmhouse door and asked if they had a room.

Prior to that the peasants of these impoverished mountain regions lived lives that were indeed nasty, brutish and short. Lower down the climate and conditions were just sufficiently strenuous to bring out the best human qualities in them but not so hard as to demoralize them completely. Right up near the top the struggle for existence was so hard that, like the lichens and the stunted trees, they just existed, but little more. They were not helped by the often necessity of that inbreeding which produces cretinism; while deficiencies of diet produced afflictions like goitre.

The English knock at the door changed all that as if a magician had touched the hovels of the high Alps with a wand.

Probably the stupid peasant asked the initial Englishman so little for his night's lodging that the guest, ashamed of his own wealth amid so much poverty, threw down more coins than was necessary.

The Englishman went home and told his young friends at the Universities about the unspoilt climbers' paradise he had found, so ridiculously primitive and cheap. They listened and some of them went to the same place. Frau Schwyzer in the hovel received them with a happy smirk and her nubile daughter with a titter.

The peasant Schwyzer himself scratched his head and probably the term "mad English" was coined when he foregathered with other farmers in the market town inn and described how his wife had made more money in a week by letting a room to these foreigners than he had made from his smallholding in a year.

The other Bruegel characters listened and the true Swiss hotel industry was founded.

Of course it was not so simple as that. Owing to her geographical position at crossroads of Europe, and to the barrier of the Alps between Italy and the rest of the Continent, Switzerland had always accommodated travellers in coaching inns. The Church had made a specialty of hostels in the high passes, even developing a Swiss breed of dog, the noble St. Bernard for the purpose of sniffing out lost wayfarers from the snow, and, later to provide valuable advertisement for a well-known mark of brandy.

Then there had been the discovery in the first half of the 19th century that if water from springs was warm or had a particularly repulsive appearance or flavor it could be accused of curative qualities in the case of maladies such as rheumatism which had a strong psychosomatic background. Such waters were often found in remote areas of Switzerland, and a positive fashion for curative baths and nice long holidays could be extended there from the more famous "watering places" of Europe, nearly all of them distinguished by the significant prefix "Bad."

St. Moritz, the high queen of Swiss mountain resorts, started as all these things. It is very high, 6079 feet. Probably the ancient Romans used it as a stage. Certainly the iron and carbonic acid-flavored water on the place had a curative reputation as far back as the Bronze Age. A conventional spa was established with the opening of the Kurhaus in 1856.

But it was the English climber and sportsman who convinced the peasants of this region, the Engadine, that it was really worthwhile to encourage the wife to take in lodgers, and, in due course, to create hotels out of hovels and impudently to construct ski-lifts and bobsleigh runs right up the faces of the most fearsome mountains. A little lake could be made into a skating rink or a course for curling. It was

Curling on a perfect, icy surface in an atmosphere of sun and frost.

easier for consumptives to breathe up here so the sanatoria could be founded.

Note, however, that high mountains are to be found in other countries whereas only the Swiss made efficient most of them at first. They were the pioneers of the winter holiday; and still their accommodation and facilities are superior to those of other lands. It is only necessary to travel across from Chamonix in the French Alps to Verbier on the Swiss side to see the difference even today. It is a difference compounded of better crockery and brighter paint-work and more reliable machinery on the slopes, also of a welcome that at least on the face of it seems more sincere. Perhaps the Swiss resorts have sometimes become the more expensive, but not in actual value received for money, and lately currency inflation in the inferior lands have actually tended to give Swiss prices the edge.

Anyway, the brutish farmers accommodated more and more of the English climbers and holidaymakers and in St. Moritz transformed part of a high glacial plateau under snowcapped mountains into a little city of smart hotels and shops. Today it has in miniature all the up-to-date facilities of a Monte Carlo or London's West End. The monetary turnover in the season must be stupendous. St. Moritz, unlike some others, has never ceased to remain in the forefront of fashion. Great hotels such as the Carlton, Kulm, Palace and Suvretta display the maximum of stars, both professionally and socially. Some millionaires keep permanent suites in these caravanserais. Others have long since built luxurious chalets with swimming pools on the mountain sides at a cost of millions of francs a time (much of it spent on grandiose earth-moving operations and the construction of wholly unnatural concrete buttresses).

It is especially significant that the hotels here, as in Zermatt, Gstaad, Grindelwald and the countless other snow resorts, are often still run by descendants of the original families of peasants who put up the first bed and breakfast signs; and the accent is on that word *families*. Nearly always the owner or manager works side by side with his wife. Frequently the wife is the harder and more important of the two workers. Until recently she had no vote; and ostensibly all the decisions in Switzerland are still taken by the men in solemn conclave over carafes of white wine at café tables; but she is very, very important, and a worker without equal in the world. She has carefully sustained in particular certain charming and highly effective customs of hotel-keeping that date right back to those original lodgings given to long-limbed, Oxford-accented and tweedy climbers.

The kind of shot that makes film directors famous.

When Leslie Stephen, the Victorian apostle of a healthy mind in a healthy body (and, incredibly, the father of Virginia Woolf), was among those like Edward Whymper the writer-climber and Sir Henry Lunn (the inventor of tourist agencies who visited Switzerland annually for "scrambling" amid the Alps), he would receive a birthday postcard from the Swiss woman who "put him up." Today a great Swiss hotel will often keep birthday records from passports and surprise clients with similar if less ingenuous greetings. And it is not uncommon still for the hotelkeeper's wife to hand a guest a little parcel on parting that, undone in the plane or car later, will reveal a small embroidered handkerchief or a key-ring with the Swiss flag. Such a simple act, of warm-heartedness and commerce mixed, has even been known to evoke a tear.

The development of these resorts has meanwhile branched out like a candelabrum in several distinct directions. The archetype Moritz caters for all, from Greek shipowners who will sometimes hire an entire five-star hotel, to hard-up tourists who arrive in small cars that have perilously pulled self-contained caravans over the passes. The surrounding mountains are climbed by some with or unwisely without the help of a trained corps of Swiss guides. A great number of young people arrive by train at Christmas and their preoccupation is wholly with ski-ing and with *après-ski* sessions of wine, women and song. The Cresta Run has its international races for skeleton toboggans, and there is a mile-long bob run down to Cresta. A lot of bejewelled old people arrive just to hobble around in ski-boots made of pony skin and ski-pants that would be kinder if they were less revealing, and to sit at tables on sun-drenched terraces and watch what they can, alas, no longer achieve themselves. It is voyeurism on the grand scale and it is magnificent.

3

TOUR I

THERE ARE WRITERS WHO ODDLY REQUIRE DICTIONARIES TO HELP
them with words. One of these is Roget's *Thesaurus,* an extraordinarily
complex and methodical word list of synonyms, antonyms and terms
in association with each other. Needless to say the original Roget was
a Swiss; and his precise mentality is still that of his countrymen, who
have not yet used computers to work out the best places for individual
holidays but will do so yet.

So while a St. Moritz is more or less for everyone but especially for
lovers of the glossier magazines, there are resorts amid the snow that
suit the specific requirements of every kind of visitor.

Quiet people have always liked Pontresina in this larch-covered,
flowery Engadine of the ancient Romansh place-names. Solitary climbers
similarly mount to Piz this and Piz that from such bases as Celerina
and Samedan, while complete unspoilt holidays can still be spent by
the most exacting down the Lower Engadine where strange signs
point the way to such as Scuol, Tarasp, Vulpera and, indeed, Sent,
Tschlin and Ftan.

Until the helicopter is in general use there can be no better way of
exploring Switzerland than by car. So the Maloja road should be taken
from St. Moritz. The Romans used it as the easiest way from Italy
north. It is usually open throughout the winter. Julius Caesar crossed
it often on horseback, changing his small hacks frequently at staging
stations, sometimes quite perilously guiding his beast over what was
little more than a bridle path.

A magnificent barn below a castle in northwest Switzerland.

From St. Moritz the fine modern highway proceeds through the Upper Engadine as down a clever ladder of the land to present another of the quick and cinematic cuts from scene to scene that are indeed the speciality of Switzerland.

There is at first splendid and characteristic Alpine scenery, the clear-cut peaks of almost steel-blue jagged rock with their white of snow which bacon-streaks erratically down the gullies; the evergreen woods that creep up the bases of the mountains like a patterned map in which the true *Alps* or pastured patches, are the emerald seas; ever here and there the impudent roofs of farmhouses, barns and chalets for hire; and in the continual verdure of valleys the white rushing water of streams, the sapphire blue of lakes, and the clustered teeth of hamlets, villages, towns.

Over all the almost royal-blue sky usually hangs out its washing of flotsam cloud, unless indeed the typical modern traveller requires a beating and makes the journey at those occasional times when the high Alps are in torment. Such a time can often be found in October, when a Swiss wedding was attended in a little chapel by a lake. It rained continuously. The chapel was stone-bare save for faded and archaic paintings on the ceiling. The service was austere and the young couple were enjoined to expect only tribulations ahead. Nothing could

A little Swiss working town, nestling among the rocks.

have been more modern than the recorded folk music that was emitted by an amplifier.

Afterwards a reception was held in a remote mountain hotel, near the ski slopes where the young couple had met. The tables and the food were as opulent as in a top-ranking restaurant of Paris or New York. The company consisted of what elsewhere would erroneously be called working men and their women. Their manners and clothing were in perfect taste save when frogs' legs were served, and the bones were larger than usual, and a middle-aged male guest with wild fair hair and a long local ancestry was seen to crunch and swallow all his bones at a gulp. They were as big and hard as the bones of chickens' legs. Afterwards this man danced vigorously with his drab, old-fashioned little wife, and, after that, still more vigorously with a large dog. Someone said that the dog scented the bones, and the night's laughter began.

It continued through rich courses of food and lavish potations of wine and continual music from accordions and stamping of feet and high yodelling above the groundswell of popular and traditional song. The jolly landlord of the hotel gave excrutiatingly funny female impersonations. The dance thundered. It was suddenly two o'clock in the morning.

And guests began to depart.

But they came back white-faced. It was still raining heavily and the road was barred.

The bridegroom was a young policeman. He got into mountain gear and went out with his companions and came back eventually to say that the company must resign itself to spending the rest of the night at the hotel because there had been several landslides on all the roads leading to their lowland homes.

The merriment went down like a candle and finally guttered away into dim morning moods that revealed the diverse origins of the company. The true Swiss continued the dance and the music or purposefully played cards. Some became in various ways ill.

Just before dawn the young men came back with the news that the major landslide on one of the roads had been cleared; and several cars lined up and, in careful procession, set off down.

The truly perilous journey was undertaken only because one Swiss farmer wanted to get back to his cows for milking and a young Swiss soldier had to get back to his unit (after his first night with his young wife for two months), and because the British in the party had that typically British stupidity where real risks were concerned.

Down the long narrow road with precipices on the left side and water and rocks rushing down on the high right the procession of cars thrust several times through mud-slimed rivers that swept across and they bumped into moving boulders and crunched on rushes of stones that were water-impelled across the edges down to deep ravines below. Should an engine have stopped where the flood was axle-high a small car would soon have been rolled over and the others behind, forced to halt, would have similarly been destroyed. It was solely chance that the procession did in fact get through and arrive home at 7 o'clock of a Sunday morning—for instant sleep that was disturbed at 8 by two little girls knocking at the door on behalf of one of the numerous charities that the Swiss support because of the bad conscience given them by success.

So it is possible to enjoy dangerously bad weather in these high Alps, although the months of July, August and the first half of September are wisely chosen by those who appreciate most the paintings of the

sun, the colors that leap to life in the bright light, the unbeatable landscape of the eternal picture postcard which is Switzerland.

All countries produce attractive picture postcards in these days of
clever color photography, but only those of Switzerland approximate
the reality of the place save on a comparatively few drab days of the year.

If picture postcards are disliked then the country should not be
visited. There are many so constituted or debased by life that a film
like *The Sound of Music* is an occasion for spiritual vomit rather than
childish delight. But the wise or fortunate person who has not lost the
capacity for enjoying lovely combinations of colors and flowers and
snow against the hard-blue sky and the prettier folk and architectural
customs of his kind, including simple songs and flowers and declarations
of undying fidelity, will choose the months of almost certain good

*In the Ticino, Switzerland's Italian region south of the Alps, the vege-
tation is lush and the architecture Latin-pretty.*

weather for this run down the arterial staircase of the Upper Engadine to the Maloja Pass, Chiavenna and then by the San Bernardino to the Ticino or Tessin.

Several lakes on the way are formed by the river Inn, such as Champfèr at 5886 feet, Silvaplana, and the largest Lake of Sils, whose color is bruised green by the fist of the mountain shadows—mountains such as Piz Corvatsch which rise above it to over 11,000 feet.

The road is a white thread that runs through a fabric of landscape beauty that occasionally congeals into the man-made ornaments of resorts such as Sils and Maloja. At the top of the Maloja pass the traveller is suddenly on the dramatic edge of a steep escarpment and looks up to the extraordinary Chateau Belvedere, a folly that was started but unfinished in the 19th century by a Belgian Count. There are remarkable Alpine plants in the park of this dizzy place, as well as ten glacier-mills.

The Val Bregaglia follows, laid out deliciously at the foot of thirteen hairpins; and there are more resorts and then, swiftly, Italy.

It is not just the frontier post. It is also the sudden complete change of vegetation, from green grass and coniferous slopes to sweet chestnut and walnut and even olive trees. Soon there are not only vines but also mulberries—and peaches.

Over there is a chestnut wood which now covers the site of what was once a prosperous market town, Piuro, that, in 1618, was covered right over by a landslide. Like the one experienced at our wedding.

Chiavenna.

In the southern Alps it is frequently necessary to cross narrow strips of Italian territory. Everywhere the two countries are interlocked in this region of deep-thrusting valleys like dovetailed boards; and the experience of going into Italy is always worthwhile because it teaches the traveller so much about his nature.

Should he find the inferior edges to the Italian roads and the beautiful squalor of the towns and villages to be more congenial than those of the more orderly country he has left then he knows that in respect of control over the environment he is an inferior human being. Rushing to his own self-defense, however, he will maintain that the arts and the most worthwhile activities of the mind will flourish amid the disorders here whereas they are quite obviously killed by clinical efficiency there. The best food, he says, always comes from a dirty kitchen.

It could be demonstrated that all this is not true, that, in fact, the contributions in the arts and the humanities of very large Italy in the last hundred years have if anything been less important than those

Characteristic Swiss Italian landscape, in the warmer Ticino region.

of very small Switzerland during that time. It could be pointed out that in the old days when Italy led the world she was also noted for just that efficiency which is the Swiss characteristic today.

But such arguments are the stupid, inconclusive fruits of complete dichotomies between different kinds of people, Left and Right, Catholic and Protestant, Romantic and Realist, Laurel and Hardy, Mutt and Jeff.

It is merely a sensual pleasure to the wise to come down to Chiavenna or right to Como and to wallow temporarily in the beauty of hair let down and the astringent tang of the artist's model in the studio of disarray before returning via the Splugen and the San Bernardino passes or the short Como-Lugano road to Switzerland's newly-washed and coiffured perfection.

The Splugen and the San Bernardino passes provide the most interesting route. Right back in Roman times the Splugen was the shortest route between Lombardy and the Lake of Constance. Curiously, in view of what has been said above, the Italian side of the Splugen is the best engineered road. The Swiss side, possibly for wise military reasons, was not made so generously. In any case the traveller mounts again to high Alpine austerity. Once over the Splugen he is in Switzerland again, and soon turns left on this lofty plateau eventually to ascend by eighteen hairpins to the pass of San Bernardino, 6778 feet, a grey place of almost lunar desolation, where the ice of ages has polished great humps of rock down to a wicked smoothness and a strange lake coldly affronts the wonder eye.

It is, all the same, magnificent motoring, especially when the road falls away from so much austerity to the sudden greenlands of San Bernardino itself, the well-equipped holiday resort, and then suddenly to the Val Mesocco, where Italianate vegetation begins again and there is the extraordinary pile of that restored castle which once enabled the

One of the hairpins on the St. Gotthard Pass road.

Mendrisio in the Ticino (or Tessin), Italian Switzerland.

Counts Sax of Misox to control the region and to take toll from all travellers who temerariously approached through the gashed valley below. It is a canyon almost now, with fearsome cliffs on either side whose height is softened by lush chestnut groves that climb almost to the sky, amid which waterfalls continually dangle their ropes of defiance.

After which there are increasingly orchards and lovely villages such as Soazza with their tortuous ways and frescoed tenements, their campaniled and baroque-cluttered churches; and in season it is possible to feed off mulberries and walnuts, sweet chestnuts and figs. The vines begin to straggle and it might still be the Grisons but the Italian tongue is spoken. Soon the actual canton of the Ticino or Tessin is entered and Bellinzona is a busy, masterful town.

The Ticino, named after the straggling river that originally cut out a way up through the mountains for eventual development as the St. Gotthard route, is the Italian-speaking canton of Switzerland and is recommended to those who enjoy both the best and worst of two dissimilar worlds. The climate is perhaps the most kind in Europe. The architecture and vegetation are charmingly southern and just sufficiently time-worn and straggly to provide the artist with the colors and shapes that are most productive of inspiration. The people can be both emotional and reliable. There is order amid disorder, the tourist feels safe, and there is a complete lack of that disturbing vibrance which proceeds alike from the high Alpine regions and from the true Italian slums. An Edwardian lady novelist would have said that the place has no soul, but also it has very little cheating in cafés, disorganized postal services, raucous odors and dysentery.

It is a short but hilly run from Bellinzona to Lugano. The warm scruffiness of the vegetation eventually yields to superb prospects of the great Lugano lake, that, to lovers of the claustrophobic, Italianate sensation is still one of the most beautiful sheets of blue water in the world.

Lugano is what the tourist offices call a well-equipped town. Maybe its municipal strivings have been a little too effective, as at Lucerne and Lausanne. Perhaps the sheer perfection of sidewalks, parks, roads and great, heavy hotels has overlaid the original native charm of the place, which was essentially based on Latin disarray. So Lugano should be described as chiefly a splendid center for business and organized tours, best in spring and autumn. Antiquarians will like the 16th-century church of Santa Maria degli Angioli, along the Riva or lakeside road to Paradiso (frescoes by Bernardino Luini and Domenicus), and Paradiso is, of course, beautiful in its setting, but, like all paradises, lost.

The views of lake and high, untidy mountains are very beautiful, especially to the eyes of speculators in real estate. Hundreds of white boxes at anything from half a million to a million francs represent the final effort of the industrious Germans to conquer as much as they can of old Europe before the storm.

Morcote is a typical small town of a scented region. Set amid terraces of vineyards under a mountain, on the spearhead of a peninsula that is seductively touched by the lake on each side, this place of ancient, arcaded houses has a museum of icons.

Chiasso is, however, the true doxy of the region, down the Como road on the main Italian frontier. The traveller should pause on the way at Mendrisio and mount to Bellavista, thence by funicular to one of the most splendid prospects, that from the 5591 feet summit of Monte Generoso over the white dentistry of the Alps and the richness of the Lombard brocade.

This richness is the true root of the banking phenomenon known as Chiasso. Since the last war Italians have come here to make their

This bridge in the Ticino was built by the ancient Romans.

deposits and to become richly sound in gold or the still sounder Swiss francs. It is a small not particularly beautiful town with a bigger banking business than many a great city of the improvident Anglo-Saxon or French lands. Here and in other places of the Tessin there is orthodox investment but also much of the cloak-and-dagger clandestine.

The southwestern reaches of Lake Lugano, as well as Maggiore below Locarno, regularly resound at night to encounters between revenue men and smugglers (particularly of Swiss cigarettes into Italy). Divers with aqualung equipment have been known to penetrate with underwater cargoes in miniature submarines from the Swiss to the Italian sides.

Locarno is the Los Angeles to Lugano's San Francisco. The visitor always has his favorite of the two; and it should be noted that while Lugano could with the passage of time become a great metropolis, Locarno will always, from its geographical situation and unique climate, be just a charming, flowery town. Locarno is not on the direct route. It stands at the head of the mainly-Italian Lake Maggiore and is so sheltered there that the average temperature is 60 degrees Fahrenheit and it has more sunshine than any other place in Switzerland. There are brilliant flowers when the rest of Europe is still shivering. The mimosa and the camelia, the azalea and the wistaria, the magnolia, the aloe, the eucalyptus, jacaranda and oleander daub the hillsides and stuccoed walls with gaudy color and fill the still, soft air with erotic odors. Oranges and lemons, figs and pomegranates ripen in the open where lizards of emerald green bask and flit into invisibility and where, at night, the fireflies gleam like little memories of the day's radiant sun. Everywhere is the significant, tropic palm.

The only snag is a tendency at certain seasons for thunderstorms to rend the beauty, although even these often have the decency to operate only at night, when in any case the lovers who make up much of the itinerant population do not notice them as they sentimentally entwine.

This is traditionally a place of honeymoons and still very much a region, like Venice, where happiness, as well as convalescence, can be consummated to the shrilling of cicadas and the flitting of large, bright butterflies. The town is open, not gloomy, yet arcaded shops provide shelter from the sun and the best of northern merchandise. It is at once a Lombard town, with Italianate architecture, and a Swiss garden city, above which mountain railways and ropeways climb and a Madonna fruitfully looks down. The sanctuary of the Madonna del Sasso has two good altarpieces, constant pilgrims, and a rocky terrace with the pink-white town and the deep blue lake below.

The hotels of Locarno have always been something special, although they vary with each generation. That known as La Palma au Lac is at the time of writing quite perfect of its genre, wherein metropolitan appointments are backed by the kind of Swiss service which anticipates every need and does not wait for a tip. It is that rare kind of hotel to which the most seasoned traveller desires to return. Note that there are reduced rates between October 15 and March 15 and that at least twenty of the apartments are suites of the type that once only kings could enjoy.

The fishermen's boats on the lake are scarlet and blue and brown, with pointed prows and circular iron frames to take awnings in the dog days. Balconies have colonnades like those that support the Doges' Palace of Venice. Campaniles everywhere thrust their triangular tiled roofs through palms and pines and flowers mixed to tintinabullate the great lacustrine valley with the music of sacerdotal bells.

It is difficult to leave Locarno. The town is a little like a fairy region suspended in the not too pleasant reality of modern life. But one of the most attractive ways out is via the remarkable sub-Alpine chasm known as the Centovalli.

First an excursion is usually made to Ascona, that was once a delectable Italianate village on the edge of the lake, and that is still favored by those who remember it as it was. The difficulty is to preserve those memories through a continual horde of parked and perambulating cars. Seasonably there are really too many people in this small place for comfort.

The Val Centovalli has the sort of road that continually turns round rock faces to meet small Fiat cars speeding on the wrong side of the road, but passengers uninterested in collisions can gaze down continually at gorges and cuttings and spider-bridges and a great, dammed-up emerald pool of a lake. Chestnut woods diversify the mountainsides, and villages belong to the leprous variety still known as picturesque. Switzerland ceases temporarily at Camedo and is not regained till Domodossola has been passed and the fine Sempione road taken up to the frontier post amid the true mountains again. The fierce Gondo Gorge is here.

The Simplon Pass road should always be undertaken at least once. It is the Swiss archetype of its kind, part of the contribution of Napoleon Bonaparte to the necessary but so-long-abortive unification of Europe. The car climbs tranquilly out of the straggly southern vegetation and the heat to bare regions where the air is good and the mighty Fletschhorn points its white brush at the blue canvas sky. All the same it is good sense a second or third time to put the car on the train at Iselle and to enjoy the extraordinary 12¼ miles of dark tunnel that be-

Castle from 1641 at Brigue.

tween 1898 and 1906 was pierced so characteristically through the very base of the Alps to the completely different land of the Valais beyond.

The tunnel emerges right in the heart of Brigue or Brig (according to your French or German mother tongue) which is typical of cross-roads market towns the world over, but given especial character by its clean white buildings after Italy and by the remarkable tradition of the Stockalper family that more or less created the place and certainly left behind the triple-towered and arcaded Stockalper Palace of 1642 in the center of the town.

From Brigue some excellent excursions can be made, either by car on perfect mountain roads, or by foot in breeches and scarlet stockings. The Great Aletsch Glacier is not far away, largest in the Alps, spewed forth in an immense frozen white stream by the corries of the Jungfrau, the Aletschhorn and the Finsteraarhorn. Or the remarkable road of the Three Passes awaits, up to Gletsch and then the Rhone Glacier with its inevitable hotel and grotto in the ice, the formidable Furka Pass to Andermatt, then round by the smooth but equally spectacular Susten Pass to reach Gletsch again via the Grimsel Pass. On the way up the Grimsel are reservoirs like fiords that lead to the ghastly Totensee or lake of the dead. Here, at 7034 feet, Austrians and French so effectively slaughtered each other in 1799 that the memory remains like a chill far below the degrees of frost that are always probing. These are the true, dangerous heights of Switzerland, yet the buses of old ladies blithely scale them.

The Valais, third largest of the Swiss cantons in land area, but much farther down the league in population, is literally what it says, an enormous valley. Corruptions of the same old Roman word con-

The castles of Sion interrupt and command the broad Valais.

Right up in the clouds, excavated from the rock of the Jungfrau, one of Switzerland's highest peaks, is a modern railroad station. The Swiss have reached their summit here.

tinue in the next canton down, the Vaud, and in parts of that country such as the Vaux.

The Valais is very interesting, running southwest and then curiously northwest in a great groove of the land originally and still gashed out by water, or a single flatness between the twin walls of mountains, even more accurately like a giant fishbone lying there, the side bones of which come down in the form of smaller, contributory valleys. These probe into the main Alps on the south side and the Bernese Oberland and the Alpes Vaudoises on the north side. They end at magnificent peaks like the Jungfrau, the Matterhorn, the Wildhorn, the Grand Combin and the system of Mont Blanc.

Until recently the only inhabitants were peasants in their scattered farms and hamlets of hovel houses with strange, handmade roofing tiles of stone and wood to resist the immense forces of snow and wind. These side valleys had no roads, only mountain tracks; and the people were very like the animals who dwelt there, the chamois, hares, wild boar, bats, squirrels, marmots and hedgehogs. They lived from hand to mouth. Sometimes they represented strange enclave survivals of human races. Up the Val d'Illiez, for example, will be found to this day some fair-haired and blue-eyed people with Scandinavian names. Their great farmhouse chalets have roofs that come to peaks in the front with a marked reminiscence of Viking architecture and ships. There is a tradition that some of the Goths who savaged classical Italy were forced into this fastness and remained there.

Then the 19th century thrust its roads and railways and spirit of enterprise everywhere and the English climbers came and old methods of combating the elements like skiing and tobogganing were converted into the money-making sports that have already been described. The first mountain resorts of the Valais, such as Zermatt and Saas-Fee (wonderful name) and Villars and Leysin of the Alpes Vaudoises, were developed thus (and, of course, to provide last asylums for lung sufferers).

There have been three periods of development, up till the 1914–1918 war, when the huge drab hotels and sanatoria and mountain railways and the more old-fashioned of the souvenir shops were built, then the between-the-wars era of slow modernization and gradual road-building and construction of primitive ski-lifts, finally the dynamic epoch in which we now abide. The last has suddenly given most of the tributary valleys of the Valais at least one splendid road each that can convey cars easily to the highest regions of the Alps. A town such as Verbier, perched dizzily on the central backbone by the St. Bernard, is still as brash as any on the Californian coast, although inevitably executed in rather better taste. The staircase road to it is a masterpiece of engineering. The chalets and the shops and the hotels and the church are all briefly brand-new. The gleaming chalets like a rash seem to climb right up to the skyline of the main Alpine backbone with what could be potential avalanches among them. In season the huge white slopes are alive like an old cheese with little black creatures, some going up slowly in ant-files, others darting down from side to side, hundreds of them, thousands, and, as will be explained later, quite a few of them not international tourists, but homespun Swiss.

So it can be almost interminably fascinating to leave Brigue on the main Valais road southwest and insert the car into each sub-valley in turn. The first branching will be left at Visp straight up to Saas-Fee, a road built on the remnants of what, before Napoleon decisively cut the Simplon route out of the rock, was the only vague path between the

Valais and Italy. After high Saas the old way can be followed still to the top of the main divide at the Monte Moro Pass, 9390 feet with all Italy below.

Saas-Fee itself is the perfect winter sports station of the earlier periods but perhaps somewhat frightening to the over-sensitive in its strange high basin with the higher Alps and a glacier so near. Further up a road to the left is Mattmark of the dam and its glacial disaster. There can indeed be a sense of foreboding in these vertiginous parts where, at night, the temperature nearly always falls far below zero and the only barrier to certain death is an oil-burning central heating plant.

Afterwards the road should be followed back down this sub-valley to where, at a point above Stalden, the signs point to St. Niklaus and Zermatt.

Zermatt has, wisely or not, done its best to ensure that motor vehicles cannot proceed beyond St. Niklaus; there they must be garaged and a small train taken for the three-quarters of an hour journey, most "scenic" admittedly so long as the windows are not over-steamed by juvenile breaths, and over rack-and-pinion rails via gorges and high rock faces to the sudden, forever memorable view of the perfect peaked mountain that has cost so many lives to conquer and made so much money for a few local peasant families, the Matterhorn.

It is also the Cervin to the 65 percent of the Valais people who speak French as against Swiss German; and Zermatt (accented properly on the second syllable) the curious mountain town, so prosperous and yet so isolate, is "zur Matte" or "upon the Alpine pasture."

The central village consists of old wooden houses most of which have been constantly restored out of the money earned by smart shops in them. Above these rise the hotels that one or two local people wisely started to build in the middle of last century and have largely retained in their control ever since. Horsedrawn carriages jingle, and sturdy youngsters forever clump around with skis on their shoulders, and patinoires gleam, and the accordions inhale and exhale their reedy tunes. Overall the dangerous mountain rises to its point of doom, a phallic symbol if ever there was one, of probing, of consummation, and of the death that must ultimately reward even the greatest enterprises of the finest human beings such as the Swiss.

Around the parish church lie the more obvious victims of high endeavor, such as the three Englishmen and a Swiss guide who paid with their lives for Edward Whymper's first ascent in 1865. Whymper came down successfully, and two of the three guides, but the others fell when a rope broke. Perhaps the full story of that historic ascent can never be told, but of course a Douglas was involved as in so many great British enterprises or tragedies. (That family of the "black" Douglases, noble but lawless in the Scottish border region.)

Zermatt is still one of the most interesting places in the world to visit, but most profitably for those who can still walk and climb. The chair-fast and tottering have all facilities here but must endure the noise of those who can be energetic, also the chagrin of knowing that they cannot really participate.

In such walks as to the aptly-named Zmutt Glacier, or to the Theodul Pass, which as far back as the fourth century A.D. had a path to Italy and in fine weather has superb prospects, if never so fine as that from Monte Rosa (15,213 feet) whose highest peak or Dufourspitz is not a difficult climb and is quite on top of the illimitable world.

In such walks as to the Gornergrat, with the aid of a rack railway, a skyscraper ridge enables the wondering eye to look down and around and over a carpet in all directions of snowy mountaintops.

When the potentialities of Zermatt have been exhausted and the main Valais road regained it may be instructive for the inquiring traveller to turn right across the Rhône eventually and penetrate a little into the northern massif and so reach the ancient resort called Leukerbad, where, probably right back to Roman times, sufferers from rheumatism, gout and skin diseases have hopefully bathed in warm volcanic waters. The small spa is not of this day and age but should attract an artist of the pastiche. There are not cobwebs and hotel porters with long, straggling moustaches, but there should be. It was a distraction for milord and milady once to float semi-naked in the sulphuric baths with tea-trays like toy boats upon the water before them and goodness only knows what strange erotic ideas in their late-Victorian minds.

Eventually Leukerbad and many other of these remote places will receive their final impetus from the development of everyman's car-like helicopter. The farther sub-sub-valleys and high Alpine pastures will be reached in a quick twittering from Berne and Geneva and Zurich, probably by Hertz Rentacopters, and real estate values will swiftly accommodate themselves to the foresight of anyone who has previously bought mountaintops as a long-range speculation.

The Rhône was mentioned. To some geographers of this region it might mean a lot. It is the drainage river for the entire great Valais, and then creates the lovely Lake Léman to come before plunging through half France and making the monstrosity that is Marseilles. But it is not a nice river in the Valais. It exists and has commercial importance, but is to the asthete no more than a swift-running conduit amid ugly stones and grey sand. It is continually crossed and recrossed. That is all.

Sierre is an efficient Swiss town that retains one or two ancient buildings such as a 16th-century castle and a 13th-century tower. To the right and the left of it run roads into the mountains that have variously fertilized more resorts.

The road to the south, up the Val d'Anniviers, has not so far achieved the success of others. It leads to magnificent mountain scenery and to villages such as Vissoie and Ayer that could be and will be famous. They are worth visiting just because they often remain as they have always been, which will not be for much longer.

What can really be done is demonstrated by the other road, northwest from Sierre. It hairpins up through wonderful vineyards built upon a prehistoric landslide to what were once smooth pastures on a great mountain flank and are now mainly the almost suburban chalet development of Montana-Vermala and Crans. On the way a few may remember how the German poet Rainer Maria Rilke lived in the small chateau of Muzot. But the chalets and the ski-lifts represent an over-spreading metropolis of snow at Montana and Vermala and Crans. The contrast between this vigorous development and the ancient barns of old Montana Village on the southwestern road down is reminiscent of similar dichotomies on the Costa Brava. Yet every winter this high region brings millions of foreign exchange to Switzerland whereas, for countless preceding ages it produced only some milk, some cheese, and a thin, delectable wine.

The main Valais road regained has a further moment for the curious at the Lac Souterrain just before the village of St. Leonard. There are a car park, a ticket office, and a stretch of dark water 330 yards long and up to 24 yards wide, deep under a hill of rock. A boat.

Sion from a distance on a sunny morning might well be the Zion of the sentimental psalmist. Faery castles cap strange peaked hills in the middle of the plain and buildings of a medieval type cluster around the skirts of these ancient mothers. Not far away always are the neatest of vineyards that produce some of the best Swiss wines (red Dôles and white Fendants) and the presence also of orchards and market gardens confirms the impression of good climate here. Although so high in the Alps this Valais does indeed enjoy as much sunshine as anywhere in Switzerland save parts of the Ticino.

The Swiss German for Sion is Sitten and maybe the strange name is derived from the strategic position of the town as a place of customs

These buildings at Sion in the Valais date from 1094.

or toll. All down the main Alpine valleys of Switzerland, at the narrow parts, are these relics of the past where once clever men, especially churchmen, held the wayfarer to profitable ransom.

Now the castle of Valère at Sion is a ruin, as it was wantonly destroyed by the French in 1798, and the bishop's castle of Tourbillon, on a higher rock, is a similar witness to the revolutionary spirit of the late 18th century. It had dominated the region since the 13th century, but was destroyed by fire in 1788. The other castle, Majoria, is now an art gallery. Where the strong men once gave orders the gapers now gawk.

Sion is a busy market town and the capital of the Valais, where the inhabitants of the region go somewhat nervously to discuss their tax affairs and their motor-car licenses with officials and their health with doctors, dentists and priests. But it is also one of the well-preserved museums of Switzerland. There is a Roman inscription that is the earliest token of Christianity in this part of Europe. It has been placed in the vestibule wall of the 17th-century Town Hall. And the 12th-century church of Notre-Dame-de-Valère not only has Romanesque capitals in the choir (actual choir stalls of 1664) but also the second oldest organ in the world, dating from the 14th century. There is the Supersax House of 1505; and the Cathedral tower goes back to the 1200s. The Museum contains a marvel of Roman and Romanesque remains.

Also Sion is an excellent center for further sub-valley journeys of exploration. It is possible to proceed right up into the Bernese Oberland by the Col de Sanetsch road, passing the mountain called, aptly for our age, Sex-Noir. The development of this region and road will be increasingly important and wonderful. On the other, southern, side of the Rhône from Sion there are two very nice mountain journeys up splendid side valleys.

One runs up the Val d'Hérens via weird Earth Pillars, peaks of soil capped by protective boulders of stone, to Enseigne, La Luette and sweet Evolène, a still-primitive village where the native costumes are unselfconsciously worn, then either Ferpecle to the left or, to the right, the ultimate mountain resort of Arolla.

The other road starts the same way from Sion then branches southwest up the Val d'Hérémence eventually to survey the high wonder of the Grande Dixence *barrage*. The journey is worthwhile not only for the superb Alpine scenery but also for the revelation of how the Swiss have harnessed the melting snow of their mountains to provide light and power for their cities and towns. The Grande Dixence enterprise is only one of dozens that have been constructed in the Alps. The clever use of this water power has been partly responsible for Switzerland's modern industrial growth and relative freedom from balance of payments crises.

Now the Valais main road, once more regained, speeds flatly through stony lands of vines and orchards. There is a season when

Cogwheel railroad to Mt. Gornergrat, in the Valais. The Matterhorn is in the background.

St. Moritz, in the Grisons.

A typical farm house (Ruedihouse, 1853) *in Kandersteg, Bernese Oberland.*
Main section of Zurich.

all is a-flower with apricot. Then a later season when the farmers storm into the little towns because they are not given sufficient reward for their produce by the all-controlling modern cooperatives and supermarkets. There is a town intriguingly named Saxon. And it is gradually discovered that the stones on the surface of the vineyards and orchards are not so much evidence of Swiss poverty as of Swiss ingenuity, the outstanding mark of this sensible people. The stones placed upon the soil conserve the moisture therein from the continual, all-consuming sun.

Martigny.

Here the great Valais pauses (profitably for the inhabitants of Martigny town with its crossroads hotels and market and annual trade *comptoirs* or fairs). The main part turns suddenly right and proceeds down to Lake Léman along the banks of the arterial Rhône. Another part turns left and coils up, with magnificent motor roads, chiefly to the St. Bernard Pass and its fine traffic tunnel, but also to some famous snow resorts, and to the France of Chamonix.

The ancient Celts, first ancestors of the Swiss, had a little city below the present streets of Martigny, a town that later became an important Roman center. Then it knew the Langobards, Norsemen with their long red beards who were on their way to fertilize much of Italy and especially what is now known as Lombardy, and Charlemagne and Henry IV (impetuous towards Canossa) and Frederick Barbarossa all came there before crawling up to the fearsome St. Bernard, one of the highest of alpine passes. Napoleon was there in 1800 with his 30,000 dangerous men, who, from Aosta later, were to win Lombardy from the Austrians in the classic battle of Marengo.

It is instructive to visit the quiet town cemetery of Martigny today. It is remote from the town under a mountainside and with vegetable and flower plots nearby. Like all Swiss graveyards it is impeccably kept, resembling the burial grounds of the northeastern Scots in this respect. It will be noticed how the names of one or two families endure from generation to generation, often outlandish names betokening the mixed blood of this historic crossroads: also how short was the average lifespan of the Swiss hereabouts until recently. The climate has now been controlled by central heating and the clever chemicals of Basle, but previously it killed most people even before they reached what is now regarded as middle-age. The climate—and the habit of hard, unremitting work without too much consideration for hygiene.

The fashionable journeys from Martigny are swiftly through the St. Bernard tunnel to the Italian warmth of Aosta and Turin/Milan, or a few miles up that road and then left by a staircase highway to growing Verbier, one of the most enterprising and popular of all the winter resorts. Still farther on up this road is the spectacular Mauvoisin barrage, all in a region of increasing development where formerly there were only empty snowfields. The Combin and Mont Blanc massifs provide constant backdrops to the wonder eye.

Back on the mounting St. Bernard road again the traveller can turn off to the right and hairpin up to the small lake and resort of Champex, continuing if he likes to the ultimate of Ferret right up by the Mont Blanc system of sugarloaf peaks (that can be so wantonly pink in the setting sun), or, by returning nearly to Martigny, he can fork left up the Forclaz road, and via the Col de la Forclaz and the Trient valley not only discover the grandeur of Chamonix's surrounding peaks but also the difference between Switzerland and France, which may please or displease him according to his temperament.

Another interesting mountain road from Martigny mounts quite dizzily up the side of the great Valais leading to Lake Léman and visits more growing resorts, Salvan, Les Marecottes, Les Granges.

Indeed Switzerland is such a place that not even the widest and best motor roads can be utilized for long stretches without missing something important. The Lausanne road from Martigny down the big right-turn of the Valais is very fast but in two or three miles the traveller must halt. There is a precipice above him on the left and it is split sepulchrally to admit the extraordinary Gorges du Trient. An admission fee is paid and the tourist can venture into the heart of the mountain, looking up occasionally at the narrow blue sky between rock walls very high above him. The river Trient rushes at his feet and the air, even on the warmest days, is chill.

Then a little farther down the road there is a very beautiful water-fall, characteristically peasant-called the Pissevache, where the river Salanfe comes to a cliff edge and suddenly falls 213 feet, like indeed a bovine micturition but also an eternally fretful grey silk scarf against the stone.

And at St. Maurice, swiftly encountered after three or four miles, there is still the summit of ancient shrewdness, a place where the great valley is suddenly constricted by rocky cliffs that in the old days almost met. Augustinian monks with swords in their belts stood astride this narrow defile and took tribute from passing travellers. They did it so successfully for so long that they accumulated an enormous treasure, some of which remains to this day in the Abbey treasury for inspection by the coachloads (modern travellers who still pay tribute but in the

The vines of Lavaux above Lake Léman have been embroidered thus upon the steep, sun-drenched hillsides right back to Roman times.

form of small admission fees and money spent on nearby cups of coffee and local souvenirs).

Articles from the time of the Clovis dynasty of Franks, 500–750 A.D., and from the rich knights of Charlemagne, have still been prudently preserved, remarkably demonstrating that the Swiss are capable of saving money and keeping it in one place for over a thousand years. These were true Swiss, because St. Maurice was originally the Celtic town called by the Romans Agaunum. Maybe St. Maurice and his so-called Theban Legion of Christian soldiers were descendants of those true Helvetii, although Roman-trained in strict martial and monastic methods. Around about 300 A.D. the fierce abbot Maurice foolishly stood with his men in the way of Roman soldiers who at that time were being painfully chivvied out of Switzerland by the tall wild Germans. The Romans slew Maurice and many of his sturdy acolytes, and the Abbey, oldest of its kind, was built in memory of this "martyrdom" about the year 515.

An Abbey is still there, although extensively and repeatedly restored. It can be said that the church tower dates from the 11th century, in spite of damage by a modern landslide. The foundations of a fourth-century chapel still exist. Parts of the buildings and indeed of the town penetrate right into the rock of the high precipice that dominates the place, probably where the earliest cavemen founded our so-called civilization and perhaps an occasional dragon lurked.

Lavey-les-Bains is a strange sulphuric spa farther down the road, first developed by the Romans and curiously suspended in time. Bex, the next place, is similarly a relic of the outmoded age of the great water cure, being possessed this time of *brine* baths, but it has other industries and much old-world and pastoral charm. It is a good idea to enter Bex and take the Villars road up a delicious region of deciduous woods and peasant farms, a primitive way through a typical region of the foothills. The valley of the Avançon unravels its green skein below, down to the finished tapestry of the dead-flat plain (save where the primeval floods have left weird, isolated hills such as that which supports the ingrown, whispering village of St. Triphon and its very ancient church tower on the local black marble).

These affecting relics are really preferred to the sprawled station of Villars on high.

The mountain views from Villars and its numerous satellites make splendid postcards and the sporting snow hereabouts is nearly always certain to arrive and to transform the roads and chalets into little beauties of white icing. The mountain railways and ski-lifts take the thousands up to ridges high above the winter mists, usually into perfect sunshine, after which the thousands slide religiously down and then go up again. A bolstered figure like an Eskimo may or may not be a famous or notorious personality of television or the international marital scene. It is, to the newcomer, both splendid and exciting.

But there is not the grand character of St. Moritz here nor yet the studied, sophisticate charm of Gstaad. It is mainly a big, evergrowing

The smart mountain resort of Gstaad in summer is for discerning people even more the true Switzerland than the same region when snow-white in winter.

winter sports resort, even a residential district whence executives commute from permanent chalets to their frantic daily affairs in the plain.

Bretaye above Villars-Chesières is well worth while the subsidiary

The Emmental between Berne and Lucerne is famous for rural beauty and for cheese.

journey by rack railway because it is a high platform with the Bernese Oberland and the main Alps around and Lake Léman like a piece of fretted blue glass so far below.

There will be an intense, well-justified desire to explore that famed lacustrine region at once.

4

TOUR II

THERE ARE FEW REGIONS OF THE WORLD THAT SO CLOSELY FULFILL expectations as that of Lake Léman. In many ways it is better in reality than in the books and films and colour-prints. This even applies after many years of residence in the region. Old habitués find they need frequent holidays to get away from the crushing effect of almost too much beauty on their doorsteps, but no sooner are they away than they want to come back. Nothing, anywhere, is so good; and this applies not only to scenery and climate but also to the everyday habits of the people.

The stern efficiency of the German Swiss is hereabouts leavened by Gallic sensibility, yet it is not Latinized as in the Ticino, nor is it French although French-speaking. The shopkeepers and waitresses can smile but not too often, yet they have a courtesy and natural good taste that is lacking nearly everywhere else save in really primitive lands.

It all begins at Villeneuve, a trippery but very ancient town where suddenly the sheet of water, itself 1220 feet above sea-level, is like a sea with dim, distant horizon above which the Jura may briefly gleam. The prehistoric inhabitants of Switzerland had a settlement here.

Then as the broad road is followed round the lake it will be felt that the climate has changed, not only in the softness and tranquillity of the air, but also in the civilized quality of the urban surroundings. The same quality was once sensed on the French Riviera. Meanwhile prospects unfold of hotels and villas up to the high-treed skyline on the right and of noble mountains across the lake such as Grammont on the left, a dark pile that leads back and via other high peaks and ridges to the overwhelming glory of the Dents du Midi.

There are those who heartily dislike this eternally-white diadem of a mountain, yet for others there is none quite so beautiful anywhere else. The several peaks are perfectly balanced. It is enormous and fragile, remote and near, perfectly fashioned by the erosions of time to provide an everlasting centrepiece for the Montreux eye. Yet feminine and light like the spirit of the Savoy which extends to the southwest of it.

Nothing is perfect. The Swiss have the strictest laws to ensure that new building should not interfere with existing amenities. Before permission is given for a building there must be an inquest at which neighbors can raise objections; and if there is a majority of objections then the plans must be modified or scrapped. Yet on the high mountainside that faces Montreux near the impeccable Dents du Midi has been erected a thermo-electric power station with towers of concrete and an industrial plume of steam.

This extraordinary gaffe is, however, compensated for by the design of the remarkable slender viaduct opposite that carries the Lake Léman autoroute above the Castle of Chillon. It could have been the greatest aesthetic crime of the century but is singularly beautiful. It provides through motorists with a scenic journey of rare excitement and saves the lovely little towns of the lakeside at last from the eternal roaring of traffic so that they must gradually become favored for restful holidays again.

The brave autoroute, greatest contribution of the 20th century to man's convenience in crawling about the surface of his environment, mounts from the Valais plain by the Chillon viaduct from Villeneuve and then burrows through the mountain of Glion above Montreux. It crosses a chasm on emerging from that tunnel, using the daring if somewhat unfortunate Chauderon bridge, then thunders across what was formerly a scene of idyllic viniferous beauty to penetrate almost into the backdoor of the Castle of Chatelard (which exercised political domination over this region for centuries). It lays a band of toothpaste down on a region of orchards and crosses an even deeper canyon than Chauderon at Corsier, where, in a typical country mansion of the English shires or the Deep South the early film comic Charlie Chaplin so long enjoyed the fruits of his endeavors.

Thanks to that noble and expensive piece of engineering the trav-

eller can proceed leisurely—on foot if he still possesses the strength—
from Villeneuve around the lake road, or better still on the lake-edge
path, to the Castle of Chillon. On the way he will pass the Hotel Byron,
that still proudly points out what was once briefly the poet's bedroom.
The Castle itself is a last survivor of the lake dwellings where the very
first ancestors of the Swiss lived upon piles. It has the indefinable beauty
of extreme age and is very well-proportioned architecturally, appear-
ing small and compact but being large and heavy.

The fame of Chillon is another of those myths that represent a
nation's secret longings or values. King Arthur and St. George and
Robin Hood were invented by the English to symbolize what they
most wanted to be. The Scots saw themselves in Bruce and the Spider.
The Germans have always inwardly yearned for the strength and
heroism of a Siegfried, and Joan of Arc has been the bed-dream of
the essentially feminist French. Even modern America has created the
legend of the cowboy and the Wild West to embody its ideas of how
the typical American should be.

The Swiss folk heroes, revealing so much of their essential ideals,
are William Tell, who was supposed to have defied the ancient Austrian overlords, and François Bonivard, who, according to the popular and Byronic legend, endured interminable privations in a dungeon
of Chillon for the sake of his religious beliefs. So evidently the Swiss
like freedom more than anything else, freedom to work and worship
as they like.

It is the popular idea, reaching down deep into the national subconscious, and probably nothing will ever eradicate it.

Yet the freedom-loving Swiss have more laws, to control every
aspect of their daily life, than any other people; and François Bonivard
was in reality the prior of St. Victor's in Geneva who, by his intem-
perate utterances and quarrels with his fellows, continually asked for
what he got, the notoriety of forcing his overlord, the Duke of Savoy,
to incarcerate him in Chillon from 1530 to 1536. He was a Thomas
More without the sweetness and with no more real justification save
the posthumous fame both won by their windmill-tilting behavior
(without a thought for dependents, including, in Bonivard's case, four
wives).

Bonivard's imprisonment at Chillon coincided with the end of the
long suzereignty of joyous Savoy over the lands around gay Lake
Léman as inherited from the Romans who originally made them so
civilized with vineyards and villas and straight roads. But when the
stiff-necked cleric was released it was by the stern, sword-bearing

Bernese, who deprived the lakeside people completely of their freedom for over 250 years till Napoleon came with another yoke that was finally lifted by the exertions mainly of the British.

The poet Byron took the story of Bonivard and twisted it into a lying legend via the too-long, so-called poem *The Prisoner of Chillon,* a piece of prose cut-up into verse professing, with true British hypocrisy, the very ideals that Byron himself trampled upon in his own life.

Yet the legend of Chillon has persisted as part of the mythology of western man, and will doubtless endure because it helps human beings in their essentially grim lives at least to aspire.

There is, strangely enough, another story nearby that could equally have become part of the mythology of the people, but, significantly, has not.

From the Castle of Chillon the lake can be a shimmering sheet of water with the many-pronged crown of the Dents du Midi above, and, below, one of the world's smallest islands just outside Villeneuve. Some people still call it "Little England" because there was talk of presenting it to Queen Victoria when she visited Switzerland.

But Hans Christian Andersen, the Danish writer of fairy tales, during his sojourns at Villeneuve heard the tragic local story of how a young couple had rowed across to the small island on their wedding night and had gone ashore there. The man had not tied up the boat properly and it had drifted away. He had dived in after it and had not reappeared. The bride had spent the night alone on the island, screaming for the help that did not come till morning. Out of this Andersen constructed the rather wordy and sententious story of *The Ice Maiden.* The young bridegroom Rudy in this story plunges into the deep lake after the errant boat and is pulled down forever by the Ice Maiden there.

All very symbolic and properly ignored by the Swiss today, who, however, still go to the little island. On a recent visit two were seen behind the stone wall round the acacias that persist in growing lush on that narrow space. They were either a man and a woman making vigorous love or they were engaged in almost mortal combat.

The boat was wisely speeded away from that minatory scene towards that flat and reedy end of the lake where there are still wild woods and a bird sanctuary and a reach of quiet river, the old Rhône, that might be in central Africa—it is so overgrown and brilliant with dragon-flies and water-lilies, ducks and fishing birds—till a lagoon is reached and rock music throbs from the inevitable houseboat there.

Lake Léman is not, however, really designed for pleasure boating.

It looks a picture postcard lake but has a very different character to the initiate, being deep and subject to sudden storms, so that it might be best left to the numerous local fishermen, who know from tradition how to manage its vagaries, and the beautiful craft of the Geneva shipping lines formerly known as *vapeurs,* of which the loveliest still have perfect paddlewheels that enable them to waddle like huge swans across the blue glass and come right up to the very edge of the land and easily park at fantastic old jetties there.

The lake was until recently overcome by a remarkable phenomenon. Throughout the ages it had received the sewage and other dirty water not only of the coastal and hill towns but also of the entire great Valais region through the Rhône. This had not polluted it too much. The weight of pure water was infinitely greater than that of the human filth poured into it. But suddenly in the 1960's the population and the use of water for cleansing purposes grew so rapidly that the great lake could stand it no longer and it began obviously to become unclean. The same happened in many of the fifty other principal lakes of Switzerland; and Zermatt the proud had a typhoid epidemic which hastened things on. The Swiss characteristically put their hands deep into their pockets and acted at once. A nationwide scheme for the cleansing of waters was launched.

Lake Léman on the Swiss side now has one of the most grandiose devices in the world for protecting beauty from the beast. A huge pipe has been buried under the edge of the lake and into this all the sewage and other dirty water of the region is conducted by lateral pipes from the towns and villages above. Pumping stations force the filth along the great pipe to structures where it is separated from the water and converted into dry fertilizer. Efforts are being made to filter the waters of the Rhône as they enter the lake and perhaps eventually the French opposite will cooperate, after which it may be possible to swim safely again.

But the walker does not consider these things as he continues bemused around the lovely promenades of flowers. The grey-blue of the water reaching to the whitecapped black of the mountains opposite, all beneath the ennobling sun, is too seductive for political and especially municipal thought. Or if the föhn from hot Italy is blowing the visitor will be completely entranced by the sudden vision of the smallest details on the shores opposite which are now brought near as through magic binoculars. (He may, moreover, be affected as are many of the Swiss by this strange wind which makes some see visions and others either get a headache or feel and become rather pleasantly amorous, the women by tradition particularly.)

Montreux is really two towns on opposite sides of an entrancing bay of the lake, and the first, Territet, was long the business rival of the other, Montreux proper. Thanks to a remarkable man called Chessex it suddenly jumped from nothing towards the end of the 19th century to become almost Montreux's peer. Since then Territet has fallen behind in the tourist race but is compensated for that by a measure of the curious charm that can emanate from decay. There is still—although it may not last much longer—one of the oldest and most typical of funiculars in the world, which works on water and mounts with quaint, angled cars right up the steep mountainside to Glion. Another, even more primitive and obviously designed as a model for artists in the pastiche, climbs similarly to Mont-Fleuri, where all continues to remain almost exactly as it was seventy years ago.

Glion is time-arrested also, while at higher Caux a new religion inhabits what were once palatial hotels: and a mountain railway continues to the high belvedere of the Rochers de Naye. This is but a short travelling distance from soft, sheltered Montreux, but is 6473 feet high with the inevitable hotel and café terrace and the kind of view of distant lake and encircling mountains that cannot be described for fear of meaningless hyperbole.

It is possible to walk past Montreux and on and on, always on good paths by the perfect lake, till the road must temporarily be used from Clarens to La-Tour-de-Peilz.

Clarens is one of the most important places in the world, because it was here that Jean-Jacques Rousseau probably received the germination of the ideas in him that, as written down in his half-baked books, have completely changed the world since. It was one world order up to the coming of dirty-minded, half-lunatic Rousseau. What he wrote about the social contract and human rights and a theoretical return to nature inspired not only those who ignited the French Revolution but also the majority of liberal-minded thinkers and politicians since.

Rousseau was an ailing youngster with a divine faculty for writing good French prose and telling part of the truth about himself, one of the few honest autobiographers the world has known, who reacted against the severely puritannical Geneva of his upbringing and developed his political and social ideas out of the kind of heady romanticism that sunny days and gay young women are bound to evoke around Lakes Léman and Annecy. Above Clarens still is the woody little district where traditionally Rousseau absorbed the divine afflatus, and, thus blown up, got the idea that eventually became *La Nouvelle*

Héloise. The "Bosquet de Julie" may still be sought among the little chestnut woods there but, of course, never found; and only the red-brick chateau of Les Crêtes vaguely remembers the 18th century.

The magic of Clarens has indeed departed. In the process of becoming a well-run urban district Clarens has developed high property values but died on its literary feet.

All of this area had long been a place of refuge for writers, artists and politicians. The world owes it a lot. President Kruger of South Africa died in exile at Clarens, and later, at the other side of the bay, Mannerheim of Finland spent his last days in Territet. A generation ago it was possible to gather for a social function some twenty or thirty well-known writers who lived in the region. Then the writers, like the old ladies who supported the English church, died and could not be replaced in an increasingly illiterate age.

Clarens leads to La-Tour-de-Peilz, and La-Tour-de-Peilz to Vevey. La Tour got its strange name from the piles of the lake dwelling that eventually became the 13th-century castle with the tower. Its fame is entirely due to that lady of whom the seduced Rousseau wrote: "Louise Eléonore de Warens was a young lady who belonged to the house of La Tour de Pil, an ancient and noble family of Vévai, a town in the canton of Vaud. When very young she had married M. de Warens, of the house of Loys, the eldest son of M. de Villardin, of Lausanne. This marriage, which proved childless, was not a happy one, and Madame de Warens, driven by some domestic grief, seized the opportunity of the presence of King Victor Amadeus at Evian to cross the lake and throw herself at the feet of this prince, thus abandoning her husband, her family and her country through a piece of folly which much resembled mine, and which she, like myself, has had ample time to lament. The King, who was fond of posing as a zealous Catholic, took her under his protection, and settled on her an annuity of 1500 Piedmontese livres, a tolerably large sum for a prince who, as a rule, was little inclined to be generous."

The above is certainly a prime example of how fine writing can cover a multitude of sins.

If La Tour owes its fame to Madame de Warens then perhaps that of Vevey is sounder based. The busy market town with its narrow ways and remarkable number of almost hidden specialist shops is the world headquarters of the mammoth industrial organization known as Nestlé.

The great Nestlé building with its curve is among the least displeasing examples of glass and metal architecture and could be a worse successor to the original Vevey of the ancient Romans, an enormous villa that probably covered the entire site of the present town.

But Montreux is the best center for this area, where it extends all modernized recently on the great bed of detritus that in some primeval period slid down into the lake from the mountains that rise so steeply behind. The place is one of the world's best for varieties of small hotel, for little courtesies of life, shelter from cold winds and, in all directions, walks.

A little train can be taken up to Les Avants in the great gully behind the town. This still has only an unspoilt mountain village, the girls' school Chatelard, and, in a pink villa still strangely reminiscent of Bognor Regis, Mr. Noel Coward. A hoary funicular ascends a steep gradient to Sonloup, whence ear-popping ways mount to heights that will eventually be sheep-covered with tourists and clamorous with the noise of development, the wooded heights of the Cubly above Montreux, of Orgevaux and many future ski grounds to the rear.

The little train to Les Avants continues through a tunnel and splendid mountain valleys to Gstaad. But that famed station is best reached by a circular road tour from Montreux, first up the Valais road to Aigle and there left and eventually left again to Leysin, a place which, like Davos of the Grisons, has neatly accomplished the change-over from sanatorium to ski resort. Once there were 36 sanatoria here for the treatment of osteo-tuberculosis, a fact to which the English churchyard, opposite what was once one of the greatest of the institutions, bears silent witness.

Back from Leysin the fine mountain road soon splits into two parts. If the right-hand fork be taken it will lead first to the hotels and snow-fields of Les Diablerets, with some chalets of the famous and quite a few of the more homespun Swiss around, then to the fantastic cables and scarlet cars that ascend like spiders across abysses of rock and ice to the dizzy heights of the Diablerets glacier among its strangely shaped and needle peaks.

Next Gstaad is reached, the most perfect perhaps of all the Swiss Alpine stations, not too large, not too small, and with an atmosphere that is at once casual and luxurious. The village has not been ruined by its modernization. It is still pretty; and the restaurant terraces upon sugar-loaf eminences around yield as good a suntan in January as do Mediterranean sands in the summer. After which the skiers twist and suddenly fly away down the white slopes in all directions, making marks like the feet of birds.

Here is the language frontier again, this time between French- and

German-speaking Switzerland; and the architecture, indeed the very edges of the road and the paintwork, change. Saanen, the next village along, has a connoisseur's street of splendid ancient farmhouses in the heavy but beautiful style of the Bernese chalet. The cowbells resound over lush meadows and the local cheese grates well for fondue purposes and for the making of high, brown cheese cakes.

The cowbells of Switzerland are graded in size according to the age of the animal. A very old cow proudly tolls a very large bell indeed, and, curiously, the tones never clash but combine in a perfectly attuned symphony of the morning. Thus the Swiss once again contrive naturally to mix practicality with niceness. The beauty of their land is wholly functional and never the worst for it.

The road from here could be continued to Zweisimmen and then through the Simmental of the cheese to Lake Thun and Interlaken and, indeed, the heart of German Switzerland again at Lucerne. But this Montreux tour should be followed left by the Bulle signs towards Chateau-d'Oex, center of the Pays-d'Enhaut. It is an extensive resort that is best visited in the high season of the snow, because in the flower days of summer it can be sad with memories of Empires vanished, and also of long skirts and straggling moustaches.

From Chateau-d'Oex the Montreux road climbs over the Col des Mosses, which, only a few years ago nothing but a desolate, open mountain pass, is swiftly becoming, at 4751 feet, one of the best ski grounds of all this region, with a rash everywhere of expensive, light-brown chalets.

Montreux regained next offers a completely different experience that, for some people, will be the best of all. The road should be taken again to Vevey and afterwards the sign "Chexbres" should be followed so that the corniche route among the vines can be attained, a route that eventually traverses the famed Lavaux.

A visitor from another planet who knew naught of wine would presume when he saw this remarkable, sun-baked hillside rising steeply from the lake, the railway and the road, that he was gazing at the military fortifications of some strong, primitive people. Low stone walls contain terraces that mount very high above lake level. These are kept in immaculate condition, like neat embroidery (compared with Italy's wild disorder) and when the finished vines are cigar brown in autumn, or just a forest of black sticks in spring, the entire prospect is quite entrancing. Between hummocks of the mounting hillside will be seen churches, and villages with fairy tale roofs, famous wine names like St. Saphorin, Rivaz, Cully, and Grandvaux itself. Below the great lake is nearly always deceptively smooth with a toy paddle boat on it; and the sky above is often clear, outlining the mountains in between, from Grammont to the peaked Grand Combin of 14,163 feet.

The efficient Swiss have inevitably laced the terraces with small concrete roads so that tending the vines and collecting the harvest is no longer the slavish job it used to be. Discreet visitors may walk along these almost suspended paths amid perfect peace and the movement only of butterflies and an occasional tail flicking lizard in the sun.

The wines produced hereabouts are mainly white and not too enduring and lack the body of Villeneuve and Yvorne farther up, also the intoxicating quality of the true Valais Fendants. It is true that the quality declines roughly from east to west, being best around high Sion and humblest near Geneva. But Rivaz produces a clear, cold wine that admirably accompanies filets de perche; and the perfected vintages of the Dézaley properties in the Lavaux group are sufficiently notable to have become quite expensive. All the same it is possible to call for a carafe of the local brew in any café of the region and pay no more than half-a-dollar for what will contain neither chemical additive nor built-in headache. Swiss wines, like those of once despised Australia and South Africa, remain reasonably honest in an otherwise adulterate modern cellar.

Lausanne in such a tour as this is best skirted (by the pretty Ouchy road leading round to the Geneva autoroute). It is an extraordinary widespread city that straggles in several distinct layers up a long, steep hillside—and will be visited again when the great cities of Switzerland are properly considered.

The excellent Geneva autoroute is for those who want to reach Geneva quickly. Since there is no point in this unless the traveller has a rendezvous at the airport or with his doctor it can be strongly recommended that the inquiring tourist take the old lakeside road so that he can pause at historic Morges with its view at last of Mont Blanc—perhaps a double view under some weather conditions when the perfect mountain is reflected upsidedown in the lake—or at Nyon of the Romans and the antiquities and the old porcelain manufacture.

Then, at Coppet of the arcaded houses, there is the chateau based on 13th-century foundations that a Genevan financier named Necker acquired in 1784. While Necker the father concerned himself with the making of money and the financial ruin of France (as one of those fatal individuals called Finance Ministers) his daughter who had married a Swede became, as Madame de Staël, not only the mistress of all comely comers but also the presiding lady over one of the world's most notable salons. There are many relics of her in the chateau of Coppet still, relics of a culture that contained the terrible seeds of its own decay which we have since grown to know so well.

To complete the picture it is only necessary to take a side road up towards the Jura and briefly into France where, at Ferney, no less an architect of our disasters than the divinely tart Voltaire wrote and talked about sweet reason and a civilization which did not exist.

Geneva is another great city—indeed, until modern times an independent republic—that will be discussed in a later chapter. So it might be best after Ferney-Voltaire to return towards Lausanne, and then taste the quite different flavors of that part of Switzerland which extends from the Oberland to the old, strange mountains of the Jura. This region is as different from the others so far described as is New England from the Rockies.

The great agricultural and pastoral district that centers on Fribourg is the larder of Switzerland, and should have special charm for those who prefer soft, rolling vistas of green to the harsh primary colors of high mountains. The towns and villages are not selfconscious like those which cater specifically to tourists elsewhere. They are redolent of hard work, flowers on the balconies, hay in the barns, dung and silage, and courteous smiles that turn to sharp, whispered inquiries as soon as the back is turned.

The area has much historical interest. If the good road be taken from Lausanne to Yverdon and then on a little farther towards Neuchâtel, the traveller can then pause and muse in Grandson, where, as every Swiss schoolchild knows, his simple, ill-equipped ancestors met, on March 2, 1476, the redoubtable Charles the Bold of Burgundy, and utterly defeated him and his armored men, taking from them great treasure that is still to be seen in a museum of Berne. The rampaging dukes of Burgundy had started by quarreling with other members of their family, then with the neighbors, until, from a minor base in France they had harried and worried half Europe. They had begun to impose their vicious, beautiful Norman pattern everywhere. They were fatally checked by the Swiss with their crude swords and hatchets, and eventually only became a memory and a wine.

Grandson has a splendid 13th-century castle with four great towers. The 12th-century church of St. Jean has a nave that is typical of the time of Charlemagne. Yverdon regained can show a similar castle to that of Grandson, built in the same century by the Dukes of Savoy, another difficult, fructifying family that also plagued these parts in those days. There are Roman remains in Yverdon, and mementoes of Johann Heinrich Pestalozzi (1746–1827) another of those Swiss of the age of reason whose theories helped to create our modern world. Pestalozzi more or less laid down the principles of popular education that, in the schools of the 19th and 20th centuries, produced millions of people everywhere whose little knowledge thus acquired did indeed prove to be a dangerous thing. Pestalozzi, like Rousseau, was not himself a great success in his personal life. Why is it that we must be continually taught cooking by people who cannot themselves boil eggs?

It is pleasant always to run from Yverdon to Estavayer-le-Lac. The countryside is verdant. Estavayer is ancient and not too troubled by tourism. It is very "English" in the sense of containing many unspoilt relics from the past and yet almost deliberately not being too well known. This whole area is reminiscent of the English shires or the New England counties, rolling countryside that is made to work for an agricultural living, and places like Estavayer and the lake of Neuchâtel that seem deliberately to hide themselves away. Lake Neuchâtel is an extreme case of this English fault. It can be seen from a distance, but the approaches to the water's edge are tortuous and the final revelation is an inevitable disappointment.

The old church of Payerne nearby is perhaps this country's best example of the Romanesque. (Payerne also has a parish church that, since 1864, has accommodated tombs of the early Burgundian kings, transferred there as part of some neat Swiss tidying-up scheme.)

All of which is forgotten and nothing when the Berne road from Payerne is suddenly interrupted by the sign, "Avenches."

Here at first is a tiny old town on a hill, with some 1700 inhabitants who lead a sleepy and agricultural life, save when the motorists and tourist buses arrive in the season. But it is possible to walk from the central square in the sun and suddenly to see the remains of a Roman theatre that once held 10,000 spectators. The eyes range beyond this to the field, hedgerows and trees, the occasional farmhouses; and they see what was once the largest city of this part of Europe, a wonderful city of the colonizing Romans like Delhi as created by the British in India or Leopoldville as created by the Belgians in the Congo: Aventicum.

Only imagination can see the city now, although archaeologists can and do still dig for it. At the beginning of our Christian era it extended over those fields with noble public buildings and villas and roads of immaculate stone. There was a population of at least 30,000; and it was a large, important city even before the Romans, when the original

The Roman theatre at Avenches was once at the center of a great city, the ruins of which have long since disappeared under green farmlands save for relics lovingly restored recently (excellent museum).

Helvetii, ancestors of the Swiss, had their chief center there. Then around 240 A.D. the wild Germans came across and found that the cultured Romans had lost their virtues and were unable to fight any-more. Half of the Romans fled and the rest were slaughtered completely.

Morat or Murten is one of the most perfect small Swiss towns.

The Germans destroyed the city and afterwards the local Swiss crept back and completed the destruction, hauling away the very stones and regarding the site of their erstwhile oppressors and civilizers with a superstitious horror.

What we see of the Romans in Avenches today has recently been disinterred and dusted down. The Museum is a little model of its kind. No one is afraid of or hates the Romans anymore now; and they are a subject for delighted speculation and archaeological examination.

A magnificent Corinthian column, from the vanished forum probably, mounts 39 feet high, and was for hundreds of years known as the "Cigognier" because storks nested upon it.

The place to stay for exploration hereabouts is Morat in French and Murten in German, situated not only on a pleasant small lake with useful, simple promenades, but also on the language frontier again. Either French or German will do, and, of course, quite a lot of American is spoken. It is a perfect small medieval town with arcaded shopping streets and extraordinary town walls with ancient, red-tiled roofs, from which can be seen an infinity of prospects vert and rare. Nearby here, on June 22, 1476, the Swiss won their final and completely decisive victory over poor Charles the Bold.

The bones from the battle were long preserved in an ossuary which the invading French in 1798 took characteristic pleasure in destroying. One can only assume that their long memories had once again overcome their good taste. Unfortunately an obelisk erected on the spot in 1823 displayed even worse taste.

From Morat it is a swift run to Fribourg (save for the dangerous descending bends after Courtepin, from which the sudden views of the icy Oberland can be an often fatal distraction).

Fribourg is fast becoming a metropolis but is best regarded as an interesting old town still. It has since its foundation by a Duke Berthold of Zähringen in the 12th century been the center of Catholicism in Switzerland, and the capital of a French-speaking canton. The great Cathedral with its high tower has a renowned old organ, but the interior, like that of all Swiss cathedrals, lacks something, which can perhaps be explained as the product of those days when the Calvinists stripped away much of the "sinful" ornamentation, which was replaced but in a sense artificially.

On the other hand the renowned Cordeliers friary of the Franciscans has some splendid works of art including a predella or altar-step painting by that local artist. Hans Fries who was one of the foremost Swiss masters of the 15th century; and there are, in the Cantonal and University Library, and in the Cantonal Archives of an Augustinian former monastery in the Auge quarter, some 350,000 volumes and 16,000 parchment documents, the earliest of which date back a thousand years.

Fribourg is thus essentially for the Catholic and the antiquarian, although, in winter, a walk through the lower town, in the strange depths of the ravine cut by the river Sarine, can be forever memorable of long shining sheets and teeth of pure ice that hang from the cliffs on the eternally sunless side: an old town that also has a fine covered wood bridge dating back to 1580 and some very pretty old fountains, one being dedicated to wildness and the other to prudence.

And the connoisseur will find above Fribourg in the Forealps some excellent resorts of the Swiss growing-up period, especially near the Schwarzsee or Lac Noir at 3438 feet, where Gypsera, for example, is lazy with memories, and the Schwarzseebad offers its springs of sulphur and gypsum mixed. But increasingly the requirements of winter sportsmen and women overtake the primitive charms of all these resorts.

A prime example of what happens to real historic loveliness in an

The ancient roofs of Fribourg teach history in Switzerland. Founded by the same family that originally created Berne, Fribourg became the chief stronghold of Catholicism. Today there is wealth and industry but still the old, old ideas.

Ancient Fribourg with the cathedral of St. Nicholas.

expanding age is Gruyère, which should be visited after Bulle (an excellent market town that was almost completely rebuilt after a total fire in 1805).

Gruyère is an ancient castle and its attendant farms and houses of artisans on a conical hill amid a plain of lush pastures that still enrich the local, holed cheese. The Forealps and then the Bernese Oberland arise toothily behind it, with, predominantly, the limestone mass of Moléson. Gruyère was long a beautiful, indeed a perfect castle and village. The Counts of Gruyère commanded from it the suzereignty of all the contiguous flat lands right to Léman (but always under the final mailed fist of their Excellencies at Berne).

In recent times so many people have visited Gruyère that it has become a professional beauty like Broadway in England or St. Tropez in France. Practically every old house has become a souvenir shop or café; and the original life of the place, vibrant for centuries, has been completely overwhelmed by the marching hordes with their cameras and purses filled with nice foreign exchange.

Gruyère is still very much worthwhile visiting, but primarily as an exercise in sociological science (although the actual journey there is

Gruyère of the cheese with holes was a nobleman's stronghold on a commanding hill, and is now one of the most popular of tourist resorts.

always a pastoral pleasure, an anticipation, and then the inevitable surprise).

From Bulle the road should be taken to Romont and then Moudon, after which Yverdon, whence the signs should be followed to Ste.-Croix: so that the weird mountain region of the Jura can be explored, a region primeval of once-towering limestone peaks that have been levelled by time to roundness and flatness like the teeth of an old horse, and of dark river gorges cut deep by the running water of billions of years.

The strange Jura looks from the air or on a relief map like the Alps would look if the peaks were sliced away. A great number of parallel ranges provide a striated appearance, which is duplicated on the walls of the ravines where the successive ages of world history are clearly discernible in the different layers.

It is a comparatively unknown region to the tourist who crosses it on shallow passes of tiredness after a long French run and aims at Geneva or Lausanne and then what he regards as the real mountains or Italy. Therefore it is interesting today when there is increasing boredom in the too-familiar ways.

From Yverdon the Ste.-Croix road mounts gently to some 2000 feet at Vuiteboeuf after which the first black canyon is experienced. Swiftly the road hairpins to a considerable height above these profound Gorges de Covatannaz, which contain the distant, snakelike river Arnon, then smoothly runs along the edge to Ste.-Croix, a strange drab place on the roof of the world with small watch factories, keen air, and good food for those who have courage. Here are assembled watches often from parts made in the cottages of villages in the region. An off-beat holiday could be spent at Ste.-Croix, with excursions to Les Rasses, the Chasseron, La Sagne, the high Mont de Baulmes, and to many secluded villages of the watchmakers.

Beautiful medieval Gruyère has absolutely no automobiles.

After Ste.-Croix there are two roads to La Brevine, and the most disturbing is that via Fleurier, because of, first, the dark gorge of Noirvaux, and, second, the Val de Travers with its asphalt that has surfaced so many European roads (and with its grass-framed reservoirs and controlled river all among the lively spruce trees).

Then the road skirts France across a lunar landscape of the High Jura with the small but lofty resort of La Brevine and eventually the Lac des Brenets which is so darkly green that its depths might proceed to the bowels of the earth. The river Doubs, which waters a whole department of France, passes through it. Sandstone rocks mount with trees to the village of Les Brenets, wherein more cottage watchmakers work amid growing hotels. Thereafter the Col des Roches leads smoothly to Le Locle, a remarkable town at 3035 feet, busy with the making of watches since Daniel Jean-Richard founded one of Switzerland's principal industries there in 1705. The watch museum is interesting; and La Chaux-de-Fonds very soon takes the traveller to the heart of the matter. Tucked away at a considerable height in the middle of the Jura is the main watchmakers' center, La Chaux, a beautifully laid-out town because it was rebuilt in the age of reason after a fire that destroyed the original buildings in 1794. There is another fascinating museum, and scope for speculation about the curious fact that Switzerland's unique precision industry is a product of the French rather than the methodical German Swiss. The French-speaking people responsible were, of course, Huguenot refugees, stiff-necked puritanical folk who sublimated their bottled-up animal instincts in hard work and meticulous craftsmanship. Some of the purest and clearest French is spoken hereabouts, as by tradition the best English is mouthed at Inverness in Scotland.

Swiss history, to be demonstrated later, is a record of struggle not only against invaders but also against fellow members of the Swiss family. The modern country is a product of balance and cooperation between the various cantons, which have at last bedded down together quite well—save in the case of this Jura region with its largely alien origin. The inhabitants still struggle for the creation of a separate Jura canton, even for complete independence.

Down to Neuchâtel the road from La Chaux first humps to the Vue des Alpes—just what it says, a 4229 foot view right across the shimmering green to Mont Blanc. Afterwards there is the descent via the developing ski slopes of Tête de Ran and Valangin of the Gothic castle and, eventually, the Gorges du Seyon which are all Jura depth and mystery. Neuchâtel, at the end of the road, consists of buildings

Church of Notre Dame and the Castle at Neuchatel.

of yellow stone that creep upwards through gardens and vineyards, and of some fine ancient monuments, reminders that the city was from 1707 to 1857 most strangely part of Prussia. The awkward Rousseau was afforded sanctuary there by his German patron but soon had to be expelled once more for writing rashly and offending friends by talking about them as if they were enemies.

The Collegiate Church of Notre-Dame in Neuchâtel dates from the 12th century (although the west towers are new) and contains a remarkable Gothic mural of lifesize figures.

Bienne (Biel to the German-speaking) is a bilingual city that has gradually overtaken Neuchâtel in number of souls, especially with the modern influx of Italian and Spanish workers, and that has really beaten La-Chaux-de-Fonds for the watchmaking crown thanks to the

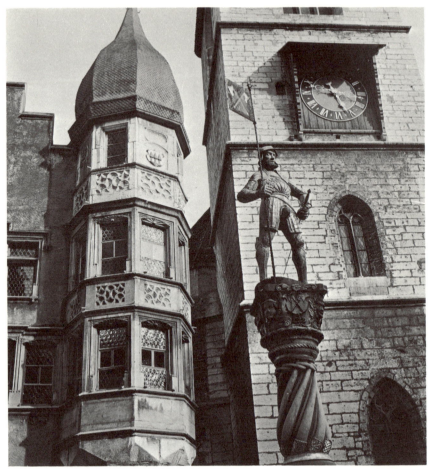

Sixteenth-century architecture in Bienne of the watchmakers.

growth of the Omega and other great factories there. It belongs to the
canton Berne, of which it is the second city, but, again, would probably
break away into cantonal independence if it could. The whole of this
region is Switzerland's chief internal headache.

But the growth of Bienne has obscured neither the beauty of its
lake nor the charm of its historic ways around the Town Hall with its
16th-century Gothic, and its arcaded Ring with lovely fountain. There
are guild houses and the wall-painted 15th-century church of St. Benedict,
also a museum that contains relics of the original local lake-dwellings,
and roads and funiculars behind to such scenic beauties as the Tauben-
loch Gorge with the river Suze and the resort of Macolin from which
a lovely landscape can be studied right across to the highest Alps.

After Bienne it would be foolish not to continue the few miles to Soleure or Solothurn, because this small capital of a little canton is architecturally and historically perhaps the most perfect town of all Switzerland. The Romans had a city there called Salodurum, and their influence has never been destroyed. The Renaissance and baroque houses and public buildings are wholly beautiful. It is a place of colored statues of knights above fountains and of such belfries as the Zetglockenturn of 1250, where a king, Death and a warrior move mechanically to mark the brilliant hours. Meanwhile the real Swiss here have never allowed the dust to collect or the stone to crumble. All is constantly restored in perfect taste, and the town is still very much as it appeared when the best of it was planned and built hundreds of years ago. The Cathedral of St. Ursus has a glittering Treasury, the ancient arsenal has one of the world's good collections of arms and armor, and the Museum has a Madonna by Holbein.

Solothurn joined the Swiss Confederation way back in 1481 and for two hundred years it was the residence of the French Ambassadors to the Confederation. Rousseau was up to his games with one of those. And today it is difficult to believe that amid such a neat brocade from the past the local people work so hard that their precision engineering is scarcely without worldly equal.

So this tour of the Swiss byways comes towards its end where it began, in the all-controlling central mountains. From Solothurn the road should be taken to Berne, deceptive like Solothurn but infinitely larger—a city that shall be written about at length later—and then to Thun at the end of its lake, the entrance to the Oberland once more.

Thun has ancient double sidewalks, one on top of the other as at Chester in England. Decorated with flowers, these are pretty; and the views of Lake Thun and the Alps can detain the traveller, but not for long. The whole district, and this includes Interlaken itself at the other end of the lake, has like the lakeside paths been a little too well-worn by tourist feet. The high mountains are over-near and they beckon impatiently. The roads to Interlaken on either side of the smooth water afford entrancing prospects but cannot detain. Interlaken is the best and worst of Edwardian England nicely arranged on the flat stretch between the two lakes Thun and Brienz, with many hotels and tearooms and shops and little parks. It is famous and the cheap tours naturally congregate there. It is also the stepping-off place for some of the most memorable excursions in Switzerland.

The Bernese Oberland is the first high range of the Alps as approached from the north and northwest. Afterwards there is a precipitous fall to the Valais and to the valley known as the Goms, from which the conglomerate merges in the northeast with the still-primitive and relatively inaccessible region of Switzerland's political beginning, high above Lucerne and southwards from that lake.

Before mounting into the central Oberland from Interlaken the explorer of Switzerland would be wise to run round the south bank of Lake Thun a little and then up to Frutigen in the verdurous Kandertal, thence by the right-hand fork to Adelboden, a mountain resort of Switzerland's middle period (although the church, dating from 1433), demonstrates the age of the settlement here). The Wildstrubel is the dominating massif, with the Lohner mountains to the east. There are hotels, shops, chalets, chair-lifts, and many walks and climbs.

Back in Frutigen a left-hand fork similarly leads through what is known as the Kandergrund via Blausee with its tinted and trout-full lake, then past the Kander Falls eventually to Kandersteg (whence cars can be taken on trucks though a railway tunnel to Brigue, and then through the Simplon Tunnel to Italy). Once again the station of Kandersteg has a period flavor, belonging essentially to the period of earnest climbers and dignified strollers. It is a long, straggling resort with its own, historic flavor. Two remarkable experiences from Kandersteg are a chair lift and walk to the Oeschinensee at 5190 feet, where a little lake is so clean and clear that the high, encircling mountains of the Blumlisalp live again within its depths—and a hard, long walk and climb to the top of the Gemmi Pass at 7641 feet (hotels on the way conveniently) whence the hardy should always continue down to Leukerbad by a pass that skirts a vertiginous precipice, often regarded as one of the most fearsome walks in the world: with the great Valais suddenly ahead and down. One passes right across the first band of the Alps and to an entirely different region here.

Interlaken must inevitably be regained. (There is no escaping it, which explains the success of the town.) Then there are two ways up to the culminating happening of this tour, one of man's most daring encounters with the dangers of his environment, a visit to the heart of Switzerland's characteristic and famous mountain, the Jungfrau.

One route is via Grindelwald, and that is perhaps the best because it takes in both the archetype of Swiss mountain resorts and its terrible but beautiful overhanging Eiger. The road is excellent. Grindelwald is still very much as it was when the great mountaineers annually assembled here. The churchyard contains the remains of many of them. Breeches and red woolen stockings are still *de rigeur*. The dignified little town is built on an eminence in the center of a great green basin of farmlands and ancient peasant houses above which three sides mount to the blue sky with mountains, that dark Eiger, then the Mettenberg, and finally the splendid Wetterhorn. Between these exude two glaciers.

The visitor can chase after those glaciers, or climb those peaks, or merely wander up and down a multiplicity of little roads among the true Alps of pasturelands, with the flowers around him in spring and magnificent mountain prospects in all directions.

The glaciers, alas, are not what they were. They have for years been receding. The Lower Glacier used to tongue its icy and fearsome way through a narrow high split in the mountains called the Lütschine Gorge. The walk to the face of the monster was bored through the rock partly and is still a chill experience, but, when the end is reached, there is now no glacier. (The latest news is that it is returning!)

There are still few better climbing experiences than those on the mountains above Grindelwald, but the actual Eiger story continues to be oppressive. Men still fling themselves at the most difficult part of the monster cliff at the worst seasons of the years and ascend with what is almost engineering equipment—and still fall.

To look upwards from a hotel balcony in Grindelwald and to regard those black mountains, among which at night are the lighted windows of a railway station (where the Jungfrau railway mounts), is perhaps to understand a little more of not only the Swiss but also the human character. Where there are mountains they must be mastered, even at the expense of life. Thus the best is brought out from a human being, and thus he can be destroyed.

He can be destroyed on the way up or he can be destroyed on the top when he has attained his ambition and found that there is no more for him but the inevitable descent.

The Jungfrau can be reached from Grindelwald by the Wengernalp and Jungfrau railways via the Kleine Scheidegg, although the more direct way for the modern pilgrims from the coaches and cars of Interlaken is on the Grindelwald road just to Lauterbrunnen, where the extraordinary railway is taken. It represents the apotheosis of 19th- and early 20th-century railway engineering. Wengen, a car-free resort of considerable charm, can be visited on the way. The actual Jungfrau section proceeds finally by a tunnel broken only by stations (with suitable pauses for stupendous views) that emerges finally 11,342 feet high, one of man's loftiest railway terminuses, at the Jungfraujoch.

This is a miniature and often subterranean conglomerate that has been constructed high up, in and on, one of the most beautiful and

A restaurant terrace on top of the world with the Jungfrau in front.

spectacular of mountains. Shops and lifts, hotels, a research laboratory, a post office, burrowed pathways greet the visitor and his money. It is like the mountain monastery of Montserrat above Barcelona but so much higher and with the religious driving force only of curiosity. In that it may of course be a cleaner place than Montserrat and it is certainly designed to afford the visitor many views of exquisitely terrible beauty at relatively low cost. There is the Ice Palace, a skating rink on a glacier. A lift ascends 367 feet to the Sphinx gallery and summit. The Jungfrau Glacier nearby can be fearsomely explored on sledge.

Between the Jungfrau and the mountain called Mönch is that yoke of hard snow, or saddle, which the station called Jungfraujoch is named after. The prospect from this vantagepoint takes in, on a clear day, nearly all Switzerland and much beyond.

A Zurich scene.
Schwyz. *The Federal Archives, Central Switzerland.*

Weggis. *Outdoor concert, Central Switzerland.*

Constellation of Scorpio, as seen in the planetarium of the remarkable Swiss Transport Museum at Lucerne.

Cogwheel steam loco of the Brunig Railway, 1909, cut away to show construction, in Swiss Transport Museum, Lucerne.

There are climbs to the peaks and a walk to the extraordinary Concordiaplatz, which is a meeting-place of glaciers.

When the visitor has finished with the Jungfraujoch he has come to the end of mountain Switzerland and he should know all. There are these wild and dangerous Alps with their deceptively beautiful inter-locking valleys of peasant farms. The Swiss, prodded to it by the British originally, have advanced into them and partly conquered the dangers, harnessed the water-power and the tourist-power of the high places, impudently driven roads and railways up the ravines and perched hotels with restaurant terraces on the peaks, strung wires with cable-cars from the tops across dizzy spaces, traced out pistes for swift descent with feet on pieces of wood, gained from it all a reputation for extreme efficiency, a great self-respect and quite considerable financial reserves.

And yet it is still only the tourist Switzerland. The real nation is elsewhere, derived originally from these hard, lovely places, but to be found in its true manifestations far, far below.

5

CITIES

OUTSIDERS TEND TO REGARD THE CITY SITUATION OF SWITZERLAND as akin to that of the United States, modern West Germany, Australia and Scotland in that the capital is only chancefully so, being a kind of overgrown administrative village compared with much larger and more important places in the same land.

This does not apply to Berne.

Washington is certainly nothing compared with New York and other great American cities; Canberra and Bonn and The Hague are artificial capitals of countries whose true great centers are Sydney and Melbourne, Munich and Hamburg, Amsterdam and Rotterdam; perhaps only Edinburgh can be compared to Berne as a capital that is smaller and poorer than Glasgow but firmly the real controlling center of the land.

History provides the proof. Since the beginning Edinburgh has been in charge, and so has Berne. There were the various Celtic and Roman metropolises in Switzerland such as Aventicum. Then Geneva, Coire, St. Gall, Zurich, Basel all preceded Berne as independent towns or towns under alien control. Berne was not founded till 1191. But Switzerland as a loosely-knit confederation did not come into existence until some time after that and then Berne soon became the natural leader, as she has remained ever since.

That is because the city was founded as a fortress by Duke Berthold V of Zähringen and he was a Burgundian knight representing a culture that imposed itself upon the architecture and the spirit of the

The Kramgasse in Berne with the Clock Tower of 1191.

place thereafter and perhaps forever. The architecture was originally and remains exquisite. The spirit is of overlords who impose wise laws with mailed fists, latterly velvet-gloved, but never faltering. The Austrians replaced the Burgundians after a time, but the original chivalric families remained and have probably never really died out.

There has been a little of geographic centrality and of playing off the monsters of Zurich, Basle and Geneva against each other. If Berne didn't exist it would perhaps have to be created. But the principal reason for the preeminence of this small capital over the large others for so long has been the toughness and efficiency of the ruling families, flamboyant once but very retiring in modern times—"Les Excellencies" as they came to be half-fearfully and half-mockingly called.

Their blood and ideas were and probably are the same as those of

other members of the same family who for centuries controlled, high
up above the mass of the population, the empires of England, France,
Spain and Germany, based originally on Norse sea-rovers, who, by
contact with Latin civilization and Christianity, evolved their extraordinary notions of chivalry (the ancient horseman's code of personal
conduct).

*The best and most memorable town view in all Switzerland is at the
heart of Berne the capital.*

It produced what was for long an efficient ruling class, but the decline of that class and its ideas has not yet been countered by a better or for that matter an equally efficient code. Its modern lack may be the most important single cause of our disasters.

Berne as a city is chiefly interesting for its architecture and museums. In a sense it is one big museum, of which the principal exhibits are the architecture, and the governmental devices that have made Switzerland unique among nations for prettiness and for freedom from disastrous external and internal wars. But care should be taken to have at least one quiet Sunday or public holiday in the city, otherwise its motorized bustle can obscure the beauty and the political interest of the place. The population of between 165,000 and 170,000 is considerably less than half that of Switzerland's largest city, Zurich, but Zurich is many times larger in area. At peak hours Berne is still a small medieval town, a pint-pot, into which the quart contents of a large modern city is poured. The city is geared rigidly to its prime task of governing the country, but has been unable to resist the temptation to develop industries all around it, chiefly in the making of textiles, machinery and chocolate, at the same time acting as a market for the agricultural produce of a lush region. Therefore it groans at times with overcrowding and the overstrain of facilities designed for a much smaller population and quieter age.

But on a Sunday or public holiday Berne is still like the City of London, a delight to the contemplative eye and a stimulus to really hard thinking about politics.

The river Aare has throughout the ages cut a steep, steep channel through the local sandstone but in a curious loop. A ridge of the sandstone protrudes from that loop and there Duke Berthold flung down his mailed glove and said to the natives: "Build me a fortress." The site was perfectly chosen. Manned by resolute men it soon became strategically almost invulnerable. There was water, there were pasture lands, there was rock, all high up and protected on three sides by the steep gorge of the river.

Then Berthold's overseers, military engineers, told the natives how to build the fortress which gradually became a town; and, like all towns based on a castle, it grew out of strength and blood into beauty. No motive for building has ever produced such dignified loveliness as the warlike instincts, crossed with Christianity, of the Normans and/or Burgundians.

The invulnerability of Berne throughout the ages, but also the innate good taste of its inhabitants or rulers, have preserved the central core of the city as it was nearly at the beginning, five or six streets that were intended to be of the traditional Roman mile length, soon known to the visitor as the Kramgasse, the Marktgasse, the Gerectigkeitsgasse, the Spitalgasse and the Nydegg-Gasse.

They are characterized by buildings of sandstone blocks resting on arcades within which the traditional shops and trades of a medieval city engage in their affairs non-stop without interference from the elements. This makes for good business and for a gnomic, fairy-tale kind of charm. Then the streets themselves often have old stone setts; and what would otherwise be their plain vistas up and down are diversified for the eye by fountains with columns surmounted by colored statues of knights, also by quaint peaked towers in which are inserted brilliant clocks.

Intersecting these main thoroughfares are primitive side streets, which in turn lead to the buildings of ecclesiastical, administrative and social function that stand on the edge of the ravine over the river, the ancient Minster, the 19th-century Bundespalast, the hotel Bellevue-Palace. Garlanded by gardens and traffic, these look down on old and modern bridges which cross the ravine dizzily.

When Duke Berthold's family eventually fell it was succeeded by others of Burgundian descent who so stiffened the resolution of the townsfolk that not even the German Emperor Frederick could subjugate the town-fortress, to which he was forced to grant a charter of self-government in the 13th century. Afterwards Berne was led by Rudolf von Erlach, another descendant of knights, to complete victory over an alliance of local country barons at the battle of Laupen, 1339. A few years later the city became the eighth canton of the young Swiss Confederation (Uri, Schwyz, Nidwald, Obwald, Lucerne, Zurich, Glaris, Berne). Indeed, it gradually became the true leader of this group; and for a long time it completely ruled certain neighboring areas such as the Vaud, till, in 1848, it was finally chosen as the permanent seat of Federal power.

The lovely buildings, decorated and arcaded, still recall the original founders and protectors of the town, who in any case cannot be forgotten thanks to the fountains, which everywhere support representations of them, all armored, shining and colored. Hans Gieng designed most of these statues in the 16th century; and today the knights and men-at-arms provide not just prettiness but also a reminder of the reality of that original and still latent power.

Then the Minster on the cliff edge, built in the final Gothic style between 1421 and 1596—although not given its present lofty tower till 1893—reminds the wayfarer of the always strong ecclesiastical props of this city, which adopted the Reformed faith in 1528 and yet has more ornate religious trappings in its old churches than most other Swiss places thanks to its strength which was able to resist the depredations of the reformers. (Indeed, it can display today much that was originally filched by the reformers from other cities, such as the plate from the treasury of Lausanne Cathedral, which is now in the Bernese Historical Museum.)

The dominating Erlach family is recalled by the Erlacher Hof, from the 18th century, that became the seat of municipal administration. After this the Nydegg-Gasse leads down to the old Lower Town, with its 15th-century Nydeggkirche on the site of a castle. One bridge not far away dates from 1460, and another, the high Nydegg Bridge, runs straight to the Bear Pit, where bears have been kept on exhibition for some 500 years. Probably Duke Berthold hunted the bear successfully in the neighboring forested region and sardonically named his fortress after his prey, which has ever since been the symbol of the city and canton.

Even today the Swiss are great hunters. They try not to shoot each other and foreigners but they mightily pursue the remnants of wild life in the many wooded lands that remain, here and in neighboring France.

The clock tower to beat all clock towers is that at the west end of the Kramgasse in the center of the town. It is known as the Zytglog-geturm and was put up in the 15th century, given its remarkable clock in 1527–30, and finally perfected in the 18th century. This tower—and others—formerly had a resident watchman whose permanent job was to regard the rooftops for fires and the surrounding hills for enemies. The tower has a carillon that plays tunes and the central clock has figures that cavort to the hours. Then there is, on the east face, an astronomical timepiece.

The great buildings of the 19th century that accommodate the Swiss parliament, the bureaucracy, their visitors and those who wish to gamble or take tea, are not offensive after the lovely central streets of Berne. They mould, if dourly, into the architectural wholeness of the place. But the Bundespalast of the two legislative assemblies, and the Bellevue-Palace Hotel, and the Casino are built in that bastard style of architecture which sought, in the 19th and early 20th centuries, to revive the best of the Renaissance period with modern trimmings; and the pastiche, like all of its kind, is without true organic life. It is, however, far less detrimental to the beauty of this fine old city than would have been a later 20th-century concrete and glass shoebox there.

The remarkable museums of Berne are indeed a significant feature of the city. The Swiss Alpine Museum is probably the best of its kind, and the same building can offer a Postal Museum, while next door is the Berner Schulwarte, consisting of books and other documents to assist schoolmasters in their handling of the young. All this is around the Helvetia-Platz, just over the high Kirchenfeld Bridge. What might be a late medieval castle on the other side of this Platz is a building erected in 1892–94. It houses the Bernese Historical Museum, which contains not only the booty captured from Charles the Bold at the battle of Grandson in 1476, but also one of the world's finest collections of Islamic remains. There are general archaeological and ethnographical items as well as the Lausanne Cathedral treasure and some exceedingly important 15th-century tapestries. The Swiss are very fond of old tapestries, as well as ancient oak furniture and stained glass. It is essentially a Gothic taste, based on the predilections of those original wild aristocrats from the North.

The central Kunstmuseum of Berne is outstandingly good for Swiss art as such, from the 15th-century masters such as Paul Löwensprung and Nikolaus Manuel Deutsch to 19th-century artists like Karl Stauffer-Bern and Ferdinand Hodler, not to mention several representatives of the 20th-century revolution.

There is a museum attached to the trades school in the noble 18th-century Kornhaus, where once the grain was carefully stored against calamity; and, near the Helvetia-Platz again, is the Natural History Museum, which, for no immediate reason that can be discerned, is notable for its collection of African desert fauna. The Swiss National Library, farther on, is succeeded down the road by a park wherein are conserved some charming species of deer.

Berne proudly houses the International Postal Union and the International Telegraphic Union and the International Union for the protection of copyright.

It is all rather dull and worthy but it carefully preserves the best of the past while contributing considerably to national and world organizations for political good, and, on a Sunday at least, it is extremely beautiful with the steel of the knights still behind it all.

Zurich is so much larger than Berne. It is in many ways a fairer, more modern city. The situation is exquisite at the end of the white-sailed summer lake whence the river Limmat emerges to be sur-

Zurich is the largest city of Switzerland with some interesting old buildings around the river Limmat at the center.

rounded by light-colored buildings with red roofs and medieval towers and spires. All has the charm of the past but in a state of up-to-date restoration. Swans float glassily here and lake steamers depart with their gilded backsides there. The Alps provide a constant if distant backdrop to the bustling scene. The visitor thinks about hotel problems if the season is crowded and about getting away as soon as possible to the Alpine or Italian resort of his choice, and, if he is a newspaper reader, about gnomes.

"The gnomes of Zurich" was a phrase that gave this great, pulsating city in our time its first real world fame in a history going right back to Stone Age lake dwellers. It referred to Swiss bankers who allegedly held the world, and in particular the formerly great Britain, to financial ransom. It was a singularly unfelicitous piece of journalistic claptrap, first because Zurich people are not in the least gnomelike in appearance, tending to be fair and straight and often tall, secondly because the place where the international bankers and finance ministers met and meet to decide what must be done about the currencies of bankrupt countries is Basle, not Zurich.

Basle and Zurich have ever been banking rivals. On the whole it has emerged that Zurich leads with head offices, but world banking as such has more or less taken up residence in Basle, which has also become the favored place for deposits of foreign wealth, being so conveniently situated just across the borders of both France and Germany.

Therefore it is totally unfair to insult Zurich with funny epithets. The directors of the great Swiss banks there have a say in international finance but mainly in the form of extending generous help with careful Swiss savings to less provident countries and people.

Zurich is almost wholly a commercial city and really always has been so, which explains why it never acquired the political and social power of the much smaller Berne. It has been concerned throughout the ages with the manufacture of textiles and machinery, with entrepot trade between Switzerland and Germany, and with keeping out of all international political situations that could possibly interfere with its busy commerce. The founders of Berne were dominating men who despised the traffic of the market place. They took what they wanted and refused to haggle or chaffer for it. They had certain ideals above or below money. (Which might explain how the gnomes of Zurich phrase arose—from a journalistic contempt for mere businessmen, visualized as stocky, bald-headed old bastards with horn-rimmed spectacles.)

No one would talk of the gnomes of Berne. "Les Excellencies"—yes.

The Romans established a military settlement where Zurich now stands and gave it the name Turicum. The lisping Celtic natives could not pronounce that properly: hence Zurich. Wild Germans ravaged the area after the Romans and many settled down there, to be conquered and organized in vassaldom by the remarkable Charlemagne, who built a great palace with fortifications. Then the Franks lost their grip and the Burgundians took over in little dukedoms and knightly fiefs here and there. They had at least nominally to kneel to the German Emperors, and the tough Duke Berthold of Zähringen, ancestor of the Berne overlord, was given the imperial stewardship of Zurich in 1098. When the Burgundians as such were defeated in pitched battles by the peasant Swiss those of them who wished to retain power neatly merged with the Swiss and in a town like Zurich so organized the local people that they were able increasingly to stand up to the Germans.

In 1218 Zurich was given the status of a free city of the Holy Roman Empire by the double-talking Germans, and after a hundred years of this status began to get definite ideas of its own, particularly under the burgomaster Brun, who forced the dominating knightly families and their financial supporters to give an equal place in the government of the city to the trade guilds. The commercial element in Zurich life was becoming predominant. In 1350 the sturdy burghers and apprentices bloodily slaughtered German imperial elements, now specifically Austrian Habsburg. Next year Zurich joined the Confederation and was besieged unsuccessfully by the Austrians, who renewed the attack in 1354.

This last siege did so much harm to the growing Zurich silk industry that the people became really annoyed. They contributed blood and treasure to the Confederate struggle so mightily that the decisive victory of the Swiss over the Austrians at Sempach in 1386 was considerably their doing. They were proving themselves to be very shrewd. One of their devices when an Austrian duke marched on them was to dress all the women of the city in men's martial clothing, thus creating such a host that the invaders turned away.

The Old Zurich War, as it is called (1436–50), finally gave the city its present freedom. The Austrians arranged with the French to help them and at the first battle defeated the Confederates, but were themselves crushed by the Swiss at the cruel battle of Ragaz.

After this Zurich settled down to a comparatively peaceful life of industry and commerce till one of its sons, Ulrich Zwingli, began as a secular priest in 1519 to preach the doctrine of the Reformation. His ardent words aroused the naturally plain-living Swiss to rise against the decadent, corrupt and overdecorated Catholic Church. Zwingli became a soldier mightily, and in 1531 was defeated and killed in the battle of Kappel against the Catholic cantons. But the resulting peace treaty gave each town the right to choose its own faith and so it has been ever since.

Zurich may throughout its history have preferred money to power, but the Zwingli episode set the tone for a certain intellectual life there that Berne has never had. Knights and burghers distrust airy-fairy thought. Businessmen often tend to subsidize it, perhaps because

Town of the Middle Ages at Regensberg near Zurich.

it can be profitable. Norwich in England and Boston in America have made enormous business fortunes partly because intellectuals have given their towns a reputation for a kind of honesty. Thus Zurich produced the pastor J. K. Lavater, the philosopher Gottfried Keller (suitably realistic), and other eggheads such as J. J. Bodmer and C. F. Meyer, also Pestalozzi the arch-schoolmaster himself. The University at Zurich is perhaps the most seminal in Switzerland, whether for good or for that disruption of the rule of law which is part of the anarchy of a civilization in decline.

But only as a thin sauce on the brave commercial dish: Zurich works from early morning till evening in modern factories and offices. One in ten Swiss belongs to Zurich. Half a million people lead the typical lives of commuters, regular hours, increasingly frequent holidays, lives led according to the old patterns, with revolutionary ideas and sexual aberrations only on the lunatic fringe.

There are nearly as many museums as in Berne. (The culture of modern Switzerland is essentially a 19th-century culture, of which the museum was a characteristic, dusty cornerstone.) Many Zurich people would, however, regard their most important collection as that

Rooftops of characteristic Zurich architecture at Regensberg.

in the Kunsthaus which comprises examples of the goldsmith's craft dating back to the 14th century.

The Grossmunster towers above the old town, nearly a thousand years old in its foundations; and it is a fine, historic church building if lacking interior decorations stripped away by the reformers, and if constantly restored a little too drastically. The Rathaus is nicely late Renaissance; the Fraumunsterkirche has been there for some 700 years; and followers of the baroque must look inside the Peterskirche.

But the architecture that best expresses the spirit of Zurich is that of the sprawling Bahnhof, and the head office of the Swiss Bank Corporation, and the hotel Eden au Lac, and the garden city factories that encircle the town like a fairy ring of sudden mushrooms. Thus there is a strange, typically modern air of impermanence here, which, however, is not found in Zurich's chief competitor, Basle.

When the traveller arrives suddenly in Basle, a city through which the frontiers with both France and Germany actually run, he cannot mistake the Swiss character of the place. It is as different from the French and German cities he has left as a crisp new Swiss banknote is different from a filthy, fragile French or a grubby piece of German paper money.

Yet it could be advanced that in many ways Basle is not Swiss at all, but an independent city-state with a national flavor all of its own, like the cities of the north German Hanseatic League or those of the individualistic Lombard plain.

This, however, is not historically valid. Basle (the anglicization of the name, which was originally the Roman Basilia meaning according to some scholars a royal residence and according to others an entrance gate, now Basel in German and Bâle in French) passed through very much the same gestatory periods as the other Swiss cities. The original Celtic settlement was transformed by the Romans into a fortress town that was despoiled by the Germans after the Latin departure and then rebuilt in its present form and dominated by the nearby Burgundians. The Habsburgs inevitably incorporated it in their Unholy Roman Empire; and the Swiss inhabitants, employing the military methods taught them by their Burgundian former masters, characteristically grumbled and fought and eventually achieved independence.

It is true that Basle did not join the Swiss Confederation until comparatively late in the day, 1501, but the inhabitants were from the beginning as Swiss as Swiss could be. They liked to be clean and efficient and to save money, and they did not want to engage in wars unless they were forced to it; and they had that deep Helvetic regard for the rule of law and the intellect that welcomed the Reformation while deploring the methods of some of the reformers. Their university was founded by Pope Pius II in 1460, but rapidly became one of the most important in the world and one of the most "humanistic," attracting to its cool cloisters some of the best brains of Europe such as the noble Erasmus of Rotterdam.

The tomb of Erasmus Desiderius, the man "who laid the egg which Luther hatched," will be found to this day in the Munster of Basle, a building softly red with its sandstone and its twin-probing spires at the cold, female sky; and near to Erasmus's suitably is the tomb of a typical Habsburg, the beautiful wife of rampaging Rudolf.

The tradition established by the Dutch philosopher has never ceased to inspire if sometimes to mislead scholars here. It is the sensible tradition of the pure intellectual who believes that good sense and decency will prevail in a jungle where the animals must by their very nature forever strive bloodily. It is a tradition that nourished the 18th-century mathematicians Jakob and Johann Bernoulli, and also in that century Leonhard Euler, who took his degree at the age of 16 and went on to lay important, dangerous foundations in mathematics and physics;

The Rhine is all to busy Basle where pharmaceutical and other factories dispute the skyline with relics from the Gothic past.

then in the 19th century came that Jacob Burckhardt who interpreted the Renaissance, and that Friedrich Nietsche who taught at Basle between 1869 and 1879 what the world was later to learn as the undeniable, terrible truth of *realpolitik.*

The intellectualism of Basle sometimes rejected the truth; and the case of Paracelsus is worth presenting in a little detail just because it reveals a weakness of the Swiss mind and method.

In the history of medicine there are only a few outstanding names, Hippocrates, Celsus, Soranus, Galen, Vesalius, Harvey, Sydenham, Boerhaave, Morgagni, Jenner, Pasteur. Among these should be included that of Paracelsus, a Swiss, as by far the greatest innovator of the Renaissance period.

He was born in 1493 at Einsiedeln; that curious religious retreat between Zurich and Lucerne whose Benedictine Abbey attracted the visitors for hundreds of years as pilgrims, and then in modern times, thanks to the writings of such enthusiasts as Sacheverell Sitwell, began to attract them again as students of the baroque. The reconstructed Abbey church, as designed by Mosbrugger and decorated by the brothers Asam in the 18th century, is for some the finest example of pure baroque in this part of Europe, and for others the triumphant apotheosis of the wedding cake. Perhaps the boy medical pioneer absorbed some of this curious atmosphere.

Anyway, his real name was Philippus Aureolus Theophrastus Bombastus von Hohenheim; and his becoming known eventually as "Paracelsus" was an indication both of a natural desire to be rid of the initial, ghastly label and of his inordinate ambition. He wrote, in turgid language, books, mainly wrong-headed, on the composition of matter; he practiced alchemy and sought the philosopher's stone; he studied in Vienna, Cologne, Paris, Montpellier, Ferrara; he visited Spain, Pomerania, Poland, Lithuania, Russia, Cornwall and Sweden; and he served as an army surgeon with the Dutch and the Venetians. He wrote: "I went in search of my art, often hazarding my life. I have not been ashamed to learn from tramps, butchers and barbers things which seemed of use to me."

He became a great doctor in 1526 when a certain Johannes Froben, who profitably published books in Basle, asked him to look at his leg. The local physicians were about to amputate it. The young Paracelsus at once saved the leg, preserved for himself a publisher, and won a reputation overnight. This was consolidated when he performed a similar, almost miraculous cure on the great Erasmus himself.

If he had only known how to handle his intellectual contemporaries Paracelsus would have had a good job in Basle for life. He was given a university chair there and at the same time appointed official doctor to the commune.

Alas he devoted his first university address to a bitter attack on the medical methods of Galen and Avicenna, the twin gods of the medical establishment for so long; and he burnt their books publicly and told the assembled local savants that they were disseminators of dangerous lies. Even worse than that he delivered his lecture in German instead of Latin, and he told the doctors that their place was at the patient's bedside and that most ills could be cured by herbs or surgery.

So he lasted only two years in Basle, went back to his poor wanderings, and died in Salzburg at the early age of only 48.

The story is worth telling because it is the story of one of the greatest of Swiss practical scientists. Paracelsus was the first modern doctor in that he preferred practical healing to mumblings from old books. The concept of metabolic disease was his; and his work in pharmacology probably encouraged the growth of an industry which today is Basle's greatest. His works on surgery and the treatment of syphilis saved thousands of lives for long generations afterwards. He was a pioneer in recognition of the occupational disease, and he traced the connection between cretinism and goitre. He invented novel and effective treatments for epilepsy and St. Vitus's Dance.

But as a teacher he came up against a wall in Basle, a city based not just on Rhine-born trade but also on respect for long-established conventions and laws.

Probably if Basle had been able to listen to Paracelsus it would have become the new capital of the world. On the other hand it might long ago have been cast in ruins by such vaunting ambition instead of increasingly becoming the paragon of bourgeois conurbations, with, today, the twin money-spinners of a banking and financial quarter similar to that of the City of London and the most modern and respected of chemical, pharmaceutical, machine-tool and electrical industries.

Provided that wars do not upset the prospect Basle has the most cheerful material future of any Swiss city. It is starting to extend and it could extend a long way into Germany towards Freibourg on the one side, and into France towards Mulhouse on the other. It is completely central to the needs of a logical European common market.

Geneva is quite different from the others. It has less than half the population of Zurich, and is smaller than Basle although a little larger than Berne. It is officially the Republic of Geneva still, and vividly French in language and culture and susceptibility to bad men who come across the Gallic border that runs through its suburbs, is fiercely Protestant in religion and puritanical in its moral attitudes. Ever since it initially rejected its international son Rousseau it has sought to become a world center of organization for human good; and it has made a lot of money out of handling and developing the products of the nearby Jura watch and clock makers. Of course it also has banks.

Possibly the most important aspect of the history of Geneva is contained in that word Republic. Today the city and its inhabitants are very Swiss, but historically they are not Swiss at all, rather an independent part of that France which still almost entirely surrounds what is one of the smallest of the modern Swiss cantons.

It was not until 1814 that Geneva joined the Swiss Confederation as the 22nd canton.

Way back in the Roman period Geneva was known as Genava, a provincial center of the civilizing Latins which rich Roman administrators probably liked for the same reason as the international bureaucrats like it now, because of its open, sunny position on the western end of beautiful Lake Léman, with its views of Mont Blanc blushing at the onset of night or just Mont Blanc gloriously white. Then when the Romans lost their nerve and went the town was occupied by the Burgundians, later by the Franks, then by the Burgundian knights again, who by 1033 allowed themselves to be profitably incorporated in the Holy Roman Empire.

Thereafter the small city was a constant object of strife between Imperial representatives, warlike Bishops of the Roman Church, and the gay if bloody House of Savoy from across the water. This continued until well into the 16th century, when the theologian Jean Calvin came to the city as a refugee from Paris. His stern doctrines, based upon the logical dislike of Rome which was already being fiercely suppressed in France, encouraged the burghers of Geneva at once to organize themselves against their oppressors and to find their first self-respect in years.

Over a hundred years later the Revocation of the Edict of Nantes made Geneva finally what it is today. The upright, strong-willed, industrious and skilled Huguenots flooded out of France to the benefit of those countries that would receive them, much as the emigration from Germany of Jews before the Second World War to the United States, Britain and other lands completely changed the world balance of economic, scientific and moral power. Strangely enough the Huguenots, although French, originated as a sect in Switzerland. The name Huguenot itself may have been derived from the Swiss-German *eidgenossen* or confederates. Admittedly puritans in Paris had started the revolt against the Catholic Church, but one of them, Calvin, had brought the idea to Geneva, in which soil it had flourished—and spread back to France.

Geneva was the brain of the Protestant religion. The French puritans did their thinking there. Translated to France, the thoughts so vibrated that Louis XIV had to be worried and cruel. The best of the resulting emigrant Huguenots naturally came to Geneva just across the border, and because the intellectual climate there was congenial. They could talk all night if they liked in Geneva, and they could worship as they pleased, so long as they worshipped according to the

Reformed Faith.

At the same time they were most of them ambitious and skilled craftsmen. They were good at anything that required precision of mind and hand, natural watch and clock makers. Later the same skills promoted important electrical industries. Other Huguenot aptitudes were for the practice of medicine and for the making of sweetmeats and clothes. And, because their religion made them at least superficially honest, the Huguenot immigrants into this land were able to succeed as bankers and as experts generally in investment, insurance and the kind of high finance that eventually produced a Necker (under Louis XVI one of the most powerful finance ministers any country has ever had). It was the same kind of phenomenon that was responsible for the Jewish financial dynasties of New England, and the Quaker dynasties among the bankers, insurance people and chocolate makers of old England.

The larger part of Switzerland speaks a kind of German, and the most extensive ethnic group is blonde-Nordic-Teutonic, however it may be called. The most orderly regions in the sense of cleanliness, bright paint and everyday efficiency are not the French or Italian speech areas. So a superficial observer might conclude that the outstanding industrial contributions would be from places with guttural names, stern, Nordic, Protestant places, whereas the French speech parts would be concerned mainly, in a thoroughly Catholic way, with the arts of living.

Yet many of the most Swiss cantons, in the sturdy, German-speaking sense, are Roman Catholic predominantly, cantons such as Lucerne, Schwyz, Soleure, Fribourg, St. Gall, Unterwalden, Uri, Zug; and the most French cantons, Geneva and the Vaud, are proudly Protestant. Perhaps the finest precision engineering is done not by the clean and efficient German speakers but by the less rigid descendants of Gauls. They represent only 20 percent of the population, but could be regarded as of key importance.

Young women continually come from the German to the French speaking parts to learn the language there, and they are willing to work at menial household duties. The compliment is seldom returned by the French speaking women, who are quite content with their own language and have ideas above domestic chores.

So Geneva and its surrounding areas profited hugely from the influx of clever, industrious Huguenots, who established most of the industries for which Switzerland is famous. It was their rare intellectual climate that could eventually shelter a Voltaire (at nearby Ferney

Geneva, the old Puritan city, still aspires to reach the sky. (The Water Fountain in the middle of the lake, and the statue called "The Breeze.")

just over the French border so that he could escape into Geneva whenever it was expedient to do so) and actually produce not only many lesser but highly cultivated mortals such as Necker's daughter Madame de Stael, but also such a transcendental world-shaker as Jean-Jacques Rousseau.

Geneva was the matrix-irritant of this brilliantly-clever, literally fundamental man. It threw him out as he deserved, but it produced him, and, through him, the ideas that brought about the French Revolution, the 19th-century Romantic movement including Karl Marx, and the principles of thought and behavior that, perhaps briefly and fatally, dominate the world today.

Soon after Rousseau the proud old city of stiff-necked Protestant democrats was rudely occupied by Napoleon Bonaparte and allowed to become just the chief town of a new Département du Léman. But from 1814 onwards the burghers took full advantage of the British-won peace. They quietly endured several characteristic 19th-century growing-pains about which the world heard and hears as little as possible. One of these, in the 1860s, actually involved an attempt at dictatorship in the city. But at the same time Henri Dunant, after recoiling from the horrors of the battle of Solferino, founded the Red Cross; and the Geneva Convention of 1864 established viable regulations regarding the treatment of the sick and wounded in war—and the same year the author of *Das Kapital* came to the broad-minded lake city to establish the first International. The workers of the world could now proceed to unite. (Shortly afterwards in Geneva they actually did so, giving Switzerland in 1868 its first, if very nearly its last, industrial strike.)

The people of Geneva were broad-minded and deeply humanitarian, but never foolish. They gave shelter to, they even produced the new ideas, but did not allow them to take active political form within their own social structture.

Modern Geneva is a bustling, sunny, sometimes windswept city of polyglots who are principally concerned with making money and enjoying the pleasures of the table, the lake and the mountains. The fact that they hospitably and commercially welcome international institutions and international bureaucrats, always with a warm, liberal flavor, does not mean that they will ever cease to become believers in the rule of law as originally instilled in them by their first masters and civilizers, the ancient Romans.

One of the principal authors of the great Geneva Convention was the civil engineer and professor of mathematics and adopted Genevan whose name Henri Dufour is commemorated on many Swiss thoroughfares and at least one lake steamer. He drew a beautiful Swiss map. When in 1847 the Roman Catholic cantons established the Sonderbund in a desperate effort to achieve the independence for which their Protestant cousins had more successfully fought, General Dufour led a sturdy army against the rebels, and, after only 26 days of clever shadow boxing, won his sensible victory.

Another citizen general from these parts, Henri Guisan, was primarily responsible in the Second World War for keeping his country inviolate as well as neutral. He stood by the principle of the alpine redoubt, appealed to the patriotism of his officers, and successfully gave Hitler the impression that to invade Switzerland would take just a little too long. Unlike many he knew who must ultimately win that war.

After which the international organizations, the tourists, and increasingly the European headquarters of many great American business corporations could come to Geneva again and work and play by the lake where the Jet d'Eau threw its phallic fountain 400 feet into the blue sky, and the Brunswick Monument recalled, on the Quai du Mont Blanc, an exile who had been so grateful to this lovely place for what it had given him that he left it his entire fortune of 20 million francs. Not many cities appear in rich men's wills. But then there are not many Genevas.

Lausanne is not a large city. If judged by extent of central shopping streets it is not even a large town. But it is the fifth most important cantonal capital in Switzerland, and has a unique character of its own

The young and the old in Lausanne.

that makes it quite different from the others and curiously influential in the land.

This character might be explained by the passage in the *Autobiography* of Edward Gibbon (referring to his Lausanne sojourn in the middle of the 18th century) that speaks of the local girls as being attractive and flirtatious but annoyingly evasive when the podgy young man made a pass at them.

Or it might be illuminated by the fact that when an oil sheikh or a pop singer thinks of Switzerland he primarily thinks of Lausanne because that is the place where he has received some of the famous Swiss medical and dental attention.

It is superficially a strangely laid-out town, running down from a high escarpment to the glittering middle reach of Lake Léman opposite the French watering place of Evian and the foothills of Savoy. There is usually a lightness in the air, a certain gaiety of climate; but if it can be very warm it can also be very cold; and high spirits tend, like poor Gibbon's concupiscence, to be overlaid soon by the real and earnest bustle of urban life.

The strange layout of Lausanne is exemplified by an unnatural poising of the town center a long hill's journey up from the lake. The shore of the lake is beautifully parked and built up with the small pleasure port of Ouchy, and it obviously should contain the main shopping streets, offices and medical cabinets of Lausanne. But it does not; and those must be sought far up on the hill but again on several layers there, one of them divided yet again by a great, bridged chasm. The real old town and core of the place, with the Cathedral, are still higher than that; and then, a weary series of kilometres farther up, are modern building developments culminating in a conurbation of bureaucrats that is suitably braced by the four winds regularly.

The reason for all this: thousands of years ago the first people in these parts were lake-dwellers. They lived in huts built on piles in the water. Eventually they were what we call Celts, who were mastered by the Romans. The town of Lausonium was built around a great villa on the beautiful lake edge. It was a place for pleasure, and as such was horribly destroyed by the German hordes who punished the dying Roman Empire in the fourth century A.D. The site was thereafter regarded with superstitious awe by the original Swiss peasants of the region; and when they started building in the area again they chose a position far above the ruins of the old Roman town, right up on the bare hillside on a mound which could not be so easily reached by marauding armies.

The typically Gothic architecture of Lausanne's Cathedral.

That is in many ways not just the story of Lausanne but also the story of Switzerland itself; and to this day the peasant will dislike the lake edge and the plain for his habitation and prefer the mountainous position that is difficult to reach. "The air is not good down there," he says, but he is not thinking just of the air.

The twin shopping centers of the town, around the Place St. François, with the delicately-cobbled and traffic-free feminine artery of the Rue du Bourg lurking behind, and around the Place Bel-Air across the bridge, are properly known, like similar shy areas of London, only to the initiate. Above these is a great conglomerate of car parks and museums, more shops, and then the ancient University. An attractive

The old town of Lausanne with the Cathedral where armed bishops once ruled the country of Vaud.

covered staircase should be ascended after the 15th-century Hotel de Ville to the five-towered Cathedral of Notre-Dame. Pope Gregory X and the Emperor Rudolf of Habsburg were there for the consecration in 1275. The proportions are fine but much of the original beauty of the great building, inside and out, has been mitigated by an amalgam of the Reformer's and the restorer's zeal. Visitors are chiefly shown two significant tombs, that of the 14th-century minstrel Otho of Grandson, and that of one Henrietta Stratford-Canning, who, at the beginning of the 19th century, was the first wife of the first British Minister to Switzerland.

But the most important building is yet to come. This is the Chateau St. Maire, formerly the Bishop's Castle, constructed 1397–1431, residence of the Bernese administrators of the Vaud from 1536 to 1798, and still the headquarters of the cantonal government.

The history of Lausanne and the Vaud is highly individual and bears little relation to that of the other little states which make up Switzerland. Sword-belted bishops more or less took over Lausanne and contiguous areas from the Burgundians in medieval times, ruling the town as a free city under the Holy Roman Empire (which, it must be insisted, was neither holy nor Roman and scarcely an Empire in the accepted sense of the term).

Then the Bernese used sharper swords, tempered by the Reformation, to evict the mitred corrupters in 1536; and they ruled the land efficiently but coldly for well over two hundred years, until Napoleon arrived and evicted them. It was not until 1803 that the land of the Vaud became the 19th canton of the Swiss Confederation; and even then it existed under the French overlord. During the 19th century it became completely self-ruling, save for the Federal powers largely exercised by Berne.

It is not difficult to understand, therefore, why the fundamentally

How the Swiss mailman sometimes makes his deliveries in the mountains.

gay people of this region, with the wine of their terrassed hillsides in their very blood, with the bright climate and the memories of Savoyard troubadours still among them, are not really so merry when analysed on the psychiatrist's couch. They have never really been free.

Lausanne is, all the same, a beautiful base for holidays with the best·of real Swiss hotels. Women can shop there for hours merrily and find modish clothing at comparatively low prices. Rich people who must spend on their ailments in the second half of their life what they so desperately earned in the first half can enjoy Harley Street standards in Lausanne with a far better climate.

But the town and the area, thanks probably to its history, has not been able to contribute men and ideas to Switzerland and the world that can be compared with the contribution of the other leading cantons. In the early part of the 19th century there was the somewhat bleak theologian Alexandre Vinet. Born at Ouchy, and died at the Clarens of Rousseau, he wrote principally about the sad matter of liberty of conscience. Then a hundred years later Charles Ferdinand Ramuz laboured at Cully on wholly local books whose themes are deeply rooted in the vineyards, but whose feeling for the primitive poetry of the region sometimes transcends the trivial.

Probably the greatest son of Lausanne was that Louis Favre who started as a working carpenter, became a public works contractor, and, by sheer pertinacity, engineering skill and originality of method, pushed the pioneer enterprises of the Mont-Cenis and St. Gotthard railway tunnels through the Alps. He finally lost his hard-won fortune towards the end of these astounding feats of the human spirit; and he died inside one of his tunnels, from an attack of apoplexy.

6

HISTORY

WHAT IS SWITZERLAND, AND HOW CAN ITS MESSAGE BE UNDER-
stood? Enough has been said of the physical surroundings now. Here is
a beautiful country in the centre of the snowy Alps, with quaint, clean
towns that have produced some outstanding people and ideas. But there
is obviously more to it than that. Perhaps the time has come to take a
closer look at what the schools call history.

History is officially defined as a continuous, methodical record of
events. It is, of course, nothing of the sort, but must be regarded as
a plastic, amorphous conception of the past that varies according to the
personal prejudices of observers.

It might be best to drop the term history altogether and substitute
for it the term mythology, understanding mythology to mean what we
want to know about the past.

The way a people writes its history is the mythology of a people,
and that is all-revealing of national character, achievement and aspira-
tions.

Thus the British laud such as King Arthur and his knights, Robin
Hood and his merry men who robbed the rich to pay the poor, Magna
Carta, the Bill of Rights, Trial by Jury, village Hampdens, one-eyed
Nelson, Factory Acts and suppression of the slave trade, wars to end
war, John Bull, Winston Churchill, a Welfare State. Most of these
did not really happen, but the British like to think that they did. The
theme is an amalgam of physical prowess and socialism.

So history is the national ideal, and, studied properly, a nation's history can reveal its significance for the rest of mankind.

What the United States of America can offer mankind is clearly stated in any cowboy film, and the entire German contribution may be studied in the *Siegfried Idyll.* America believes in the triumph of the good strong man over the bad strong man; and Germany believes in the triumph of the strong man. The fact that both are right has nothing whatsoever to do with it.

France is La France and Italy is a series of supreme achievements in the arts; and Russian history as written today, although not necessarily Russian history as written before the Revolution, reveals a strong national belief in material progress by social organization.

Needless to say, ideals are not based on facts but on the contrary. As what a nation believes is its history is never its history, so the mythology is always clearly based on what a people would like to have but sadly lacks. Physical prowess is not the mark of the modern Briton; and his socialism only leads to increasing distinction between classes. Modern America is not controlled by good strong men, nor have the strong men of Germany triumphed in the two great lost wars of that nation. The French patriotism consists of dodging income tax and national service, sending as much money as possible abroad, and refusing to work hard under any circumstances. Italy has for thousands of years been making a shambles of the beauty around her; and the standard of living of the Russian masses is still lower than that of many nations with contrary ideals.

What the Swiss like to learn about their past outstandingly is the following:

A Stone Age people of lake-dwellers were, about 400 B.C., overwhelmed by the immigration, from the west, of Celts. The Celts can be scientifically identified as ancient inhabitants of Brittany, Cornwall, Wales, Ireland, Scotland and the Isle of Man. But the modern inhabitants of those parts, and the Swiss, like to think of them as a long-headed, handsome people of warm temperament, profound intellect, and artistic ability, good at fighting if necessary, but rather unfortunate in major wars.

These Celts mixed with the Stone Age aboriginals to produce the Helvetii which the Romans found when they arrived marching during the final century B.C.

The true facts about the great emigration of the Helvetii from Switzerland into France and their return will never be known. The Swiss tradition is that the Romans somehow tricked them but that they gloriously survived. The Italian tradition is perfectly written down in

Julius Caesar's *The Conquest of Gaul.* Caesar maintains that the Helvetii, warlike but living in a small, poor country, cast envious eyes on the agricultural richness of Gaul, particularly the great Roman Province therein. They decided at last to emigrate en masse out of Switzerland into what is now Provence. They packed all their goods, put their women, children and old people into carts, burned their property to the ground, and trundled around Lake Léman and through a Jura gap into the promised land. Caesar had already fortified the Rhône gap and gathered his legions. He told the Helvetii that they must return home. The Helvetii refused, and were finally met in battle at Bibracte in Burgundy, 58 B.C. They were defeated, and forced back into Switzerland, and made to rebuild their towns and villages. Caesar says there were 368,000 of them originally but only 110,000 at the end.

The Swiss eventually acquired out of this the tradition of a supremely brave if simple and unaggressive people who could even stand up to the might of imperial Rome. Is this right or wrong? It does not matter. That is how the Swiss felt and still feel. They fight no wars. They recoil from bloodshed and place supreme trust in the rule of law. But they have been very brave and they could be again.

The Romans occupied what is now called Switzerland for some 500 years. Undoubtedly they gave the country the bases of its present civilization. Theirs was the rule of law and the communal system of local government. They built roads, walls, bridges, aqueducts, temples, villas. They introduced sanitation, piped water, and habits of personal hygiene. They taught the Helvetii how to cultivate the grape and make wine. Maybe they introduced a money and financial system—and 500 years is a long time, far longer than any modern power has occupied its colonies.

But the Swiss, like the British, were able soon after the departure of the legions in 401 A.D., and the invasion of northern Switzerland by the Germans in 455 A.D., to wipe most of the true history of the Roman occupation off their memories like something unpleasant, that in retrospect must be forgotten to be endured. All traces of the conquerors were obliterated save the name Romande for the French speaking part around Lake Léman, and for the Romansche and Latina dialects in the high mountains of the east: also that overwhelming respect for a rule of written law.

And a link with Rome was maintained through the Christian Church, although even that irked increasingly till it was summarily cut by the zeal of the Calvinists.

After the Romans came the Germans from the east and the Burgundians and the Franks from the north and west. They divided Switzerland into lordships and took tribute from it and ruled it sternly for some six hundred years more, until what we now call the Austrians concocted their Holy Roman Empire and took over the suzerainty of all the Alpine lands. The Swiss were downtrodden more than most by these tough men, centering around the Habsburg family, because the founder of the Habsburg dynasty and the Empire was technically a Swiss himself, Count Rudolf III, the ruins of whose ancestral castle may still be seen at Habsburg near Brugg on the road from Waldshut to Berne. He was particularly good at appointing businesslike bailiffs to rule over his territories and extract the utmost in taxes from them.

Real Swiss history thus begins in 1291 when the people revolted against the Austrian bailiffs and the Perpetual Pact was drawn up and signed.

We have the actual document to read today, like Magna Carta and the American Declaration of Independence; and a meeting of representatives of the forest cantons of Uri, Schwyz and Unterwalden did take place on the famous Rütli meadow opposite Brunnen, on the southern shore of Lake Lucerne. They entered into a verbal agreement which was eventually written into the Pact. The Pact stated that the peoples of the forest cantons, because of the difficulties of the times, would act together to defend the region against the hostile acts of others. They would appoint a judge who would be paid to settle disputes, and really difficult disputes would go before elders of the community. A common law would be established. Criminals would be punished.

That was really all. It said nothing about the bailiffs or the Imperial yoke generally. It was just a matter of internal reorganization in the wildest, most inaccessible region of Switzerland. It was indeed the birth of the modern Swiss nation in that the three cantons eventually became the four, and the five, and the six, until, six to seven hundred years later, there were twenty-five of them. Only in folk memory did Switzerland emerge from the womb as a fierce, independent state in 1291 at Rütli. Only in idealistic retrospect and the later writings of the more dubious kind of scholars did a nation begin when the Austrian bailiff Gessler forced a Swiss named William Tell either to bend the knee to his would-be masters or shoot an apple off his young son's head with a bow and arrow. The legend says Tell did not fail in his aim. Gessler asked him: "What would you have done if you had missed and had killed your son?"

Tell showed Gessler another arrow. "I had this ready," he said, "for you."

Whereupon Tell was seized and taken across the lake in a boat, but a storm arose and only Tell could navigate the boat. He was freed to do so, and leapt ashore eventually to escape and ambush Gessler and his men, and to destroy Imperial castles at Zwing-Uri, Sarnen and other local places. Part of this is written in the 1470 *Obwalder Bundeschronik*. In the 16th century one Agidius Tschüdi of Glarus rewrote the legend without any knowledge of the 1291 Pact, and dated the revolt about 1307-8. When the German poet Schiller came to write his *William Tell* in 1804 he got his "facts" from Tschüdi's unreliable book.

The legend of Tell has done for long generations of Swiss what the legend of David has done for the Jews and the legend of Arthur for the British and the legend of George Washington and such as Wyatt Earp for the Americans.

Yet the sturdy peasants of the forest cantons did get together and sign a document of cooperation in 1291, and they must have had brave leaders, and all kinds of interesting incidents must have occurred in the struggle that followed.

There is no doubt that there was a struggle. The Austrian bailiffs were not going to allow the natives to make and enforce their own laws. They must have sent men-at-arms to teach these impertinent peasants a lesson. Anyway, after some 24 years of this kind of confrontation, there was a pitched battle between oppressors and oppressed. The men of the three forest cantons, probably aided by jubilant youngsters from the Zurich region and the Grisons and Berne-Fribourg, met the Austrians on the boundary between the cantons of Schwys and Zug at Morgarten by the little lake Agerisee. It was November 15, 1315. The Imperial forces were completely routed. The Swiss had for the first time in over a thousand years defeated their masters in open battle.

If those crude, rude young peasants had not fought so bravely or so fortunately at Morgarten in 1315 the eventual Switzerland might never have come into being. One certain law of so-called history is that nothing succeeds like success. The decisive martial victories of the Jews over the Arabs in our time cannot be denied and *must* attract respect, adherents and an eventual nationhood of wide proportions. The success of the three cantons, now to be known as the *Eidgenossen* or Confederates, at Morgarten in November, 1315, led first to a renewal definitively, on December 9 at Brunnen, of the Perpetual Pact. Three years later the burghers of Solothurn were inspired successfully to resist a siege of their town by the Imperial Duke Leopold I. Eight years after Morgarten the shrewd knights of Berne decided at least temporarily to ally themselves with the Confederates. Lucerne joined up in 1332, Zurich in 1351, Glarius and Zug in 1352, and Berne joined finally without reservations in 1353.

This agglomeration of widely-separated and often totally different city-states was not accomplished without difficulties. The burghers of Zurich had to combine against the aristocratic families and the business-men of the city who were in the Imperial pay. The Confederate knights of Berne had to fight a decisive battle at Laupen against the Burgundian nobility of the region and of Fribourg. There was a "Bloody Night" at Lucerne in 1343 when the townsfolk finally destroyed the Habsburg supporters among them.

This is all what the schools call historical fact, but of course it is not all quite true. For example, what the books rarely emphasise is that the bubonic plague arrived in Switzerland during this 14th century, and not only in Switzerland but also in Germany and France. The Austrian and Burgundian armed forces were decimated by that Blackest of Black Deaths and the will to power of the Habsburgs was strongly affected. The Swiss towns and villages and farms rapidly lost as much as two-thirds of their populations. There were 14,000 victims in Basle. In some places (such as Villeneuve at the head of Lake Léman) local Jews were rounded up and burned alive because the ignorant people thought that they were responsible for the disaster. But the Swiss peasantry, particularly in the high mountain valleys, tended to survive the plague, both physically and mentally, more than the townsfolk, and particularly the softer-living Austrian aristocrats and local feudal nobility.

The feudal nobility of the Swiss regions was eventually overturned by the peasants and burghers at the point of the sword, but it was *La Peste* that prepared them for the slaughter and for the change of a complete social system. The more or less classless structure of Swiss society emerged from this period of natural revolution.

The final day of the old nobility was July 9, 1386. The men of Zurich had marched on the Habsburg defenders of Rapperswil; the men of Schwyz had impudently taken Einsiedeln from the Austrians; and Duke Leopold III of Austria assembled a great army, bright with the banners of the remaining owners of local castles, which encountered the Confederates at Sempach, a few miles from Lucerne, off the Olten road. The Austrians were completely defeated once again, and Duke Leopold was himself among those killed.

Sempach was important. Two years later the men of Glarus fought a similar battle at Näfels and destroyed one of the last Habsburg hosts

—there were eleven devastating attacks, commemorated to this day by eleven memorial stones and an annual procession, the Näfelser Fahrt—and without a doubt the Austrians were now morally as well as physically defeated.

In 1394 the Holy Roman Empire formally renounced its claims to the suzerainty of the forest cantons and of Lucerne, Glarus and Zug. This was known as "The Twenty Years Peace." Much of Switzerland was, for the first time in its history, more or less free.

But what the Swiss most like to remember of this vital era in their history, after the William Tell legend, is the death of Arnold von Winkelried at the battle of Sempach. The story goes that the Austrians stood so compact with their spears out-pointed that it was impossible to break their line. Young von Winkelried threw himself on the spears and allowed several of them to be thrust into his body, so that, when he fell, there was a gap in the line through which the Swiss could pour. The story may or may not be exactly true, but it is what the Swiss like to know about their past; and it has never ceased to inspire the otherwise quite unwarlike youth of this peaceful little country.

A village between two lakes in the Engadine.

In the succeeding century there must have been, among the peasant and burgher leaders of the confederated cantons, some minds of considerable political importance, because continual negotiations between the various areas gradually led to such an enlargement of the Confederation as to make it increasingly strong in diplomacy and difficult to attack. Appenzell, Aargau, Thurgau and many small districts right up to Lake Constance adhered. The Upper Valais rose against the saintly bishops who had governed them for so long on behalf of the House of Savoy. Even Mulhouse in France asked to join. The first meaningful Swiss penetrations were made into the upper Ticino. The men of Uri started this, and occupied the Val d'Ossola. Later Uri and Obwalden bought Bellinzona.

But in 1436 there was real trouble again. The Empire had long plotted a comeback. It could not endure the thorn in its side of the unconquerable little Swiss Confederation. Vienna, in return for a quid pro quo that need not be discussed here, obtained the help of a strong force of French mercenaries known as *Armagnacs*. On August 26, 1444, these marched over the frontier and, at St. Jakob an der Birs just outside Basle, encountered a force of Confederates and defeated them. Fortunately the Armagnacs were more anxious to take their spoils home than to fight the Confederates in the unpleasant mountains. At the same time a conflict had flared up in and around Zurich. The Austrians, considering that the moment was ripe for their comeback, advanced into Switzerland and finally met the Confederates at Ragaz in 1446. The Swiss were victorious; and, as winners of the rubber, secured a peace that confirmed their right to self-government.

But not necessarily their independence.

A theorist might well explain the undoubted phenomenon of rich, neutral, comparatively classless Switzerland in terms of two features of that country's history.

Switzerland until the 19th century had no central government completely in charge of its external affairs and owing no allegiance to an outside power.

And the long struggle against the Austrians eventually destroyed almost completely those families who aped the lives of the French, German and Italian nobility, families who were allied physically and spiritually to the overlords of Austria, Burgundy and Savoy. So that afterwards there was no aristocracy in Switzerland, whose eventual complete freedom had been won by a peasants' revolt. In any case aristocracy remained at heart a dirty word; and when the burghers of Zurich, Basle and Berne became millionaires they took care to remain simple folk on the outside, as they remain to this day.

In March 1474 another peace treaty with Austria was signed. The Empire recognized the Confederate territories as such. *But* the Confederates, by their very act of signing, continued to recognize the Empire. It was no longer to interfere with their internal affairs, or to tax them, but it was still the dominating power of the world. It bore the same relation to little Switzerland as the modern super powers bear to their neighbors. It had the money and the bombs.

Trying to be diplomatically clever and to offset the Imperial power, some politicians of the Confederates temporarily allied their loosely-knit states to the France of Louis XI. Part of the bargain was an annual supply of soldiers, the first mercenaries, who spread to many lands and at least once, as in the Milanese wars, had to fight against each other. (But probably the wise old men round the wine tables in the cantons thought that it was better for the self-confident young men to do their fighting abroad than at home.)

But almost immediately the crack of the whip came again. Representatives of the Emperor conferred with representatives of the Confederation and suggested that the Swiss should combine with them in a punitive war against Charles the Bold of Burgundy. It paid the Confederates to fall in with this plan. Charles was a dangerous wild animal, always prowling around the frontiers of the Confederation; and, as the last great flareup of the Burgundian power, might well have conquered the existing world if not stopped at this point.

It was not for nothing that he was called Charles le Téméraire, because the Burgundian was evidently among those who still tended to underrate the military quality of Alpine peasants. He advanced with a considerable army into the country and got as far as Grandson on the southwestern reedy shores of Lake Neuchâtel before the Confederation deemed that the moment was ripe for a decisive engagement. Burgundians and Swiss clashed head on, and the Burgundians, on March 2, 1476, were so completely routed that Charles had to run for his life and leave all his treasure and artillery behind.

It was a great victory but not decisive. Charles ran but regrouped and must have held the pursuing Swiss at bay, because on June 22 he had an effective army again, reinforced from Burgundy, and was able to offer battle once more near Morat or Murten by the open lake of that name. The Swiss won hands down and had so many Burgundian bodies to dispose of afterwards that eventually an ossuary was built to contain the bones.

Charles made his final escape and had a few more months of boldness before the final battle of Nancy where he was killed. The Imperial forces were responsible but a strong force of Swiss, fighting under Duke Renatus of Lorraine, contributed to the elimination of what had hitherto been Europe's third dangerous power.

There was a short period now when the Swiss went to war on their own. It was the only occasion in their history when they were so un-Swiss.

The Milanese had not liked the comparatively peaceful penetration of the men of Uri into the Leventina part of the Ticino. They had particularly disliked the overwhelming little victories won by the Swiss when there had been occasional armed clashes. They could see that if this sort of thing was allowed to go on then eventually the Swiss might penetrate into Lombardy itself. So they sent 10,000 armed men (with a stiffening of Swiss mercenaries) up the mountain valley to encounter and eliminate the interlopers.

The encounter took place on December 28, 1473, at Giornico, a few miles up the winding road and river from Bellinzola. The 10,000 men briefly fought just 600 mingled Swiss and local men and were routed.

Thereafter the Confederates lost their heads. They supported the men of Uri strongly and began methodically to conquer district after district south of Bellinzona. In the next 25 years even the Pope became worried. The belligerent Swiss came down as far as Pavia, and Novara of the plain. Their penetration southwards was enthusiastically aided by men of the remote Grisons, who had always been at odds with their fellow mountaineers of the Tyrol.

It all came to an end in 1515 with the battle of Marignano. The Swiss were bady defeated for the first time (if the clash with the Armagnacs at St. Jakob in 1444 be regarded as a minor engagement) and, not only was the legend of their invincibility destroyed, but their wise men were confirmed in their opinion that a small confederation of mountaineers could not afford to be drawn out of their fastnesses into foreign adventures.

It was, and probably still is with the Swiss as outstandingly it was with the British in many of their overseas adventures and with the Americans in Vietnam. There comes a point when military lines of communication are stretched too far and even the bravest, most powerful armies are weakened fatally by sheer distance from home bases.

Add to that the fact that Switzerland is one of the most beautiful countries in the world. Whoever lives there, even to this day, is rarely happy when abroad and deprived of panoramas, the pretty vistas, the

Ferdinand Hodler, one of Switzerland's most characteristic painters, thus depicted part of the battle of Marignano (after which the Swiss resolutely turned away from foreign wars of aggression).

companionship in peasant inns, the sound of cow bells, the peerless snow in winter beneath the deep blue skies, and, in spring, the flowers everywhere.

Similarly the Russians suffer unbearable homesickness when away from their frozen winters, illimitable forests, and thousands of miles of sad, unique plains. Everywhere else is so completely foreign and far away.

To conquer foreign lands and to occupy them lengthily it is necessary to be driven to it. The most dangerous peoples are those who issue forth in a spirit of dissatisfaction with their own backyard.

So the end of the Milanese Wars in 1515 was also the end of Swiss external belligerence. The Confederates moved towards the policy of armed neutrality that gradually became the leading Swiss contribution to the philosophy of international affairs.

Meanwhile there had been the Swabian War of 1499. Once again Vienna had shouted its Imperial orders. The Swiss Confederation might have been recognized as "independent," but the Imperial Chamber of Justice was still the ultimate legal authority in that part of

Saas-Fee, a typical Alpine resort of the Valais.

Europe. Certain taxes had still to be paid. Pressure had been exerted particularly on regions near Austria such as the Grisons, not then part of the Confederation, which joined in, helped to defeat the Swabian League, and secured many Imperial concessions by the Peace of Basle.

After Marignano the Confederates decided there must be no more foreign wars; and to complete their stern decision, the product of victories but also of defeat, they signed in 1516 a pact of "perpetual peace" with France.

The legend is that Switzerland thereafter turned the sword into the ploughshare and became the first nation in history successfully to disengage itself from the follies of war.

What actually happened was that the martial energies of the Swiss turned inward and the 16th century was largely devoted to often quite bloody internecine conflicts. In 1519 a secular priest named Ulrich Zwingli began to preach the doctrine of the Reformation at Zurich. What he said about the necessity of throwing off the religious domination of Rome appealed to Schaffhausen, St. Gall, Basle, Berne and the Grisons, but was rejected by the four forest cantons as well as by Zug, Fribourg, Solothurn and the Valais. (Note that Geneva did not come directly into this conflict as it did not form part of the Confederation.)

In 1529 the cantons that wanted the Reformation engaged in what is known as the First Kappel War against the staunchly Catholic cantons as above and they won. The resulting peace treaty more or less said that the Confederation should be Protestant.

Two years later the fighting broke out again in the Second Kappel War. At Kappel on October 11, 1531, Zwingli was killed at the head of his belligerent congregation and one more resulting peace treaty granted each town of Switzerland the right to choose its own faith. It was of course a victory for the Roman Catholics but also for commonsense; and Switzerland's comparative freedom from intolerance ever since may be derived from that otherwise tragic moment when the high-minded preacher from Zurich was struck down mortally as he strove against the centuries-old domination of papal Rome.

Curiously enough the Swiss Guard of the Pope had, only four years before, died almost to a man in defense of their master when Imperial forces had attacked and sacked the Holy City.

During 1526–1536 the strong, warlike families of Berne marched across the green farmlands and down to the smiling terraces around Lake Léman. The country of the Vaud, as it was then known, was partly ruled by aristocratic representatives of the House of Savoy and partly by sword-bearing bishops. Both had been seduced by the climate and by the length of their rich suzerainty, and they soon fell or ran before Nägeli and his stern burgher-knights. The Vaud became a Bernese colony and remained so until Napoleon came.

Nägeli and his tough men at the same time helped Geneva finally to rid itself of the martial and religious domination of the neighboring Savoyards, a task that was suddenly made easier by the preachings of Calvin. This preaching inspired the townsfolk to fight for their religious independence and their mercantile freedom, an irresistible duality of motive as always. Berne thereby consolidated its conquest of the Vaud but was quite unable to digest Geneva itself, as it had doubtless hoped, with the result that even to this day the Vaud and Geneva, forming parts of the same national whole, are sometimes almost like foreign neighbors to each other.

Yet as Berne and Geneva were confirmed permanently as distinct, self-governing states by the 16th-century religious wars, so they laid the firm foundation then of what has proved to be a perpetual alliance against the real strangers. This was actually put down on paper between 1584 and 1586, when Geneva, Berne and also Zurich resolved "perpetually" to stand together against the machinations of the Roman Catholics, who, at the Council of Trent, had developed the notion of a Counter Reformation, with positive steps against recalcitrants to be taken by such resolute representatives of the old order as Cardinal Borromée. The most serious result in Switzerland was the "Escalade" of December 21, 1602. The forces of Savoy attacked Geneva and were finally repulsed.

When the Thirty Years War broke out (1618) as an initial result of the inevitable defenestration and declaration of independence in Prague, the Swiss Confederates tried very hard to maintain their new policy of complete neutrality, and would have been successful if the Imperial armies under the Duc de Rohan had not entered the Grisons in order to improve their communications with Italy. The local peasants inevitably fought back, and found an extraordinarily powerful leader in a hitherto mild pastor of one of their village churches, one Jurg Jenatsch. At the head of his rough little army this bookish man harried the colorful Imperial forces and then put them to flight. By 1639 the Grisons had demonstrated to the world that they were masters of their own mountains—and the brilliant Jenatsch had been assassinated. In 1648 the Peace of Westphalia ended the Thirty Years War; and it contained the usual clause, recognizing the independence of the Swiss Confederation.

Till Napoleon came Switzerland had to endure mainly internal rumblings. Small fights took place between Protestant and Catholic villages, and between peasants and the last of the feudal gentry. The Confederation formally signed an alliance with Louis XIV in 1663. In 1685 the Edict of Nantes was revoked and the Huguenots came massively to Switzerland. The principality of Neuchâtel became, in 1707, part of the dominions of the King of Prussia, against which event the Bernese vainly intrigued. In 1715 the Catholic cantons had the temerity to enter into a separate alliance with France; and between 1721 and 1784 there were numerous anti-aristocrat flareups in the countryside. Small local heroes like Major Davel in Lausanne, Pierre Péquignat in Porrentruy, and Samuel Henzi even in Berne represented a deep movement in Switzerland that was soon to become

The postal coach (with passengers as well as mail) speeds through the Val d'Anniviers.

a social cataclysm in France.

Switzerland was one of the first countries both to throw off the Roman Catholic yoke and to break the power of the old feudal order, although these upheavals were not so much philosophical as commonsense reactions against the centuries-old nuisances of the Habsburg Empire and allied Savoy.

What the Confederation still lacked was a central government. The future might have been doubtful indeed for this essentially anarchic collection of city states with their profound religious differences— had it not been for the French Revolution and the emergence of that unifying man, Napoleon Bonaparte.

Paradoxically the first act of the French Revolution saw Swiss soldiers heroically defending the old order, the stand of the Swiss Guard at the Tuileries against the invading rabble. Doubtless the more idealistic and simple-minded of intellectuals in Geneva and Basle applauded for a year or two even the worst excesses of the French assassins. Some of them actually worked secretly with the revolutionaries of Paris to overthrow their own social system.

But when the French general called Bonaparte rudely occupied the Val Tellina in 1797 and incorporated it in a new Cisalpine Republic, going on to rape in turn the Vaud, Solothurn, Fribourg and even *Berne,* there must have been a change of heart.

Or were the excellent Swiss at this period, after so much internal bickering allied to the emasculating policy of external neutrality, no longer capable of standing up against a foreign foe? Where were the men who had fought off invaders so bravely and won independence for their land? Where were the rolling stones from the grim mountain tops upon the dangerous valleys below? Napoleon, save in the Grisons, missed most of that. He was very lucky.

Undoubtedly the Swiss had been emasculated at this period by internal quarrels and by the new intellectualism of their leaders, but the principal reason why they did not stand and fight the French was that they genuinely believed, as did so many people at the end of the 18th century, that the Revolution had brought about a fine, new world order and Napoleon was merely an honest soldier who was dedicated to achieving the triumphant freedom of decent, ordinary people.

What Napoleon did at once was to dissolve the Swiss Confederation and replace it by an Helvetian Republic, centralized and with the latest (French) revolutionary institutions. Also he completely annexed Geneva, the Jura and Mulhouse.

Whereupon the Swiss of the mountain regions began to stir.

It was too late for them to drive the invaders out of Switzerland, but they could make matters difficult for the French occupiers of their own mountain valleys, and they soon did. The Helvetian Republic, prodded on and supplied by France, had to mount several expeditions against the loyalists. In 1803 Napoleon sponsored the Act of Mediation in an effort at once to make Switzerland a viable

Confederation again (nineteen cantons, now to include Aargau, St. Gall, Grisons, Ticino, Thurgau and the Vaud, but excluding the Valais which was to remain permanently French because of the Simplon road which was being constructed, and also excluding Geneva as another wholly French possession). The reorganization was also meant to please the rebellious mountaineers and perhaps bring them into the fold.

Meanwhile some of Napoleon's wars had actually been fought on Swiss soil to the great despoilation of the land, and thousands of young Swiss had been conscripted into the Imperial armies. Eight thousand lost their lives in the retreat from Russia alone. The scene is vividly painted by the German writer Reichard in 1803: "Where are Helvetia's glories?" he asked. "Where the trophies, the pride of courageous ancestors, the well-filled granaries, treasuries, and arsenals? Where the countenances radiant with joy, with proud content and the sense of independence? Where is the flower of her youth? Where are the lasting works of her industry? O, wretched land, trodden underfoot by pride and despicable deeds of violence! O, Switzerland, once happy and prosperous, now desecrated by the atrocities of war, ravaged by discord!"

When Wellington defeated Napoleon there was behind the scenes a rush in Switzerland to pick up the fallen trappings of power; and once again the decent, ordinary folk were not quick enough. They woke up one morning to find that in many places the old families formerly allied to the German Empire, to Rome and to Savoy had taken over local government control.

Then, far away, the Congress of Vienna admittedly recognized Swiss independence and neutrality, but carved away certain former parts of the Confederation, in Savoy and the Ticino. The ancient Jura bishopric of Basle was handed over to Berne, creating a Jura separatist movement which is still a source of trouble. Geneva, the Valais and Neuchâtel became a permanent part of the Confederation, but lands were lost undoubtedly—in return for minor gains such as the creation of strange free trade zones in France around Geneva.

Yet the legacy of the Napoleonic period was not wholly a mixture of temporary physical ruin and a dangerous putting of the clock back towards the domination of the land by castles and cathedrals. There is no doubt that while Napoleon ravaged Europe he also went some way towards unifying it and gave lands as far apart as Sweden and Portugal the benefit of many similar wise laws, structures of local government, and social habits. Not since the Romans had Europe known such an essentially civilizing hand. That it had also been a cruel, destructive hand was ironically incidental.

The German and Italian speech areas of Switzerland today are out-wardly German and Italian but their institutions and habits tend to be French, or at least like those of France based on what the Italian Bonaparte thought was Roman. Roads are important, and strict, all-embracing laws derived from the Roman system. The grape is the source not only of conviviality but also of wisdom. Each able-bodied man bears arms, or at least keeps them at home and knows how to use them. Buildings are heated by pipes from a central source. Sex is quite a different thing from what the strait-laced Americans and British glorify and fear. There is garlic on the breath, and a touching belief that once a matter is inscribed on the tablets it is settled.

And the strong French influence continued. Fifteen years after the battle of Waterloo there was another revolution in Paris, and when they heard about it the Swiss were many of them encouraged to strive against their own forces of "reaction." It was the time everywhere when universal suffrage suddenly seemed to be the certain way to the new Jerusalem. A document called "The Memorial of Kusnacht" was drawn up by a gathering of Swiss "liberal" elements, and it demanded "popular sovereignty by popular representation." Almost simultane-ously the "patriciats" or conservative ruling families were overthrown in Thurgau, Zurich (the day of Uster), St. Gall, Lucerne, Solothurn, Schaffhausen, Aargau and the Vaud. New constitutions were devised and adopted in these cantons which provided for regulated elections based on a more or less popular suffrage. Characteristically the Swiss hedged these around with checks and limitations. Not every adult got the vote, not by a long way, and no women. It was given chiefly to what might be described as "burgesses"—adult men who had either been born in the place or admitted to burgess status after rigorous examination.

In 1831 the brothers Schnell had the courage to challenge *Les Excellencies* of the heartland Berne. They called together a popular assembly at Munsingen outside the city; and the patrician families yielded to a new liberal government.

Very soon many people had second thoughts. It was not a sinister re-emergence of former oppressors so much as a bourgeois and peasant fear of too rapid change allied to the discovery that some of the new men did not know their political job. Zurich recalled their right of center politicians in 1839, and in 1841 Lucerne changed its constitu-tion back to what was already being known as "conservative." There was a lot of trouble in Lucerne. Such a smiling, eye-on-the-main-chance holiday town as this was eventually to become had at that period an atmosphere often of the Parisian barricades, but with right-wing Catholics to the fore. In 1844 Lucerne actually brought the Jesuits back; and the same year a skirmish near the frightful gorge of Trient overturned the "revolutionary" forces in the Valais and allowed the cantonal government to be traditional for a long time afterwards.

Next year there was renewed provocation of Lucerne by a body of what we would now call leftist sympathizers. They marched on the city but were soon sent home; and the chief effect of their militancy was to knit the Catholic cantons together in what became known as the Sonderbund, or Separate League.

Switzerland could now have split into two countries permanently, if it had not been for characteristically stern action by Berne and the military skill of that ingenious man and mathematician Henri Dufour. Berne proposed an entirely new Federal constitution, also the expulsion of the designing Jesuits, and, of course, the suppression of the Sonderbund. Dufour was appointed general of the Federal forces; and in 26 days, without an important engagement, he routed the uncertain army of the Sonderbund under General Salis-Soglio.

That was 1847. Next year representatives of all the cantons gathered in Berne and the new constitution was adopted. Berne became the Federal capital. This more or less established the Switzerland of today. The actual constitution will be examined in another chapter, but in 1848 the principal effort of the politicians was to stop the Protestant-Catholic and Liberal-Conservative bickering permanently by a system of balancing laws that would give the Federal Government certain powers but reserve others to the cantonal governments.

A particular problem at this time was what we know now as the calm city of Neuchâtel with its intent tradition of watch and clock making as the end-all and be-all of life. In 1848 Neuchâtel was still technically a principality. A republican party took over the government that year, but it was an uneasy situation for a long time, until, in 1856, the old order suddenly came out and briefly struck down the defenders of the constitution. The Federalists counterattacked and there was an uneasy moment while Prussia distantly growled and remembered its former powers over the canton. Napoleon III intervened. It was rather like a Kennedy–Khrushchev confrontation in a Cuba of those days. It gave everyone a fright—and it was the end at last of the civil wars.

That did not mean the end of a healthy political strife, but only of the recourse to arms as a means of settling disputes. From 1856 right up to 1870 there were many arguments and reversals of ideological fortune. At Solothurn in 1856 itself a strong movement developed on a proper democratic basis to curb the powers of the liberal-radicals. Between 1861 and 1864 Geneva had to deal with the dictatorial Fazy. Basle—the country canton, not the town—had the brilliant idea in 1864 of the obligatory referendum allied to the right of initiative. In the years up to 1870 the same idea was translated into permanent law by Thurgau, Aargau, Solothurn, Lucerne, Berne and Zurich.

And already the Federal Government at Berne had begun to establish permanently the pattern of the new Switzerland. An important law was that of 1859, which made it illegal for Swiss to fight in foreign armies. This finished the long-dangerous mercenary system. Henri Dunant's aforementioned Red Cross in due course gave Switzerland a means of helping humanely in wars without fighting, a means indeed of allaying an uneasy conscience and of teaching men everywhere that man's inhumanity to man must eventually stop. In 1866 many people wanted the Federal constitution revised so that the central government would have stronger powers on a par with other countries, notably the United States of America. The country rejected these proposals; and similar revision was turned down in 1872; but in 1874 a watered-down version was nationally accepted, and the Federal Government became more of a real national government at last.

During 1870 and 1871 Swiss troops for the first time manned the frontiers in full fighting kit while the Franco-Prussian War raged around the country. It had the delicate task of admitting and interning the 100,000-strong army of the hapless General Bourbaki; and learned much of what modern mobilization meant and how nervous the situation of a neutral Switzerland must always be during a real international conflict.

In 1871 a movement known as *Kulturkampf* brought about the downfall of a liberal government in Lucerne. The same thing occurred four years later in the Tessin. The traditional forces of the right were once again triumphant.

All the same the Papal Nuncio was told politely to leave Switzerland in 1873, and *Kulturkampf* itself was finished as a movement by 1883, at which time most people were really more interested in the second great National Exposition that was being held in Zurich.

The talk in the 1880s was all of alcoholism. The country was becoming really prosperous. The Franco-Prussian War had brought big orders for new industries. Mass production methods and machinery had arrived from America. The word "tourism" had not yet been coined, but increasing numbers of monied British in particular were regularly visiting the country on the heels of pioneer alpinists from Oxford and Cambridge. Everywhere hotels were being built; and it was being found by the Swiss that they had a natural skill for commercial hospitality in all its departments. The money brought by the visitors represented useful invisible exports, so that Switzerland could begin to import more than she physically exported and thus improve both her capital resources and her standard of living. The visitors hogged the local wines and the natives watched them and began to drink too much themselves. This disturbed the strong Puritan element in the population; and thousands of names were written down in 1885 by earnest, worried people on referendum sheets to demand *a law*. The law was passed, regulating the sale of liquor, and was added to in 1887, but the problem remained largely unresolved. In 1908 absinthe was completely banned.

The Ticino knew vicious political conflict in 1890. A majority of the people, or a majority of the politically-conscious people, wanted the ruling Conservatives out but could not achieve the necessary turnover satisfactorily, whereupon the Federal Government intervened and introduced the system of proportional representation (which had already worked quite well in Neuchâtel). The basic trouble was the emergence of a real radical party in the Socialists (founded 1888) and the development of an arrangement between the Liberals and Conservatives to keep these underdogs at bay. Proportional representation seemed to offer a way out of the impasse. It was interesting, but probably the Third National Exposition, at Geneva in 1896, occupied more talking time.

This was, all the same, Switzerland's great era of socialistic experiment. A lifetime before the British Welfare State, and much longer than that before America's first anti-free enterprise rumblings, Switzerland was experimenting really hard with the theory that all social problems could be solved by simple State intervention. Only distant New Zealand, a very similar small, mountainous, but economically favored country which had weaned itself completely from the old aristocratic order, could be compared with the Swiss Confederation as a pioneer pink.

In 1898, for instance, a law was passed to nationalize the five principal railway companies. In 1907 the control of money was invested in a National Bank. In 1912 there was instituted a kind of partial national assurance against sickness and accidents. Innumerable little laws were passed to regulate almost every aspect of human life.

Upon the outbreak of the First World War the Swiss simultaneously put their three-pronged plan into action: Strict neutrality was proclaimed; the Army was mobilized; and Red Cross aid was given to wounded and to sick prisoners of both the Allies and the Central European Powers. And the plan worked. For four agonizing years the Swiss at once lived upon their fat and prayed that the strategy of the conflict would not move in such a way that one or other of the combatants would have to march across the lowlands or obtain control of a main Alpine pass. By good fortune it was unnecessary for the Germans in particular to violate this brave neutrality, and the long moment passed. Already Switzerland was becoming an international safe deposit, and both warring sides had an interest in keeping the little country inviolate as a hedge against defeat. It was also a useful central post office, both for exchange of communications, and for spies. Somerset Maugham in *Ashenden* very faithfully described later the extraordinary life of an Allied agent in this uneasy vacuum at the dead center of the storm.

Undoubtedly Switzerland thanks to her neutrality made immense gains out of that war. She did not lose her best young men, nor did she spend four years flinging expensive metal into other countries. She was able to do various kinds of business with all the combatants; and her fair land, her factories and her *amour propre* were intact at the end so that she could get away to a new start without terrible wounds to impede her.

It was, however, by no means all honey. Since the economy had grown fat before the war on the basis of export-import on an unnatural scale, it was hit really hard by the isolation of the war. Switzerland, being among the least self-sufficient economically of all countries, with few natural resources as yet, had as was said to live the four years on her accumulated fat. Many, many great enterprises, particularly in the departments of tourism and international business, lost too much money and never properly recovered but were replaced afterwards by others, run by different men. Many families of substance had sunk to the lowest social class after that war.

The young men were not lost but on the other hand they were not weeded out by the grim agent of natural selection, and this left the country with many who did not properly belong to the changed, modern world. The same applied to the untouched factories and institutions.

Yet Switzerland did manage that war very well, and continued to make the very best possible of the resulting peace, which, like all peaces, was in many ways an even more unhappy trial for the nations than the actual armed conflict which had bred it. The first Swiss trial occurred in 1918 in the form of a general strike of workers. This was dealt with in what was becoming the characteristic Swiss manner. The police firmly prevented the strikers from going too far, and the police were staunchly backed by the Federal Government. Then that Government partly pacified the strikers by instituting a 48-hour week in all industrial enterprises, and countered the growing strength of the Socialists by introducing proportional representation on a national scale. This brought together the strength of the anti-extremist vote.

Then Switzerland at once reaffirmed its perpetual neutrality and joined the new League of Nations and gave it a splendid home at Geneva. It also nourished the infant International Labour Office, and, later, not only the Locarno Pact of 1925 that was meant to fix permanently the frontiers of Germany, France and Belgium, but also the Kellogg Pact of 1929 (as an international renunciation of the utilization of force in world disputes that was, unfortunately, far beyond its eventual time—and toothless at that).

During the economic crisis of 1922 there were a lot of unemployed in Switzerland, but hard work yanked the country out of that trouble as it did similarly after 1929, although it was necessary to devalue the Swiss franc in 1936, not because of its weakness as such but because the currencies of its trading partners had so gravely depreciated by comparison with the franc that Switzerland was placed at a grave disadvantage in her international business affairs. Nations could not afford to buy from her as their own currencies were so weak.

The Second World War for Switzerland followed almost exactly the pattern of the first. There was in the country at times a strong consensus of opinion which believed that Britain and France would be defeated and that arrangements should be made to deal in due course with triumphant Axis powers. This kind of thought was countered by the entry of the United States of America into the conflict. Switzerland owed her commonsense and inviolate emergence from the Second World War more than anything to that General Henri Guisan who began by encouraging a strategy of national defense based upon the principle of the Alpine Redoubt, with immense installations and stores dug into the high mountains for an indefinite stand there if necessary, and then went on to issue the splendid *Rapport du Rutli*, in which he appealed to his officers to remember their glorious past and be prepared to fight to the end for their country. Guisan was splendidly in the tradition of the great folk heroes of this land. He had exactly the right touch; and it is quite possible that if Hitler had decided to devote a couple of hard fighting months to taking the rich Swiss cities of Zurich, Basle, Berne and Geneva with all the valuable treasure in the banks and useful armament factories around about, and then to seizing one or more of the important Alpine lines of communication with Italy, he would have suffered far more from the adventure than he would have gained. Even in the similar mountainous country of Greece his troops were delayed dangerously. Guisan's Alpine guns and Guisan's resolution would have made the high passes very expensive to traverse, particularly in winter.

As for the great railway tunnels through the Alps, they would have been blown. A Swiss friend of the writer's actually stood when young at the Ticino-side entrance of one of those tunnels with the dynamite handle never far from his hand, always awaiting the telephone and radio instructions from the northern side. "After a few months of that," he said wryly, "I began to realize that if it did become necessary for me to blow the tunnel then it was highly unlikely that my little contingent would emerge safely from the disaster. But it didn't make any difference. It couldn't. Orders were orders."

The Swiss emerged from that war with that wonderful spirit intact, a spirit that makes nations great and that will eventually be all humanity's only hope. Switzerland did not enter the "peace" with the other kind of mentality, the mentality of the decadent peoples which says "We have been betrayed and from now on we think only of ourselves."

Immediately after that war Switzerland at once introduced a system of old age pensions (based actuarially at first on contributions not on needs) and prepared regular Swissair flights between Zurich and New York. She joined UNESCO and the European Organization for Economic Cooperation. She went on to welcome Geneva summitry and to enter into an atomic pact with the United States and to climb Everest second after the British. Her new world status was underlined by transformation of Swiss legations abroad into embassies. She refused votes to women on the national plan but allowed them for cantonal elections in the Vaud and later in other cantons.

Thirty years after the outbreak of the Second World War it could be said of Switzerland that her people had perhaps the highest standard of living and the greatest wealth in the world per head of admittedly small population. Her currency, the Swiss franc, had no world equal for strength. She had great problems, particularly those posed by the enervating effects of prosperity and by importing great numbers of alien Italians of the south and Spaniards to do the dirty hand work that was becoming increasingly repugnant to such a rich people. But even these she was manfully and successfully tackling as they came up. Rigorous military service was maintained to prevent the young men from becoming too soft. There was what amounted almost to a folk movement towards new ski grounds each winter. Every child was equipped with an expensive ski outfit at an early age. Previously the sport had been for rich strangers but by the 1960s it had become the weekend play of the Swiss themselves, and of all the young Swiss, not just an upper class.

And a law was passed which suddenly limited the number of foreign workers who were allowed in the land. Thousands were sent back; and there were affecting scenes; but it was done, and a greater eventual tragedy was averted by this typical firm, Swiss action.

To say more at this juncture would be to usurp the job of tomorrow's writer. An outline of some facts have been given with some interpretations. Much of it is maybe mythology, but for patriots it is Switzerland.

7

THE WORKS

UNIQUENESS IS THE PREROGATIVE OF EVERY ORGANISM, BUT SOME are just that more unique than others. Thus Switzerland has, during the long years already recounted, developed certain ways of life that are worth studying not only because they tend to be different from those of other countries, but also because they might well be emulated elsewhere usefully.

If the human race founders it will be due to failure in the face of certain difficulties, such as the control of the savage animal in man. How can violence best be mastered or diverted into harmless channels? What is the prescription for original sin? How can the liberty of the individual be equated with the safety of society?

There are great nations of huge basic wealth and promise, such as America and Russia. The kind of freedom allowed in the one also permits gangsterism, racial warfare, industrial disputes that cost more than they gain for either side, and could lead to world war with weapons that might destroy all. The kind of suppression of individual liberty in the other cancels out enterprise and hope, while it brings out the human worst in the stern controllers of the land, who must terrorize the people with police and prisons and who must inevitably use eventually the weapons that might destroy all.

The vast population of Chinese follow the compulsive Russian method; and the very strong and ingenious Japanese people deliberately choose to follow the same dangerous path of imperfectly controlled individual freedom as the Americans.

150

Britain, Germany, France and Italy suffer perhaps forever from the deep wounds of their stupid wars. Britain tries to maintain the high standard of living of an Imperial power and at the same time to finance a social revolution. It no longer has the Imperial wealth necessary, and it refuses to do the necessary work to replace that wealth. Germany makes the money but is cut in half by its history and still probably believes that it can eventually fight its way out of its problems. France, although ruined by its wars, remains convinced at heart that there is no country to equal France, and therefore cannot properly cooperate with others for the future. Italy, knee-deep in its own ruins for centuries, allows its wonderful capacity for hard work and good design to be emasculated by an equal division of its people into those who pray to Catholic idols and those who pray to Communist idols.

There is obviously no hope for any of them unless they change their ways; and this extends to the satellite countries such as those of the former British Dominions and Colonies, those of Eastern Europe, those of South America and the so-called Afro-Asian bloc. These satellites variously follow the larger nations that give them the most money. With a few exceptions they tend to favor military strength and jungle ethics as the only viable policies in an imperfect world.

Meanwhile intelligent young people discuss how those ways can be changed, and many of them see no hope save in what virtually amounts to nihilism. By destroying all existing institutions and returning to the beginning, they vaguely feel, it might be possible eventually to build up something completely different and better. This has the merit of rather good fun while it lasts. Destruction is one of the more pleasant occupational diseases of childhood. Also it is a method of lunatic despair.

How much better to study hard, to make analyses of what went wrong in the past and of what works well in the present, and to seek to change institutions and social habits according to the results of that survey!

This book has been written with the object of demonstrating what Switzerland can offer to such a student and reformer in terms of better social, political and economic methods—and what has been said about its scenery and arts is but the backdrop to that larger drama.

A little country consisting largely of fearsome mountains stands neatly at the crossroads of Europe. It has always benefitted from the east–west and north–south traffic that must pass its way. It has always been able to take toll of that traffic, and also, like a man sitting in a small office, stretch out a hand in any direction and do business.

At the same time the nature of the country has forced the Swiss to work rather harder than many other peoples. There is no easy digging of lush soil here. Vast mineral deposits do not make mushroom fortunes. A soft, warm climate does not allow men to laze in the sun and occasionally feed themselves with tropical fruits.

Then, that desire to be complete masters of their own land has always been strongly imbedded in the Swiss character. The people, thanks to their physical toughening from the hard environment, do not make easy slaves.

In order to make a good living out of a poor land and to maintain the utmost of personal freedom demanded by their temperament, the Swiss have evolved by a long process of trial and error certain methods that might well give hints to those who are so disastrously floundering elsewhere.

Firstly and foremostly they have taken a realistic view of their natural resources and opportunities and have not made the mistake of trying to achieve what is outside their class. They have limited ambition to the possible. After two thousand years of hard work over half the productive land is still covered by grass. Only a very small percentage of the land is allowed to grow grain. The grass is turned chiefly into milk through the agency of carefully-bred cattle. Even the beef is young and milky. The great cheeses of Switzerland evolved through the centuries as the most practical way of getting an all-round food from a peculiar land. In the 19th century it was realized that a valuable export industry could be developed not only in this cheese but also in condensed milk and chocolate. The little Nestlé came down from Glion above Montreux to start a small factory in Vevey that became one of the world's largest corporations, and his methods were swiftly followed by many others such as Tobler, Lindt, Sechaud, Cailler.

Nestlé extended into canning and frozen foods, then rationalized ultimately into what amounts to a financial holding company. Wise Swiss in modern boardrooms had observed that the days of mere chocolate making were over and that Switzerland's future might lie more in clever financial control than in manufacturing for glutted markets.

The vine was always a favorite cultivated plant in the suitable areas of the Valais, Vaud, Ticino, Neuchâtel and the Rhine valley, but as soon as it was discovered that Swiss wines were not good travellers the Swiss relegated viticulture to a comparatively low place in the national product. They did not, and they never will, allow sentiment to interfere with economic reason. That is one of their success secrets, and it is one that could be more widely shared. Half of Britain in the 20th century, for example, was trying to make a livelihood out of producing what it was no longer meant to produce.

Two favorite occupations of the Swiss women in the old days were weaving and embroidery. Out of that came important industries of the eastern part of the land in particular, at the beginning of the 19th century when modern machine methods could gradually be adapted to the ancient skills. Switzerland developed textile mills that could produce some of the finest cotton piece goods in the world; and the Schiffli embroidering machine for some time gave St. Gall a unique industry. But as soon as the taste for embroidery declined, and King Cotton was dethroned by the mixture of Asiatic competition and the invention of artificial fibers, then the Swiss switched. They turned their limited resources and energies to what would continue to pay— the new textiles, and particularly·artificial silks.

They were similarly swift to observe that the heavy industries of the 19th century were to be superseded economically by lighter fabrications of new metals and synthetic plastics, and that the motive force was to be electricity. For the first time in all their history they could see the possibility of making some practical use of their hitherto inconvenient melting snows and grey rocks. These might actually be transformed by new techniques into valuable natural resources. The pioneer hydoelectric works of the world were thus developed in Switzerland and the first really clean, comparatively noiseless factories. Railways were electrified far in advance of those in most other nations. Aluminum was soon recognized to be the basic modern metal.

"It is not remarkable," said a Swiss, almost in apology for these developments. "We are a miniature country with no real wealth save that in our native endeavors. It was necessary for us to keep in the forefront of technological progress."

He did not add, in his modesty, that Switzerland was not the only country in the world with poor natural resources but had been one of the few to do something about it. Others, he could have added, had been content to be regarded as undeveloped nations and to leave their development to the charity of countries such as his own which had not only worked hard but also used their brains and worked in the right way.

One of the few traditional Swiss industries which has not been

Within the Clock Museum at La Chaux-de-Fonds.

basically modified or bypassed to keep in step with the times is the watch-making of La Chaux-de-Fonds, Bienne, Neuchâtel and Geneva. But the machine tools used and the type of movements and outward styles offered have been constantly changed.

Indeed the outstanding industrial difference between Switzerland and many other old industrial countries is that Switzerland keeps at all costs up-to-date. This takes money and courage. The Swiss have a heritage of courage, and they have usually had the money also, thanks to hard saving and wise tax laws.

Every true Swiss knows, thanks to an imbedded folk memory of thousands of hard winters, that it is necessary to put aside part of the product of work for use in an emergency and also for the purpose of rebuilding houses and industrial plants. Thanks to this trait the country developed gradually the world's most efficient and modern banking system, together with a currency that could be trusted more than most.

Maybe the engineering, especially the machine tool works of Zurich, Winterthur, Baden, Geneva and other places were not deliberately developed for military purposes, but they did develop in such a way that Switzerland would derive great sustenance from them if engaged in war. Neutrality is a word completely without teeth in a real emergency. It can be proclaimed to the high heavens and ratified by a whole library of international treaties, but when a determined aggressor wants to pass that way he will take no account of words—only of men and guns. And if he did indeed respect Switzerland's "neutrality" he would also be respecting the engineering industries of Zurich, Winterthur, Baden, Geneva and other places. These have been maintained in the forefront of technological progress. Some of them produce what many experts regard as the best guns in the world, also excellent tanks and other warlike vehicles. The would-be aggressor considers that Switzerland not only maintains a citizen army of considerable strength but also possesses factories that can make superb weapons for that force.

Doll automaton in the Museum at Neuchatel.

He is inclined to say: "Perhaps we had better respect that 'neutrality' after all."

The modern growth of the chemical, particularly the pharmaceutical industries of Basle is very remarkable. The efficiency and cleanliness of the Swiss has here been allied to a tradition of chemical healing that dates back to Paracelsus and beyond. In the second half of the 20th century these industries rapidly became among the most important in the world, and were suddenly responsible for saving more lives and allaying more suffering than all the bleatings of the philosophers. And it gradually transpired during this time that some of the raw materials for the chemists could be found in the hitherto useless mountain regions of Switzerland itself. This pointed the way to what may eventually be a major breakthrough.

Switzerland's economic difficulty has always been the necessity of importing foodstuffs and raw materials. More than half the industrial output of the country has had to be exported to pay for those, and even that has not been enough; a debit balance on this visible account has had to be met by earnings from the tourist trade, international banking and insurance, and investments abroad. It has been remarkable always that the country in spite of this has, unlike similar others, kept out of debt and consistently paid its way, accumulating rich gold and other monetary reserves that have usually backed the nation's note issue by nearer 150 than 100 percent.

All the same, it has been a continual worry and strain, which would be immensely relieved if the scientists could find chemical combinations in the mountains that would replace imported raw materials and even foodstuffs. What the great Basle pharmaceutical manufacturers such as Ciba-Geigy and Roche have been doing might well lead to this eventually.

Probably an immediate cause of war is often balance of payments difficulties. It is not the root cause (that proceeds from the very nature of man) but pleasure-loving countries that cannot afford any longer to import their pleasures have been apt throughout history to fight their way out. Undoubtedly the end of the great stupid export-import race would also be the end of many international stresses and strains; and if Switzerland could eventually become self-sufficient thanks to the ingenuity of her chemists, then she would have one of the greatest of all lessons to teach the world.

A more immediate lesson is taught by the Swiss national money and tax systems, that, as has been said, have made possible the almost unequalled growth (per head of population) and continual modernization of industry.

It is impossible to equip factories without money. If this money is to be obtained from abroad then much of the profit from those factories will eventually be lost. If the money is to be raised at home then there must be inducements for the people to save it. The tax system of Switzerland provides one such inducement. It has been cleverly devised so that, on the whole, it favors the man who spends less. The tradition goes back to the ancient sumptuary laws of Europe and to the rapacious tax gatherers of the Habsburgs and Bourbons who jumped upon a man as soon as he made a display of wealth. And the Swiss system remembers how the peasants were often willing to lose their lives rather that pay away the product of a year's hard work in the high mountains to cruel Austrian bailiffs. To this day it is not easy to increase or put over new taxes in Switzerland. In a too-typical nation of the western world such as Britain there can be Budgets often more than once a year in a crazy attempt to stop inflation by heavier taxation, but the people do not complain of those taxes as such. The traders put up prices to equal the new taxation and the people strike for and obtain higher wages to pay the increased prices. The inflation continues and no one is better off. Indeed the country as a whole is worse off, because its higher-priced goods cease to be competitive in export markets. The ordinary folk of Switzerland do not necessarily realize this. They just remember how their forefathers suffered; and they do not like taxes. Of course it is necessary for the Government and the cantons and the communes to have money, but they are never going to get it easily if the Swiss people have any say in the matter. Thanks to the peculiar electoral system they do have such a say, one that can hold up new tax proposals almost indefinitely; and it so happens that this say is exercised chiefly by the most responsible members of the community. According to the constitution the 25 Cantons and half-Cantons each have their own tax laws, and cantonal taxes, for example, play a larger part in Switzerland than the taxes of the individual states in America.

Because the politicians know that the people actively resist new taxation proposals they tend to confine these increasingly to what the economists call indirect levies. The result is that the average Swiss probably has less deducted from his pay packet than most other peoples. Thanks to the indirect levies, on sale of goods and on capital, he pays quite a lot in the long run, but he does not immediately feel it so much as those peoples who are subjected to heavy income tax and death or succession duties. And if he restricts his spending and does not flaunt his worldly possessions then he can put aside a substantial surplus each year. The emphasis of this is to make him work hard and not be extravagant with the product, much of which he invests in the least conspicuous of ways, such as savings deposits, the interest on which is not declared by the banks for taxation below a certain annual sum, and such as tax-free Swiss franc foreign bonds (that tend to be oversubscribed immediately, even though the interest rates are comparatively low).

Three other features of the Swiss taxation system must be carefully noted by foreigners who want to learn from this clever little country. Laws against tax evasion are severe, but the evader is not subject to the same severity of *criminal* law as elsewhere, while the institution of the tax amnesty gives him a chance at regular intervals to put his affairs in order if his evasion has indeed become criminal.

Then the laws relating to death duties on estates are so devised that families can continue to build up and prosper even after a series of leading deaths. This is achieved by the simple method of levying duties on deceased estates according to the degree of relationship of the successors. These vary from canton to canton, but run something like this: if the estate of a father passes to his children they may have to pay only a very small percentage in succession duty, maybe as little as two or three percent; but, if the estate passes to strangers then they may have to pay a comparatively high percentage, perhaps as much as 25 percent. Wives and mothers tend to be treated rather harshly in this scale of relationship, according to the canton in which they live. Overall, however, no one in Switzerland pays anything like the taxes that have crippled hard-working families in America or completely destroyed a social class in Britain.

Humble people in Switzerland can be seen to enjoy the fruits of parental frugality; and they continue the good work themselves for the sake of their children.

This makes for an extraordinary contentment and stability in the country, although admittedly it can be tough on those who do not work hard and prefer having a good time now, or those who choose the wrong parents.

The third feature of the Swiss tax system that is highly important to the economy of the country as a whole, and that might well be emulated more frequently elsewhere, is the special concession to foreign residents and corporations.

This again varies from canton to canton. In one canton, Zug, and in the Principality of Liechtenstein (which partly shelters under the Swiss umbrella), the nice fiscal accommodation of strangers is a leading industry of the land.

Anyway the grant of highly favorable tax conditions not only induces wealthy people to bring their fortunes and their spending power to such cantons as the Vaud, which do not have strong native industries and require money of that kind during the off-seasons for normal tourists. It has also had the powerful effect of inducing some of the greatest corporations in the world to transfer their head offices for fiscal purposes to Switzerland—and inevitably of persuading some to do more than that. Geneva particularly has benefitted from the system. A considerable number of American corporations conduct all their European business from Geneva, thanks to, in that order, the favorable tax system, the central position of the city within Europe, and the availability there of highly efficient personnel and services.

These sensible tax laws of Switzerland have, moreover, encouraged the growth of an almost unique banking system. The native Swiss have been persuaded by comparatively low taxation to save their surplus money and to employ the services of originally homespun banks to invest it sensibly. Foreign persons and corporations coming to the tax havens have similarly required guidance and fiduciary services, so that the Swiss banks have grown enormously and have had the money to develop some very remarkable techniques, all based on low interest rates and on charging fairly and on a percentage basis for each separate service. Minimal interest is actually paid on current accounts; this is offset against charges at the end of each half year; and as a result the average current account costs little or nothing to the client. Similar accounts at many American and all British banks would cost the client at least $100 or anything between £25 and £50 a year.

Side by side with this wise banking the Post Office runs a form of the giro system that enables the public to pay all its monthly bills simply, swiftly over the counter, and without any cost whatsoever. The Swiss pay their bills with cash in this way. They queue each month in the Post Offices religiously and to an observer from abroad who has experienced difficulty with the collection of debts, it is a sufficiently affecting sight.

The Swiss pay their bills because the system is easy and inexpensive, and because they wisely dislike being in debt, and because strict methods and laws make it difficult and expensive for them to owe much money for long. Bills arrive with the legend "Delay of payment 10 (or even five) days," and perhaps with additional threat of a small sum to be added to the bill if unpaid after that time. It is a well-known fact that with Swiss bills you cannot win. You always have to pay them and do pay them and they are very nearly always correct in their figuring. It is best to settle them at once without giving overmuch thought to the matter.

The system is very modern and streamlined in its technique but exceptionally old-fashioned in its spirit. All the emphasis is on care before making a purchase and then, when the purchase is made, paying for it as swiftly as possible. The reward is financial stability and often a pile of trading stamps which can eventually be exchanged for a set of fish knives, unless a small, immediate cash discount is preferred.

Another effect is that neither the buy now and pay later in installments, nor the credit card systems have ever taken strong root in Switzerland. The hire purchase debt per head of population is substantially lower than that of most other western nations. Switzerland as a whole saves the money first and then buys. Her economic philosophy of life thus tends to be somewhat at variance with that of, especially, Britain and America and their hangers-on.

Whereas economic progress in most countries is always severely limited by the amount of credit available, and it has been necessary to invent highly dangerous systems of credit-creation that inevitably burst sooner or later like the bubbles which they are, in Switzerland the frugality of the people and the tax system have always made sufficient real money available *in advance* for all developments. An impecunious Briton or debt-heavy American gaze goggle-eyed in Switzerland at new blocks of expensive flats that remain half empty for several years, till gradually they are filled with purchasers at the right price. The Swiss can afford to keep their investment thus tied up. They literally have so much money, the kind of money other western countries could have had if they had similarly worked hard and saved hard.

This has on the whole been the Swiss rule for more than 100 years now, save for periods of great privation during the world wars; and, judging by the appearance of the great solid houses in towns like Berne and Zurich and Basle, the country has always been financially strong save during those war periods. It is possible that it will remain so indefinitely. On the whole countries do not change basically with the years, even though they may pass through great convulsions. Russia will always be Russia. Australia will always be Australia. There is a basic character, derived from the first settling families and the effect on their descendants of the peculiar environment and climate.

With each generation the older Swiss say "it is nearly over. We have had the best of it." But strangely the young people grow into hard-headed canny Swiss and the best becomes even better each generation.

Many considered there was great danger to the Swiss way of life in the arrival of hundreds of thousands of Italian and Spanish workers to relieve the labor shortage of the 1960s. Very soon the numbers of such immigrants were strictly limited by law and thousands were sent back home. But wiser observers had already been able to see that the Italians and Spaniards, far from bringing alien cultures into the country, had swiftly become even more Swiss than the Swiss. The mythology of a country, and its basic habits of life, are so extremely strong that they endure through wars, revolutions, vast immigrations of aliens. Ideas are always more important than men, and are even more enduring and irrepressible than viruses and bacteria. So far no antibiotic has been discovered that can kill a philosophy of life.

The Swiss philosophy can be studied in certain of its political products, notably the constitutional system of the country and the method of dealing with labor disputes. Probably the essential stability of Switzerland owes much to these dry-as-dust but eminently practical systems.

The outstanding feature of the constitution is the way it balances different forces in the state, and, more or less by setting them off against each other, preserves a state of affairs in which there can be no excess.

The English essayist Joseph Addison wrote in the 18th century: "Were the Swiss animated by zeal or ambition, some or other of their states would immediately break in upon the rest. But as the inhabitants of these countries are naturally of a heavy phlegmatic temper, if any of their leading members have more fire and spirit than comes to their share, it is quickly tempered by the coldness and moderation of the rest who sit at the helm with them."

That is one explanation, and it has a certain validity, but there are other countries, like Britain, where the inhabitants are similarly half-phlegmatic and half fiery but where the stresses of political life are far from balanced against each other: where politics is continually a class or race war, and where handfuls of fools are allowed, by the system, to ruin the endeavors of all.

Let us glance briefly at the actual constitution of Switzerland, as codified chiefly in 1848 and 1874.

It sets up a federal state of 22 sovereign cantons, sovereign in that they were self-governing and exercised all rights save those transferred in the constitution to the central government, known as the government of the Confederation. The cantons elect their assemblies and pass their own laws and conduct their own affairs like independent countries, even some little cantons that have less population than comparatively unknown American cities—save for those items of business that are expressly reserved in the constitution to the central government of the Confederation. And such items are notably internal and external security, diplomatic relations with other powers, the control of money, the railways, the post office, forestry, hunting and fishing, hydroelectricity, the douane or Customs, and non-local matters of justice.

This is obviously a method of giving local people the illusion of self-government but reserving real power in central hands, and yet, it is not quite that. Further provisions in the constitution, those that control parliamentary representation and the passing of laws, actually make it very difficult for the central legislators to interfere with everyday life in individual cantons without express local consent.

Firstly supreme legislative power is vested in a Federal Assembly or central parliament that is composed partly of a National Council which is elected by the whole nation, and partly of the Council of States which is elected by the individual cantons. This Federal Assembly passes the laws; and the laws are administered by a Federal Council, the cabinet or true government, seven people from the Federal Assembly who are elected for four years and who in their turn elect the President of the Confederation from among their numbers, a President who holds office for one year only.

A semi-dictator would find it practically impossible to impose new laws and regimes suddenly on the Swiss. He would be impeded by the multiplicity of elected bodies whose majority vote he would have to obtain; and then he would finally come up against the twin obstructions of the Referendum and the Right of Initiative. These last are Switzerland's most important contributions to the science of modern government.

The law of the Referendum states that if 30,000 active citizens or at least eight cantons sign a valid request then the central government must ask for a popular vote relating to Federal laws or decisions.

The Right of Initiative states that if the signatures of 50,000 electors are appended to the request then a partial or total modification of the Constitution can be demanded and must, after certain discussions and safeguards, be effected.

The executive politicians of Switzerland have always feared these constitutional checks and done their best to avoid provocation of the electorate to such an extent that the checks may be invoked.

It is a highly complicated modern system, as if devised by the best brains among political scientists, but actually goes back in its essentials to the earliest days of Switzerland and to what is one of the purest systems of democracy the world has ever known. The peasants acquired a spirit of sturdy independence by clambering about on mountainsides and then having to deal with armored men who came to collect taxes for Emperors. They met on the Rütli meadow in 1291 and drew up their Perpetual Pact. They went on meeting, and so arranged their national constitution eventually that nothing could be decided unless it was thoroughly discussed and agreed upon at grass-root level.

This applies not only to local and national politics but also to all kinds of affairs, commercial, social and of the family. A meeting is arranged around a café table. Several demi-litre carafes of white wine are drunk and the talk may continue for an hour or two. At the end a decision is reached which has majority agreement.

Is this wholly democratic in that it invites and allows the participation of every person in the community? No, it is not. It is *selective* democracy, the only kind of democracy that has yet been found to work lastingly and satisfactorily. The all-important voting right is accorded in local body, cantonal and federal elections only to male adults either born in the commune or canton, or accepted as voting burgesses after careful examination. It is possible to live and pay taxes in Switzerland for years without any kind of civic or voting rights whatsoever. The only crack in this severe system recently has been the gradual accord of the franchise to women in certain cantons and local districts, but, of course, only women who are responsible burgesses of the district.*

The unique nature of Swiss democracy is thus that it has been kept, right back to the beginning, in the hands of the real Swiss. Immigrants are gradually admitted to this inner governing elite, but only after years have passed and the newcomers have almost become Swiss themselves.

With such a constitution it might be thought that legislation would sometimes be nearly impossible. Often it is. Certain fundamental issues of modern life have had to be shelved in Switzerland because they cannot be dealt with by the too-complicated law-making machine. But this has at times been a great advantage to a country that otherwise might have been emasculated and ruined like others by the combination of industrial disputes and uneconomic welfare schemes.

It is also paradoxically true that no country is so tightly-governed by *petty* laws. Codes have been drawn up and ratified by parliament to control innumerable small features of everyday life, from the letting of apartments to the breeding of dogs. It is true in Switzerland, and

* *On February 7, 1971, a national referendum at last accorded the federal vote to women, by a roughly two to one majority.*

it is a weakness of the way of life there, that when a question comes up for discussion the first remark is, not the justice or equity of the matter, but what is the law relating to it. On the whole this system works well. Most of the laws are sensible. It is not wise to allow young children to operate elevators, and there is a lot to be said for forbidding this by strict regulation. But sometimes reliance upon written rules can be stultifying, out of touch with reality, and by no means an encouragement for the citizen to think hard for himself.

On the other hand the large body of laws and regulations relating to industrial disputes and to the syndicates or trade unions do work extraordinarily well. They are too complicated to be discussed here, and it is probably no use their being copied optimistically by other countries, because, as will be shown in a minute, they spring directly from the Swiss character and way of life.

Basically the relations between employers and workers are controlled by laws that enforce independent arbitration. Such laws do, however, increasingly exist in other countries where industrial disputes multiply each year at fearful cost to the community. It is quite obvious that laws are no good unless respected by litigants. Workers and their trained advisers in other countries often have no intention whatsoever of respecting any laws or conciliation systems that might prevent them from beating the bosses at all costs in the struggle for more money and better hours, conditions and holidays.

If men passionately believed they had an inalienable right to break into each other's houses and steal then all the anti-theft laws and enforcement agencies would be unable to prevent their doing so.

It is not just the system of industrial laws in Switzerland that gives this country a unique national freedom from crippling strikes and lockouts. It is the belief of the individual man and woman that it is more sensible for employers and workers to cooperate than to fight to the death. Months, indeed years, of discussion may precede changes in wages and conditions. The discussion can be hot on details. But fundamentally it always ends in a sensible, mutually-helpful settlement.

Moreover, an essentially serious people have no time for frivolities like disputes over tea breaks or lavatories; and publicity is disliked until a settlement can be announced.

Swiss workers would stare if it were suggested that they paralyze their industry with a national strike because operatives in a remote machine shop had some trivial grievance. And the responsible newspapers of the land would refuse to make front page copy of such a disaster if, by a miracle, it did occur. The newspapers, like a majority of the Swiss individually, are still quite patriotic.

To be patriotic means to love one's country. It is a sentiment that has been almost destroyed in our time elsewhere by nationalistic wars and their aftermaths, and by the sneerings of those intellectuals who have a deep fear of being forced to sacrifice their unlovely lives in order to maintain the liberties of their native land. Nothing, repeat nothing, can be done with a populace that has lost the art of patriotism. Ask men in the decadent countries of this world why they act so and they reply "Why should we act otherwise? Who will thank us if we sacrifice ourselves? What did it avail my stupid old father?"

The Swiss have never been like that, not even during the hundreds of years of their history when their country was continually torn by wars. They have always had that peculiar mountaineer's brand of patriotism that proceeds from a mixture of intense pride in the beauty of the place and of the knowledge that they must stand together and help each other in an emergency or there is no hope for them. It is also a kind of patriotism that produces lovely, sad songs.

Put in another way, both employers and workers in Switzerland have always realized, to quote the handout of a leading bank, "that their common interests are more important than their differences, and thus, for decades, social peace has reigned, making it possible to raise the standard of living of the entire population successively to a level well above average."

At the time of the writing of this book there is virtually no unemployment in Switzerland, and all other economic graphs climb fantastic mountains of prosperity. Both exports and imports have steadily risen for a decade; and, while wages have gone up in the same way, both consumer and wholesale prices have lagged a little behind, giving the people a better life all the time.

And although there are many factors responsible for this felicity the basic one is indeed the sensible and above all the patriotic attitude of the Swiss people towards their communal responsibilities.

One evening the writer rushed into a supermarket just as it was closing. In the butchery department the men had just finished putting the meat away and washing down the immaculate counters. "Is it too late to get a couple of chops?"

"Why not?"

The young butcher grinned pleasantly as he opened the refrigerator and took out a best-end of mutton, and began to cut it up.

"You are very helpful, and I am extremely sorry to put you to this trouble at such a late hour."

"No trouble at all."

"Where I come from I'm afraid I wouldn't get that sort of response."

"Why ever not? It's business, and that's what we're here for. If the firm does well then so do we. If we all do well then Switzerland does well. No problem at all."

Just like a theorem demonstrated by Euclid.

8

ART

THOSE WHO LOVE SWITZERLAND HAVE FREQUENTLY TO COUNTER the accusation that it is a cold, perfect country without a single important contribution to art. Such accusers imply that art should be the major occupation of mankind, and their accusation is meant to condemn Switzerland completely. Holbein, Witz, Füssli and Hodler are forgotten completely, or the remark is made that Holbein was really a German; and even those who know most about the latest are the first to forget that Paul Klee, Charles-Edouard Jeanneret-Gris ("Le Corbusier") and several others such as Giacometti were Swiss. Great writers are artists, and how different the world would be today if it had not been for the Genevan apostle of permissiveness and of the so called rights of man, Rousseau!

The Swiss cultural contribution is, if anything, outstandingly remarkable for a country of its size, lack of great, displayed wealth at the top, and slender population.

Admittedly it is a different kind of contribution from that made possible in other countries by the patronage of kings and aristocrats. It is the sort of art that might be expected from an essentially virile if normally pacific race of mountaineers who have always preferred short haircuts to flowing locks, and to this day speak with the greatest pride of *simplicity* in their lives and surroundings.

There is always a distinction to be drawn in other countries between art at the top and at the bottom. The aristocratic tends to be exotic and the popular to be childishly crude, a product of the state fair and naive mind. In Switzerland there has been throughout the one art, that of the undivided, almost classless people. The qualification "almost" is used deliberately in this case because no society can be entirely without division. Roughly the Swiss are composed of lower simple folk and upper simple folk, not according to their incomes but according to their tastes. A small farmer is extremely musical and collects heraldic window-panes and forces his children to undergo all the rigors of the higher education. Whereas the extremely wealthy owner of a famous factory may live privately like a peasant according to the values scheme of a healthy animal.

The people of Switzerland are proud of their great art galleries, of

Very old houses in the Zurich region are decorated like this.

St. Lucius Shrine of 1252 in the cathedral at Chur or Coire.

their open, modern minds and their effort always to be new and up-to-date in appreciation and in their environment. But fundamentally they are not much different from the paleolithic founders of their essential culture: a race of simple country folk who like first to keep their surroundings neat and clean, and then, when they have time, embellish them a little in a decent but primitive way.

It was thought that the origins of a characteristically Swiss art were to be found in what the Romans, Burgundians, Austrians and Savoyards left behind. It is now known, from discoveries in the Wilkirchli cave, also at Cotencher, and in the Kesslerloch and Schweizerbild, that the high valleys of the Alps were settled long before those moderns, and that the tastes of the people go right back to stone age ancestors who lived high in primitive wooden huts with wide roofs just like those still used by the peasantry of the upper Valais pasturages and those of the remote Grisons.

The Romans and subsequent conquerors of the land left behind overtones of difference, but the true Swiss art has remained fundamentally a peasant craft, uncomplicated, clean. The straightforward portraits of a Holbein, the austere architecture of a Corbusier, the in-

The finest architectural style of the Engadine.

spired infantilism of a Klee are all in that very ancient tradition still.

Because of this strong tradition (which is felt in his bones by every Swiss) there may be traced the further peculiarity that great isolated works of art are rarely to be found. The cultural achievement of the country does not reside in an altarpiece here and a cathedral there but in the general extremely high standard of all artistic and particularly technical endeavor. Switzerland indeed is like the Cotswolds in England where every gatepost is lovingly fashioned and each stone village is a lasting delight.

Right back to Roman times, indeed, this country has correctly considered a work of art to be not necessarily just a studio painting or sculpture but also a wall, a bridge, even a road. The original Roman roads over the St. Bernard, Julier, Septimer and Splügen passes remained for the Swiss as supreme examples not only of technical but also of aesthetic endeavour. And somehow to this day the selfconscious showpieces of churches, castles and great houses, devised cold-bloodedly by professional architects, are less impressive in Switzerland than the whole villages, towns and workaday buildings that were erected by now-forgotten local craftsmen as part of a living, organic process.

When Montaigne wrote in 1580, and Fynes Morison in 1594, that the very farmhouses and stoves, the fountains and humble, arcaded shops of Switzerland were surprisingly beautiful, they were observing what we must now recognize as a unique phenomenon. Goethe wrote in 1775 that Berne was the loveliest town he had ever seen; and any unprejudiced traveller who has visited every country must agree today that none is really so beautiful as Switzerland. Others, like New Zealand and the Americas and Austria and France, have equally fine mountain landscapes but not the perfect domestic architecture, exquisite arrangement of streets and vistas in towns, absolutely unerring taste in decoration, typography, floral embellishment—together with solidity and extreme efficiency of construction. Others like Holland and Belgium and parts of Germany often have equally attractive domestic architecture but in flat, uninteresting surroundings, or, indeed, in an environment of distressing muddle and dark despair.

Among the buildings of Switzerland that have so graciously and properly evolved throughout the ages are the town halls, the granaries, the guild houses, arsenals. These have been built and tended with the same energy and care that in other countries have created the royal palaces and seats of government, because in Switzerland they have each expressed the self-importance and ambition of little, more-or-less-independent states.

Above all the farmhouses have grown as works of art, in many different styles according to local taste (and extending into the so-called towns, which were originally, and still often appear, just collections of lovely farm buildings erected side by side for safety's and efficiency's sakes).

Way back in the 16th century travellers were already noting with considerable surprise that most of the farmhouses in Switzerland had the glazed windows that were elsewhere confined to the seats of the mighty alone, also that they actually had fine wooden floors whereas in France, Germany, England and Italy not only the rural but also a great proportion of the urban population had to make do with beaten earth that was sometimes strewn with filthy rushes.

The regional variety of farm building in Switzerland is again quite unique, especially for such a small country. As has often been pointed out, no other land displays such an extreme multiplicity of regional taste, echoed in the many, many local dialects and styles of costume.

Deep in the heart of the Alps, high up, the architectural style is squat, wooden, varying locally according to the length of the horizontal timbers used. In that ancient town of Schwyz, so near to the beginning of the Confederation, there are superb town houses that represent this primitive style as embellished by subsequent art.

This four-square wooden hut with the necessarily overhanging roof of rough-hewn wooden or stone tiles was influenced in the Grisons by

A farmhouse of the Bernese type in the Emmental.

Italian modes from over the divide until the characteristic rural buildings became high and pink-faced with small, decorative windows, but still the great, snow-resistant roof with the overhang to keep the thaw away from the walls.

Further down northwards, in the areas near Zurich and to the northeast, the mountain refuge with the roof like a broad-brimmed hat was influenced by the Scandinavian habits of Norman predators in Europe, especially the use of lathe and plaster and half-timbering, so that the rural architecture of these parts of Switzerland is rather like a compromise between the chalet and the timbered houses of old London, the west of England, Normandy and parts of Germany.

But each little canton or part-sovereign state has its distinct peculiarities of building. Small Appenzell, for example, has for centuries built its farmhouses with façades consisting entirely of long rows of windows —and the people of the Engadine have always specialised in deeply-recessed windows that are surrounded by charming sgraffiti.

Needless to say the noblest and most imposing style is that of Berne, a sort of composite of the others but with great overhanging and curved dewlaps over the front elevation from the wide roofs which give it a wholly characteristic appearance, especially when the dewlaps are painted yellow and the rest of the timber frontage is varnished brown amid rows of windows and balconies with scarlet geraniums. There are roads from Berne to Lucerne and elsewhere through the Emmental that, in suitable season, traverse villages that have no equal in all the world for splendor of bucolic architecture and for sheer color. All the farm buildings are here clustered under one great roof, and there are side balconies, and brilliant coats-of-arms upon the walls or hanging in the fantastic filigree of ironwork, while the flowers are cultivated in every nook and cranny to provide the lipstick on the lovely, simple face.

Each Saturday afternoon the inhabitants of the villages spend an hour or two at vigorous sweeping of the ground in front of the great houses, so that neither a reproach nor a leaf remains for the douce and blue-serged Sunday.

How narrow, and yet how nice of them, especially for the visitor who likes his holiday to be a change from the untidiness and human squalor of his workaday, northern life!

High up on the Jura between Berne and France what was originally the squat mountain hut of Switzerland becomes a similar structure of ancient stone, whereas in Neuchâtel under that Jura, it is suddenly very modern in appearance, almost a bungalow surmounted by a long roof.

Ancient peasant architecture of the Valais.

The chalet as such is claimed as an original development by the Vaud, where apparently it was first built behind Montreux. Now the original, functional mountain box of wood has become a true cuckoo clock without birds, and might well have been transported originally as a style from the Black Forest in Germany where the cuckoo clock was first evolved. This is a development which is best at its pretty-prettiest, when new or newly painted and beflowered, but apt to be ugly in age like a woman who foolishly clings to the prettiness of youth amid her wrinkles.

In the many great side valleys of the Valais there is a plethora of architectural variation again, sometimes stony and drab, often colorful and Italianate, absolutely paleolithic in old Montana and at high places like Saas Fee, where roofs seem literally to crouch under the impending blows of avalanches: and at Champéry up the secluded Val d'Illiez, suddenly blossoming into perhaps the finest sub-species of all, where great roofs advance to bird-beak or boat-prowed points that recall the Vikings who, by tradition, came curiously to rest, a small tribe of them, in these mountain parts after sharing in the destruction of the glory that was Rome and Cisalpine Gaul.

Round the Geneva end of the lake an architectural curiosity is the development of the gutter and not the gable side as the main elevation. But hereabouts, as in the comparatively modern tourist towns of the littorals, towns like Geneva itself, Lausanne, Montreux, Interlaken, Lucerne, the indigenous style of Swiss building has been overlaid by the predominantly French methods of Mansard and other artists of the chateau-cum-wedding-cake school, interrupted incessantly today, alas, by phallic absurdities that only recall an inevitably lesser Manhattan.

The glories of the true Swiss domestic architecture are matched inside the houses by all the characteristic appurtenances of folk art. Only in England and Holland are the bygones (to use the proper technical term of the antiques merchants) so various, well-made, and beautiful.

The Alpine districts specialize in chip-carving of Celtic and Romanesque provenance mainly. Lower down the great farmhouses have panels and staircases and furniture that testify to the skill of a people who have consistently made the best of the forests that originally surrounded them. The work done in the 17th century particularly advances from crude joinery almost into what the furniture experts call cabinet-making, and branches out into styles that are peculiarly Swiss, multifarious and ranging from the rococo paint of the great cupboards of Appenzell and the Toggenburg to the chaste bare walnut in the French style of Berne. All is embellished with the bold and lovely ceramics that will be described in another chapter, and decorative ironwork, and strong, lovely utensils of copper, brass and pewter.

It is a curious commentary on the Swiss character that the furniture and metalwork are not polished, and that this does not proceed from dirtiness or laziness but from a feeling that a high, lustrous surface might imply dangerous ostentation.

An English couple who came to Switzerland and polished their furniture and were gently reproached for this by their Swiss neighbors had the dangerous idea of similarly endowing their lavatory seats with a

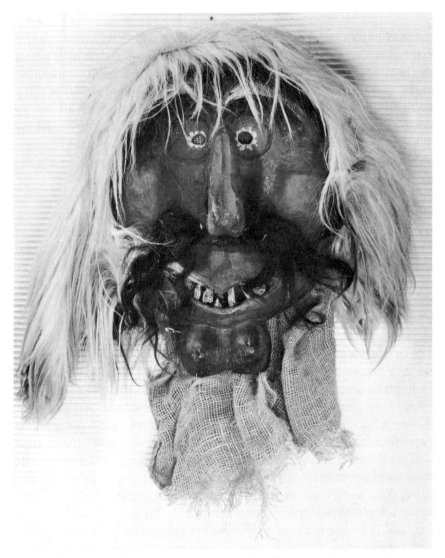

Up in the mountainous Valais they made these masks, once the true, humorous folk art of a region where life was "nasty, brutish and short," now expensively collected by connoisseurs.

bright, waxen patina just for the fun of it, and perhaps that joke went too far.

Two items of the rural interior are notable in this country. One is the heraldic stained-glass windowpane. The art of coloring glass was originally developed to extreme fineness in the Gothic period here. Early specimens at Berne, Wettingen and Konigsfelden are extremely important in the history of art. Then as the country almost chancefully developed without a true aristocracy, so the ordinary people took to heraldry as a means of developing a suppressed but inevitable desire for class distinction. The family was the only important social unit, so it was proclaimed in its importance through the medium of a heraldic device for all, down to the meanest lines of day laborers.

Thus heraldry became in Switzerland universally indulged; and in the 16th century a custom developed of bestowing gifts of the "cabinet pane," a small piece of stained glass showing the coat of arms, flanked by supporters, of the recipients' humble families. White engraved panes were developed in the 18th century. Even today the heraldic panes are proudly displayed, but have also become the subject of valuable and often Transatlantic collections.

Thus the most republican and democratic of nations must pay its inevitable tribute to the desire in man for protocol and precedence, as the Americans and Australians who have proudly banished titles must, nearly all of them, try to claim English or European lords as ancestors.

The other unique Swiss contribution to the domestic interior is the curious, hideous mask of the central cantons and the upper Valais. These are made of painted wood and fabrics and hair, ugly as gargoyles,

A village of typical Engadine architecture.

Beautiful statue of the Virgin from about 1400, at Sion.

and closely resembling the masks worn by witch doctors in Africa and the Pacific. Do they provide one more evidence of the common origin and remarkable wandering of races? Such masks are worn for festivals and kept proudly on walls and chimneypieces. They are so demoniacal in design that an observer must naturally think of some deep preoccupation with deviltry in the soul of Germanic man.

A lovelier product of the essential artist in the native Swiss is the cow-bell, ranged in sizes for use on animals of different ages, and, by some unknown magic of euphony, providing not only a way of tracing his beasts for the herdsman of the mountain pastures, but also a veritable music of the spheres across the flowered valleys and Alps of shining May. There is no sound more likely to evoke a tear, in visitor and exile alike, although this has been known to become a tear of vexation for the kind of tourist who can never sleep well in a foreign bed.

So we must continue to the more conventional manifestations of aesthetic man in Switzerland, and must briefly note (in architecture) that outstandingly interesting examples of the church buildings of the Dark Ages exist in Coire, St. Maurice and other places, and that, outside architecture, the Swiss were particularly good during this obscure period at the allied arts of calligraphy and cartography.

After which the Romanesque period left behind some characteristic churches and sculptures and illuminated MSS and primitive paintings. And Gothic art completed the cathedrals, the sculptures, and provided most of the extant castles.

It should be felt, however, that the Swiss adopted but could never, by their very nature, make the most of these alien styles: and the important point to emphasize is that the buildings of the Middle Ages in this country, apart from the houses of the people, are chiefly notable for their *situations* rather than their architecture and interiors. The flair of this people has always been for arrangement. The castles are almost more striking than any other in the world—from a distance. They are placed so well, both aesthetically and militarily, usually on hills so that they can be seen from many interesting angles. The picturesque effect is all. A nation of essential artists has been preparing the scene: the cathedrals of Geneva and Lausanne high above the narrow streets, the Valère at Sion with its dramatic outline over the plain, even the Temple of Montreux in placid piety like a mariner's church guarding the town, the Grossmünster of Zurich and the Minster of Berne and a hundred Alpine chapels that look so extremely charming in their dominance of the landscape (but, close up, are often too plain if not drab for serious attention, while the interiors of the greater buildings are just what might be expected after a really efficient reformation).

Then rather unexpectedly, in the first half of the 18th century, some true architectural glories of the world were produced in Switzerland thanks to the patronage of the Catholic Church. Specialists in the baroque, such as the Beer, Thumb and Moosbrugger families, were

Perhaps the most beautiful ecclesiastical interior in the world, that of the baroque Klosterkirche of Einsiedeln.

brought from Austria to build the splendid "hall" churches at Rheinau and St. Urban; and the summit of this extraordinary activity was the abbey of Einsiedeln by Caspar Moosbrugger with the interior, decorative aid of the supreme Asam brothers. Perhaps there is nothing quite so beautiful in the world as the carved and painted, enfoliated, swagged and luxurious decoration of Einsiedeln inside. The proportions are just right. Moosbrugger was supreme at this moment. And the Asams were at last given enough money to make the baroque method come off, a question of all or nothing. There is a point with over-decoration where its very excess is irresistibly lovely, and that is what, remarkably, happened here. It was probably one of the best investments the Swiss Catholics ever made; and it paid them to loosen their purse-strings.

So much for the buildings; and it is now necessary to consider the individual pictorial artists.

The first, and still perhaps the greatest Swiss artist was Konrad Witz. Does the reader know him?

He worked at Basle from about 1400 to 1447, and by at least one of his productions should be considered among the important painters of all time. That is the altarpiece in Geneva which contains, in the part known as *The Miraculous Draught of Fishes,* what is not only the first landscape painting in art history and the progenitor of Switzerland's most frequent school, but also a superbly modern attempt at humanistic realism.

Exterior of Einsiedeln's baroque masterpiece, as executed in the 18th century by Caspar Moosbrugger.

At the back we see the landscape above the south bank of the Lake of Geneva exactly as it was in the 15th century, with the Salève, the Voirons, the Môle, and the white Mont Blanc system as final backdrop. The fields and farms and trees are as neat as anywhere in Switzerland today. The fishermen in the boat are human beings, and the scarlet robe of Christ provides such a splash of attractive color that ever since the tint has been similarly used by best-selling artists. Not only is this the first true landscape painting; it is also the first time mountains were taken seriously by a painter.

The depiction of scenery for its own sake is thus an original Swiss invention in the history of art: and throughout successive centuries it suitably became the aesthetic specialty of this land, running side by side with a similarly original development of the art of cartography. The very best early maps were Swiss. Then, finally, both came together in the Swiss color print, which has few if any equals, right up to the present day when commercial color-printing from superb photography is better in Switzerland than anywhere else in the world, with the picture postcard in its apotheosis as perhaps an art-form of permanent importance.

The picture postcard as produced in Switzerland today may eventually represent this age far more adequately—and acceptably—than the temporarily inflated products of professional painters.

As for the maps it is only necessary to regard the *Plan of Zurich* of Hans Leu, executed about 1497, which is in the National Museum; and early panoramas of that town by Josias Murer and of Fribourg by Sickinger. Then Johannes Stumpf preceded Saxton, Speed and Blaeu as a pioneer, fine cartographer of the 16th century.

A Basle publisher, Matthäus Merian, much later commercialized his personal craze for collecting views of cities and rural scenes. The copper engravings that he commissioned laid the basis of a unique Swiss contribution in a byway of art, so prolific that in our time an antique dealer of the English West Colony could make a good living out of specializing in old Swiss prints alone.

Konrad Witz at the very beginning not only painted the first important landscape. He established what was to become the characteristic Swiss style or method in pictorial art. This was the method of simple realism, based on accurate draftsmanship, that continued with Niklaus Manuel of Berne, an important man and sparetime artist who in the 15th and 16th centuries, with Urs Graf, Hans Asper, Hans Leu painted in what was known as the *lansquenet* (or military) school, a hard, vigorous product of the contemporary wars, strongly realistic and leading inevitably to the summit of Hans Holbein.

Holbein was born in Germany, 1497, and died at London in 1543, but came to Basle as a young man, where he enjoyed the patronage of an informed middle-class and became thoroughly Swiss in his deliberate, naturalistic method. He was almost as good a draftsman as Dürer, without the Germanic darkness, and he was a much finer artist in his interpretation of character and in the essential harmonies of his compositions. This Renaissance man is still among the greatest of all portrait painters; and when he came to the English court of Henry VIII he found immortal subjects. It is undoubtedly true that Basle, the great humanistic city, completely made him.

A Tobias Stimmer of Schaffhausen was in the 16th century sometimes almost as good as Holbein, whom he closely resembled. It is necessary to see his murals on the house called Zum Ritter in his native town. Meanwhile Hans Fries executed some noble altar pieces; and the typical Ticino painter of the period was Bernardino Luini (see his frescoes in the church of Santa Maria degli Angeli at Lugano).

It is now necessary to jump to the 18th century. First came Jean-Etienne Liotard of Geneva (1702–1789). Not only did he become one of the most popular portrait painters of his day in Paris, Rome, Constantinople, Venice, London and Amsterdam, but at least one of his paintings, *The Countess of Coventry* in La Musée d'Art et d'Histoire at Geneva, is timeless in its sweet simplicity and utterly modern in method and color.

Salomon Gessner (1730–1788) and Anton Graff (1736–1788) were minor masters who led to what will be the increasing importance of Johann Heinrich Füssli or Fusely of Zurich (1741–1825). This eventual Inspector of the Royal Academy in England, and close friend of William Blake, had real genius. He was at the same time one of the finest draftsmen ever, but his increasing importance will be derived from the extreme fire and swirl of his true Romantic feeling. The woodenness of the Classical era was completely renounced by this great innovator, whose free style, like that of his less sane friend Blake, lies at the basis of all so-called modern art. Then there was extreme pictorial beauty in all that he did. The Kunsthaus, Zurich, has his typical *English Lady of Fashion*. This is derisive, careless, mobile, utterly beautiful.

Then in the 19th century the painters of Switzerland became supreme among people of artistic talent in their land. The mood of the century was inimical to architecture, which was temporarily a matter of city hall classical, a style that could inspire no one and remains not so much a blot on the land as a constant aesthetic reminder that income tax must be paid. But the painters somehow escaped this Victorian blight of the artistic soul. Possibly the best of them at first was that sensitive Vaudois type and pupil of Ingres, M. C. G. Gleyre (1806–1874). The lovely Genevan landscapes of Barthélemy Menn (1815–1893) have a Corot quality; and Arnold Böcklin (1827–1901) was the most ardent Romantic of them all, strongly influential on the modern school of nature painting as completely represented by Alexandre Calame of Vevey (1810–1863), who with François Diday of Geneva (1802–1877) for the first time depicted not just Alps and sanctuaries but also the terror, the lyricism, the quaintness and the profound emotional impact upon modern man of rock peaks, snowfields, bleached pines, rushing torrents, edelweiss, gentian, wild cyclamen, iris and narcissus.

An old Swiss maiolica plate.

And out of this came a flood, particularly encouraged by the copper engraving technique developed by one of the artists Aberli, the method of the so-called *vedute,* whereby the landscape was etched in outline on copper plates and printed from them, after which the prints were tinted by hand. Suddenly the Alps were on the walls of the world.

Today the true *vedutes* by the best masters are sufficiently rare to be extremely valuable, while they have a small and permanent place of their own in the history of art.

So extensive was this aesthetic business of the Alpine 19th century that monoliths like Turner and Ruskin were ponderously moved to make the rough voyage across Europe in an attempt to cash in. It is amusing to study the contrasting results. Turner dissolved the Alps in an eternal, sanguinary sunset. The first of the true moderns among painters, he evidently sought to give at least the impression of profundity by usefully evading his true artistic responsibilities. Then the eunuch Ruskin prissily endeavoured, without great success, to make exact scale drawings of everything within sight. (Courbet the Frenchman, who was similarly inspired to visit Switzerland at this time, was much more successful in his highly-disturbing paintings of the time-eroded Jura.)

In the second half of the 19th century the paintings of Paul Bodmer of Zurich were popular locally but earned no wider fame. Eventually they should enjoy some international recognition. Bodmer painted with simplicity the everyday scenes of his beautiful country. His mind was as primitive as his style, and the result should eventually appeal to re-actors against 20th century novelty and carelessness in painting. The detail known as "The Song of Home" from his fresco in the Basle Gallery is, to the truly modern mind, quite delightful.

The Berne and Zurich Galleries should be visited for a different experience, that hard impact which comes from the work of Switzer-land's greatest modern painter, Ferdinand Hodler (1853–1918). If Hodler had worked in Paris or New York, or if he had had the good fortune to be a refugee Austrian or Czech, then his world name would have been more important. He was one of the most impressive figures in modern art, personally as well as in his pictures. His temperament accorded with the climate of his mountain land. He was strong, yet subject to föhn-like moods of clarity and deep depression. His style combined the Swiss naturalistic method with the exaggeration of *Art Nouveau* and not a little of the symbolism of a Blake (who should be regarded as one of the most important pictorial artists produced by the British people).

Within the world-famous 18th-century library at St. Gall.

But words can only befog the vision of the true connoisseur, who is best advised to study at least a reproduction of the famous Hodler interpretation of how the Swiss regard their outstanding folk hero, William Tell.

Here is no noble American-type man, forced by a tyrant to shoot an apple off his son's head and subsequently constrained to lead a rebellion. Here is a fearsome giant, a monolithic monster of masculinity who stands foursquare and quite immoveable in the path of the invader. Every true Swiss would be at heart the Hodler Tell; and the harsh architectural structure of the true symbolist picture is such that an idea is forever frozen stiff therein: the idea of freedom. To all aggressors of the world it is intimidating. At the same time it is one of

How the great Swiss painter Ferdinand Hodler saw the true strength and formidable terror of the Alps.

the most nationalistic pictures ever painted. Other monumental works of Hodler in the Berne and Zurich galleries may one day be regarded as of high significance in the whole history of art. In the meantime any would-be invader of Switzerland should thoughtfully study them.

The money, the pride and the efficiency of modern Switzerland are the products not just of geographical chance and hard work but also of ideas as expressed by artists who, if they had belonged to a larger country, would be among the most important in the world.

Perhaps a note should be added about the builders of the Ticino. This canton is Swiss in allegiance and method of organisation but Italian, or specifically Lombard, in its cultural origins. It has produced some great painters such as Luini. Its rural arts and crafts are delightful, from the remote farmhouses with their Roman tiles and arcaded galleries for the hanging of corncobs to the loggias of villas and small churches (repeated nobly in the streets of Lugano).

But the builder-architects of the Ticino provided the outstanding contribution. The vestibule of St. Peter's in Rome was the work of Carlo Maderno, also the Palazzo Mattei and the church of Sta. Susanna.

Then the Villa Falconieri at Frascati, the Palazzo Barberini and S. Andreas delle Fratti in Rome were built by Francesco Borromini from the Ticino. At Venice the Sta. Maria della Salute, and the Pesaro among other palaces, were the work of Baldassare Longhena; and the Doges' Palace at Genoa was built by the Ticino-man Simone Cantoni. Most of the plasterwork in the baroque building of 18th-century Italy, Germany, Poland and Russia was done by the wholly inimitable craftsmen of this part of Switzerland.

9

THE TABLE

EACH COUNTRY GOES TO THE DEVIL OR SPENDS ITS MONEY IN ITS own way. The characteristics of a nation are revealed by what the people do on their days off. By and large the Swiss overtake each other furiously and often disastrously on roads in new, small automobiles, briefly emerge to slide about their mountains on skis or to lie in the sun by lakes and swimming pools, and then, almost with audible sighs of relief, sit down at well-appointed tables to eat and drink.

The table is all-important in the Swiss way of life, and, these days, chiefly the table in svelte restaurant or under the Campari umbrellas of cafés. Formerly it was the table in the home that chiefly counted, but mother prefers to be taken out in an age when girls refuse to do domestic work, and the motor-car has provided an easy means of transporting families to eating-places whose average standard is higher than that of any other country. Right up on a mountain top will be perched a restaurant whose appurtenances and menu are as good as those in the expensive quarters of New York, London and Paris but much cheaper and very much cleaner.

It has been explained before how Swiss democracy is chiefly a matter of sitting around a café table and talking.

The actual tables are not so interesting as they might well have been, and only rarely does one come across such a piece of furniture that is worth studying for its own sake. The infinite variety of the tables of England, for example, is not to be found here, the gate-legs, the Pembrokes, the supper and sofa tables and the consoles, Sutherlands. Thus it could be noted here that the Swiss are not an antique-minded people. They like to be up-to-date, and a great deal of their eating furniture is now metal and plastic: and constantly renewed. The same applies contemporaneously to tableware. *But,* the tableware of the Swiss throughout previous ages constituted one of their principally important contributions 'artistically.

All civilizations are ultimately judged by their ceramics, for the simple reason that only pottery endures when the centuries have trodden human artefacts underfoot and when the corrosive chemistry of time has done its worst. The shards of Ur remain when other traces of the proud Chaldeans have gone.

Swiss tableware started with a single large dish that was placed in the center of the table, heaped with food, out of which the primitive family ate with hands. The custom of eating cheese or meat fondue from a communal vessel is a survival of this old roughness.

The first platters were of earthenware, lead-glazed a somewhat repulsive green or brown with metallic oxides. In the 16th century the crude Swiss potters started to color-glaze selfconsciously in the decorative sense, sometimes scoring the soft body with a pattern before firing. And they began to make drinking bowls and cups, jugs and small plates in competition with the makers of treen, or wood-ware, and the ubiquitous pewterers.

The big potter's breakthrough came in the 17th century with the development of faience, pale red earthenware covered with a tin glaze, and at Winterthur in Switzerland certain families—notably the Graafs, Erhardts and Pfaus—began a craft that was to last for some 130 years. In the Swiss National Museum one of their spice jars goes back to 1592, and there is an armorial plate dated 1607. Vast numbers of these plates were made, nearly all decorated with crude depictions of fruits and with the coats-of-arms that were proudly displayed by even the lowliest families. The four colors of the Winterthur potters were blue, green, yellow and manganese violet. The earliest work was crude and ugly, decorated with lighter-green spirals on a brownish-green base. Later the backgrounds were lighter and the decorations more elaborate, and the wine-jugs, particularly (pewter-capped), can be very interesting collectors' pieces.

The Swiss have always liked to embellish their workaday surroundings, which is why theirs attracts or repulses as a supremely "pretty" country; and thus the potters of Winterthur turned early to the making of faience tiles, not only for the decoration but also for the actual construction of *stoves.* The most glorious of these 17th-century stoves, green-glazed and brightly-painted, are for avid collection today.

The 18th century was, however, the age of the potter's apotheosis; and, contemporaneously with the great developments of the ceramic art in Germany and France, Italy and England came the typical Swiss contribution. This proceeded not from the patronage of kings in cities as elsewhere, but from small peasant potteries in country districts, especially in the rural canton of Berne and the great valley known as the Simmental, where three villages—Langnau, Heimberg and Blankenburg—for some reason or other outstripped all the others in sheer primitive artistry.

Very early Langnau is too primitive to be beautiful, but the products of this small peasant pottery from about 1720 onwards are more attractive in their way than much-vaunted others such as Hispano-Moresque ware. Incised decorations of flowers, fish and animals stand out against a light ground. Religious or satirical sayings are inscribed and long-forgotten celebrations of marriage are remembered. Then there evolved a characteristic Langnau type of bowl, chocolate brown with light dots or marbling, and even plastic figures most cunningly molded by hand and affixed.

A great Simmental maker of stove tiles was Abraham Marti.

Blankenburg pottery in the 18th century was characterized by a white ground on which paintings were done in blue, yellow, violet and a brownish-red. The figures are delightfully out of drawing always and very attractive to the modern taste. The potters themselves did the drawings boldly, and fortunately did not try too hard.

Two families, the Flückigers and the Herrmanns, were responsible for the development of the Heimberg pottery near Thun. They specialized after a time in chocolate-brown pieces on which bright colors were oddly superimposed. Figures with fantastical costumes, and broad jokes were painted upon this base.

The methods of these Simmental originals spread to many other parts of Switzerland, even to the Ticino, where they produced particularly the charming wine jugs known as boccalini.

During this remarkable 18th century the characteristic wealth of the ordinary Swiss, thanks as always to hard work and saving, was able to pay for a complete revolution in table habits. The single great dish was for once and all put aside in most houses and the potters were encouraged by the new demand to produce many kinds of sophisticated eating contrivances, small and large round and oval dishes, jugs of various dimensions, pots for condiments and sauces. The ever-improving ceramic materials were used to make decorative pieces, candlesticks, figures, containers for fruit and sweetmeats. The potters sent spies to learn the latest methods in Dresden and Paris but also developed their own. They learnt for the first time how to use reds properly and how to scallop edges and paint flowers correctly.

This painting became the hallmark of good Swiss pottery and porcelain. It exhibited always an innate native good taste: never brash, never gaudy. The typical product had a cream or white ground, looked basically clean and fresh; and the pure background was kind to the colored depictions thereon of lovely flowers, quaint peasants in their paysage, leaping deer, birds of blue. It became a most desirable style, contrasting in its simplicity with the over-elaborate products of the great German factories and the extreme artificiality of the contemporary French product. Neither was it such a slavish copy of the famous German and French marks as was the English and Italian of the period.

It is true, however, that in Switzerland as in the rest of Europe few of these enterprises endured notably beyond the 18th century. The Simmental potters worked only for two or three generations. Berne itself had two notable factories. One of them, under the bailiff Augustin Willading, lasted just from 1758 till 1763. The other was started in about 1760 by Lieutenant-Colonel Franz Rudolf Frisching and had a working life of only some 17 years, during which it employed not only Adam Spengler of Schaffhausen but also Daniel Herrmann of the great Heimburg family.

Berne pottery of the period, sometimes marked with the letter B, was decorated chiefly with simple flowers most accurately painted, the favorite being sprays in what was known as the Japanese style, with the chrysanthemum predominant. At that time a lot of Chinese and Japanese pottery was beginning to reach Switzerland. The colors of these Berne pieces are as brightly fresh today as when originally painted, thanks particularly to Herrmann's scientific techniques as described by him in a recipe-book that has been preserved.

Then the Berne potteries produced a large number of the characteristic Swiss stove tiles, particularly the Frisching concern (whose flowered specimens are among the best ever done and infinitely finer than the Dutch).

What a sad commentary on the commercial folly of high artistic endeavor is the history of most of the best potteries and porcelains! Possibly the apex of faience in Switzerland was Lenzburg between Zurich and Berne, where Markus Hunerwadel and Adam Heinrich Klug in 1763 founded an enterprise that lasted just four years, but, in that time, produced sufficient fine pottery to last collectors and fill

Intragna—Ticino. Baking of bread, Southern Switzerland.

Native costumes. Dames de Sion *in the Valais*.

their books for hundreds of years. It nearly all had hunting scenes, and the entire history of the chase in Switzerland (a chase that is as popular among the ordinary people today as it was in primitive times) may be studied on a representative collection of lovely, creamy Lenzburg, all kinds of huntsmen, all kinds of game: only the connoisseur must always be careful to differentiate between the true Lenzburg and the very similar work done by a pottery at Künersberg in Germany.

A second faience factory was started at Lenzburg in 1775 and lasted till 1790. It was controlled by another fine painter of pottery, Jakob Frey, but the products have not the extreme importance and individuality of the true early Lenzburg. Single plates often have the mark LB. Frey particularly liked large zinnias surrounded by butterflies.

Two more Swiss potteries must be mentioned. That at Beromünster near Lucerne was started in 1770 by a young man of 26 named Andreas Dolder, a Swiss who had probably received some French training. He specialized in curved fluting. His work displays the curious asymmetry of what was one day to be called *Art Nouveau*. When he found that most of his orders came from the wealthier families of Lucerne he removed his atelier to that town (1780) and there, until the short end of this period, he executed particularly some of the best-ever flower painting on fluted jugs and sugar bowls particularly. (Usually marked with an M for Münster.)

The other faience factory is that started at Schooren near Zurich in 1763, and it is important not just for the large amount of pottery it produced with considerable commercial success, but also for its eventual making of the important Zurich porcelain.

Zurich was curiously started by a learned local committee: with such members as the artist Gessner and that Adam Spengler who had worked with Frisching at Berne. (Spengler's son Jean-Jacques subsequently joined Duesbury at Derby). A shop for publicity and retail purposes was opened at the Münsterhof in Zurich city. There was nothing original in the typocal rococo of the work produced. The faience was very similar to that of the other Swiss factories. But Zurich (marked with a blue Z beneath the glaze) was perhaps the most commercially successful of all the potteries. It produced a vast amount of tableware and tiles—even work of pipe clay and the soft porcelain known as *pâte tendre*—before it turned to the true hard paste porcelain that made its real and lasting name.

This porcelain is like a refined version of Swiss faience, with the same cream background and charmingly painted flowers and scenes and only the most tasteful addition of rim gold. It cannot bear technically comparison with the best of Meissen and Sèvres or even of Capo di Monte and Chelsea, but it has a unique Swiss charm, that of the dairy; and, because of the scarcity of fine pieces today, it is extremely valuable.

The *pièce de resistance* of Zurich is undoubtedly the Einsiedeln service, still to be seen in the "zur Meisen" guildhouse of the Swiss National Museum. This was made to the special order of the city of Zurich for presentation to the Prince Abbot of Einsiedeln in 1774 in return for his hospitality to Zurich delegates during an important conference with representatives from Schwyz. Everything is here that an 18th-century table could need, and the outstanding feature of the porcelain is the lovely, delicate flower painting.

The Zurich enterprise eventually began to lose money and was closed in 1790, at the graveyard time of great potteries everywhere. The reason for this and the other numerous failures was that the spirit sustaining such artistry had failed. An age was ended by its own over-civilization (which prevented it from fighting successfully against revolutionary forces).

The other Swiss porcelain, that of Nyon near Geneva, actually limped on till 1811; but when Napoleon came to Switzerland and the Swiss found that their vitals had been sapped by over-success and they could no longer resist new ideas and harsh invaders, then there was no longer the economic climate nor the spiritual incentive to produce fine work. Not until a century later did many of the arts and crafts properly revive, and never again did they reach the heights of that wonderful second half of the 18th century.

Two Germans established the Nyon factory in 1781, the painter Ferdinand Müller from Frankenthal and a young man, Johann Jakob Dortu, who had married his daughter. This young man provided the brains, but strangely steered the style of potting and design into French rather than Germanic hard-paste and painting so that the best Nyon became very similar to Sèvres, although sturdier and less decadent in appearance (not so stylized and lacking in spirit, still often with a peasant crudity).

Once again the principal products were designed for actual use on the table, tea, coffee and dinner services, much embellished with gold upon the immaculate eggshell hard-paste, and for a long time to be the great snob possession of western Switzerland. A blue fish is the mark on Nyon porcelain, which is now much sought after by the wise connoisseur.

The Swiss love the arts of the table; and to this day it is more satisfying to eat and drink in Switzerland than almost any other country. France might be supreme but only at outrageous cost. Switzerland is still relatively cheap. It is possible to buy a good meal with excellent wine there at less cost than in Britain, Germany or the United States. Italy runs Switzerland close but not with the same high, average standard.

In order to accommodate international tourists the Swiss have developed two distinct cuisines. The first is international. Half the tourists and half of the Swiss also eat what is most favored in Paris, New York and London. Perhaps the steaks are a little more tender and nicely grilled, and the chips are finer and more tasty, but basically they are cooked in the same way as their counterparts in other popular parts of the world. The standard was set by such as the original Ritz, who emerged from his native Valaisan village to found the best hotels with the best restaurants in the world. It is maintained today by hotel schools which are just as serious in their methods and approach as are the great technological foundations elsewhere. And the tradition is sustained by the inevitable volume of petty Swiss laws relating to food and wine. Above all no adulteration and very little artificial coloring are permitted in this country. There is thus less chance of being poisoned by food or wine in Switzerland than elsewhere, although on the other side of the coin it is true that the regulations sometimes tend to emasculate the joys of the table, especially in meat, which is not so full-blooded as it might be thanks also to the basically milk-type of the native cattle.

The second kind of Swiss cuisine, loved exceedingly by the other half of local diners and by the more discerning and courageous among visitors, is that which is indigenously Swiss alone, and can be first explored over the border from France and Germany in Basle, which probably offers a wider variety of native dishes and wines than any other city, from the Romande, the Grisons, the Ticino, and then from all the country districts ranging from Lake Constance to the Jura.

The sausages called Chlöpfer in Basle, a variety of saveloy or *cervelas*, are probably the best of their kind in the world. The gastronome would wisely eat excellent salmon from the Rhine here, and possibly Schweinspfeffer or jugged pork. (Swiss pork gets better every year.) Coffee would be taken with Gugelhopf. The gingerbreads of Basle are, of course, without equal elsewhere.

In Zurich it would be a characteristic marzipan Leckerli, while the Zuger Kirschtorte or cherry-tart, with great gobbets of pure, cow-flavored cream would accord well with the perfect, strong coffees of these parts. Meringues, similarly lush-creamed, and sandwiched with

"Tirggel," a Zurich specialty, of sugar, honey and flour.

ices made genuinely from milk, are much favored here as in all Switzerland (particularly in that lovely hill fortress of tourism called Gruyère, where they have long been a chef's specialty).

In Zurich some of the best restaurants are to be found in the old guild houses. An excellent food of the town is Zürchertopf, meats with rice, and the local Leberspiessli, or spit grilled liver, minced, mixed with flour, shredded and boiled.

Then, travelling through the magnificent sceneries of original, central Switzerland, the experimenter with food will wisely call for jugged chamois of Schwyz, after the characteristic Käsuppe (cheese soup). He will toy with Pantli and Knackerli in Appenzell, and will greatly enjoy the fish dishes particularly of Zug and Lucerne—barbel from the lake of Zug and perhaps a giant pike from the lake of Lucerne. Always he will find splendid trout; and Lucerne will additionally yield him a tasty patty of mushrooms and herbs called Kügelipastete. (This town is also very good for cheesecakes—and occasionally, of course, for cheesecake also.)

Eastern Switzerland is notable for its soups; and Lake Constance and the Rhine provide a plenitude of fishes. The visitor should try the restaurants of such small towns as Arbon and Stein-on-Rhine. The smoked Gangfisch of Ermatingen is a rare experience indeed. Sausages are very good and various hereabouts. Up in the Grisons hangs the Bindenfleisch, fresh meat that dries in the mountain air to a paper-thin quintessence of its original self, and one of the unique delicacies of the world so long as it is properly handled and presented. It should be eaten with wholemeal bread and washed down with red local Veltliner, particularly the varieties known as Montagna, Sassella, Grumello and Inferno.

One of the real Grisons delicacies on a Sunday in season for the local folk who throng the sympathetic dining-rooms of local small hotels is a Gitzi of young goat, taken with Polenta or maize-meal pudding.

The local dishes in Geneva and around about have an inevitable French flavor, the sauces being exceptionally good, such as the Geneva sauce that transforms trout into *ombre-chevalier,* and (especially upon the Vaudois shores of the lake) the tartare sauce that transforms crisp-brown fillets of perch into tongue-teasers of a very rare order indeed (washed down with cool, clear Rivaz, a perfect workaday wine of the Vaux).

The Genevese have an important dish, which the visitor should bravely experience if he can, that consists of leg of pork prepared in Madeira. They can also be proud of their baked crayfish tails and morels on toast and of their principal local sausage, the *longeole.*

The Vaud offers specially a succulent *saucisse aux choux,* best eaten on the same plate with a completely different *saucisson de Payerne.* Ham is excellent in this canton; and the recent flood of Italian workers has encouraged the making of mild local salami and pizza that are admirably adapted to the northern taste. The pork in Madeira here becomes a steaming dish of pig's trotters (*pieds de porc au madère*).

Above all the Vaud is the true home of the *fondue.* As said before, this dates back to the days when a family economically used only one dish on the table. It continues to be an ultra-democratic way of getting together over a meal, the basic Swiss method of social life and politics, and is marvellously convivial so long as the diner is not afraid of dipping his breaded fork into the same bubbling bowl as his companions. It is important, by the way, not to lose the bread in the bowl, lest a fine of a bottle of wine be imposed. Of course this is a local joke and nothing could be kinder than the attitude of the Swiss as hosts, especially at the *fondue*. If the stranger can properly share this dish with his Swiss hosts then he belongs at once to an intimate fellowship—and is probably given the greatest privilege of all, the right to scrape the savory, toasted, almost toffee cheese at the eventual bottom of the bowl.

A local white wine is drunk before the *fondue,* but the true Vaudois prefer to imbibe only a small glass of kirsch while eating. The secret with this dish, during the preparation and ritual consumption, is to avoid what could cause indigestion. And the classic recipe is diced or shredded cheese or cheeses of the Gruyère type that should be melted gently in the traditional earthenware and thick-based pot while a little local white wine and a little flour are stirred in. A flavoring of garlic and kirsch is added; and when the bubbling mixture has a smooth consistency it is ready.

Cheese is, indeed, the most important of all Swiss foodstuffs. The people long ago learnt that it was their best way of getting good sustenance from the mountain pastures in a form that could be stored for winter. The Swiss owe much to their cheeses, which range from the basic Gruyère type, strong flavored, pale colored, punctuated by small holes, to the luscious cream variety of the Jura known as Vacherin (recognizable immediately by the slight flavor of pinewood, derived from the local containers of bark in which it is packed).

Emmental, from those rich farms of the great Bernese valley, is a Gruyère with larger holes, a milder flavor, and a richer color.

The Bagnes and Conches cheese of the Valais are allowed to ripen longer than Gruyère and Emmental, and therefore cut well and melt nicely in the famous *raclette* of the canton, one of the simplest dinner dishes ever invented by man and yet one of the most effective. A cheese is cut in two and the inner surface warmed at a fire until it melts and can be scraped on a plate and eaten with boiled or jacket potatoes, gherkins, and several small beaker glasses of Fendant.

The *plat Valaisan* is meanwhile a tasty dish of cold meats and sliced sausages, including the delicate local *jambon cru,* uncooked but well-smoked ham; while this canton grows excellent asparagus and fruit. These seemingly spring from the actual glacial stones or dried riverbeds, but the soil is richly fertile underneath and the stones have actually been placed there laboriously by hand to conserve moisture in the hot days when the Valais has, indeed, right among these very high and remote mountains, the best sunshine record of any part save the Ticino.

Piora and Muggio are the principal cheeses of that excellent, warm Italian part of Switzerland. Sprinz is like Parmesan; and all in their

The perfect pastoral scenery of the Emmental, home of the holed cheese.

hardness are suitable for grating into soups, a zuppa pavese, a minestra, or that excellent tripe soup called busecca.

The mixed grill of the Ticino is famous, and the visitor should never fail to call for fritto misto allas ticinese. If there at the right time of the year he should also be sure to sample a dish that consists of baby asparagus (the field type) with a fried egg. Then a sausage here is made from the rare, herb-fed flesh of a local, half-wild pig. All the best Ticino foods and drinks have indeed the subtle flavor of the herbs and spices that constitute a natural benison in this hot, dry land. The peasants themselves have been basically nourished throughout the ages by their cheeses and the rich polenta with its buttercup color, and, if possible, on certain days the rareness of game. The lakes and the rivers can sometimes be nearly solid with fish. Pasta in all its Italianate variety combines with a delicious light bread to absorb the potent, slightly-sweet local red wines. The expresso coffee is almost as good as that of Milan, and should be taken with a glass of grappa, the true spirit of the warm land.

Indeed the drinker is strongly advised never to avoid Switzerland these days. Once upon a time he would have scorned this country with its primitive beers and raw aperitifs and wines that would neither keep nor travel successfully. France was all, and after France the Rhineland and perhaps Tuscany. But times have changed. An English expert of the true college-cellar type, than which there is no connoisseur of wines more prissy and ritualistic, remarked recently that to obtain an honest vintage these days it was necessary to go as far as Australia. He meant that the wine producers of Europe were increasingly doctoring their harvests in a kind of decadence of the art. Thanks to strict laws that are largely observed by a naturally law-abiding people, the humble and fragile Swiss wines are now often better to drink than the famous products of France and Germany. The after effect is what counts, increasingly with the age of the drinker; and a Swiss wine still disturbs neither night nor digestion. (Swiss beers have meanwhile improved greatly; a lager type, they are now better than those of many other countries.)

The foreign legend that there is only one Swiss wine, that called Neuchâtel, is a curious travesty of the truth. The various Neuchâtels are good and accord well with the food and climate there. Above all their dry, cold substance is meant for fish and *hors-d'oeuvres*. The best is Auvernier; but it should be understood that what is known as Neuchâtel also comes from the slopes of Bienne, and might be better described as a Bernese lake wine; also that it can be nicely red, from the Pinot noir grape. The connoisseur also knows Schaffiser, Twanner and Champreveyres.

The very best wines come from the Valais and the Vaud; and first place should be shared by a Fendant such as Les Murettes or Château Conthey, and by an Yvorne such as L'Ovaille or Cymaise. The expert would choose as runners-up a Dézaley called Médinette or a simple Villeneuve from the cave of the wine producers' association.

The old saying was that broadly speaking the wines improved as the valleys from Geneva by the lake were mounted, until at length proud Sion in the heart of the true Valais was reached. That is still true save for the exceptional circumstances of the Monts de Lavaux and Yvorne-Villeneuve. The wines of La Côte, from the Jura foothills between Geneva and Lausanne, are light, white, dry and ordinary. Then between Lausanne and Montreux there is the remarkable terracing of Lavaux, which since Roman times has laboriously known the grape above the reflective shimmer of the enormous lake; and here certain vignerons, such as those of Puidoux in Dézaley, have brought their husbandry to such a pitch of perfection that climatic difficulties have been overcome

Gathering the grapes on unique Lavaux above Lake Léman for the pure white wine of the region.

and the resultant wines have a perfection almost unequalled these adulterate days. The sun shines down, and then is reflected upwards from the lake. There are views of the Grand Combin, of the Dents du Midi, and then of Grammont opposite, upon which the ever-changing pattern of the melting snows in the spring traditionally tells the vigneron when to set about his various tasks. Among the descend-ing vines, neat as a market garden, patterned like a piece of celestial embroidery, black in spring, green in summer, dotted with yellow plastic containers in early autumn and with the blue cloth of bending backsides, the work continues above interlacing strips of concrete service road that affords some of the most perfect walks any tourist could desire, until in late autumn there is the best color of all, a kind of Sienese brown gradually changing to that of a well-toned cigar, when the wine is at home at last in the great casks of the stone, arched caves that burrow beneath the almost military-style houses of the growers, in which sensible folk sip samples on Saturday afternoon and talk with great laughs and order their eager dozens at only a few francs a generous Vaudois-style bottle.

The Dézaleys are the best and most expensive, but Epesses, Cully, Rivaz, St. Saphorin, Chardonne each in turn yield a slightly different sensation and flavor. Montreux afterwards has turned too many of its once excellent vineyards into residential districts, but soon Villeneuve compensates for this desecration and continues to produce a remarkable light white wine that is traditionally recommended to all those ageing men who start to suffer from affections of the *vessie*. Then on the way to Aigle westwards there is on the left, hugged in the arms of the mountains, the sun-trap enclave of Yvorne. The vines here are the best-tended in the world, and of recent times this care has been rewarded by such a remarkable improvement in the quality of the local white wine that most Swiss, at least, must acknowledge its perhaps supreme position.

After Yvorne and Aigle there is not much of importance until Martigny is reached at the parting of the Alpine ways. And here we come seriously to the subject of Swiss red wines.

In former days, apart from the characteristic Dôles of around Sion up the left-hand valley of the Valais towards the Simplon, the red wines of Switzerland were not very good or plentiful. Recently, in response to changing taste, the vignerons have struggled hard everywhere to produce more red and rosé; and all the way up from Geneva these darker wines are now increasingly found. But it is really not until Martigny is reached that they can be taken at all seriously. Up the mounting Chamonix and St. Bernard roads from the right of Martigny are choice vignobles now that can offer some splendid light reds, somewhat similar to clarets but thinner and with just a soupçon of Italianate douceur.

If the main valley be followed to Sion then of course the real Dôles will be found, more like a Burgundy than a Bordeaux when Pinat noir in origin. They are aromatic, full-bodied, the Gamay, the Mâconnay, the Côte d'Or, and are accompanied by Johannisberger-type wines, by Muscats and Malvasiers, and finally the golden-brown Glacier from the highest vineyards in Europe above Stalden.

But Sion is also the capital of the great Fendants, still for many the very best of Swiss white wines because of their curious (and dangerous!) effervescent quality. If you are excitable or melancholy a good Fendant may indeed mount quickly to your brain and subtly fan the flames of ardor or despair. The wine is very slightly aromatic, full-bodied for a white, and is rich in sugar content although by no means sweet. By comparison a Sauterne is, to a sophisticated palate, quite undrinkable.

The best red wine of the Ticino is the Nostrano, particularly that from Gordola. We have spoken also before of the red Veltliner of the Grisons; and every other canton can offer at least something local, such as the Meiliners and Stafners from the lake of Zurich district, and the Bereckers and Altstatters of the Swiss Rhineland.

The true Swiss and particularly the hand-working folk drink all these wines in the same casual way as Americans drink highballs or English bureaucrats and strikers drink tea. Wise visitors share with them a unique pleasure and gastronomical sensation (saving themselves a lot of money thereby). Alas the half-sophisticated among the Swiss tend to replace their local bottles with imported brews for reasons of pure snobbery; and each year more French and Italian and Spanish and Algerian wine is brought into the country wholesale. This is regrettable. Every country, every district should drink its own wine; and the man who permits snobbery to interfere between himself and his table is a fool and likely to lose eventually both his money and his digestion.

But the mass of the Swiss people can be safely left to work out their own destiny in this matter. They have always found the best solution (to use a typical Swiss phrase) in the past; and they will most certainly continue to spend some of the best and most productive hours of their life at the well-appointed, all-significant table.

In a bistro of Vevey is a table inscribed "Jean-Jacques Rousseau sat here," or words to that effect. Undoubtedly he did, but not, unfortunately for long. If he had only stayed at that table, gently drinking the local Chardonne, then the world might be a less hate-ridden and ungovernable place today.

10

IMMIGRATION

THERE IS LITTLE DOUBT THAT THE MOST SUCCESSFUL COUNTRIES have always been those that have periodically admitted influxes of new blood. It might even seem that nations are like animals, the breed of which is best improved not by inbreeding but by judicious outcrossing from time to time. And Switzerland is an excellent example of this. She has retained from the beginning a hard core of what might be described as indigenous Swiss, whose characteristics never cease to provide the main pattern of the land. But, right back to Roman times and beyond, she has frequently allowed the stranger to settle among her.

Save for the Roman conquest this has always been a matter of free will on the part of the Swiss. They have chosen and carefully controlled immigration.

The principal foreign admixtures in Switzerland of recent times have been from lowly hand-workers and from more or less wealthy expatriates. The first has been by far the more important ethnically speaking, although the more leisured strangers have had a strong financial and social influence.

There is no doubt at all that the future of Switzerland may well be changed by the recent enormous immigration of Italian and Spanish workers particularly. It has been described before how the Swiss have vigorously backpedalled and may seem to have the foreign flood under control, but there are already so many Italians and Spaniards in the country thanks to the recent wholesale admissions that the most violent expatriation of many of these will not be able to counter the great dilution of the traditional Swiss blood that has taken place. (A politician named Schwarzenbach recently launched an "initiative," leading to a referendum that was narrowly defeated as a result of which the Government increasingly restricted the percentages of foreign workers, but it was already too late to make Switzerland wholly Swiss again.)

Undoubtedly Switzerland will in the future have to be regarded as much more of a Latin country than it was in the past. This may well be not altogether a disadvantage. The imported workers are vigorous in many ways. They are strong, ambitious, artistic, clever. Their home countries were formerly the most important in the world; and perhaps they have learned not to make the mistakes that resulted in the downfall of those countries. As in the case of all striving immigrants they may be guided by the essential Swissness of Switzerland still into less foolish and warlike paths than those which ruined their homelands. It may well be that the new Swiss laws will prevent the Latin immigrants from swamping the native goodness of this rare country. But there is all the same no doubt at all that Switzerland will be, for better or worse, a little less inflexible, a little less blonde, indeed a little less Germanic. The given and the surnames will be increasingly Mediterranean. There will be rather more excitability and innate artistry and what might be described as the Roman Catholic values; rather less phlegm, thoroughness and what are regarded as the Protestant values.

Perhaps the most important question, in the purely material sense, is whether the adulterated Swiss will continue to retain those indomitable characteristics that for centuries warned off the invader and, more recently, have enabled this country to preserve an armed neutrality inviolate. It may at the time of writing be an open question, but it should be remembered that for every unwarlike Italian immigrant there has been a potentially unyielding (in the military sense) Spaniard.

The second possibility is that the increased Latinity of the land may affect its hitherto immaculate scheme of business ethics; but, once again, the pessimist might consider that the Spanish half of the great immigration derives from an essentially honest people for all their Iberian faults of religious intolerance and proneness in certain circumstances to what more northern peoples regard as cruelty.

It is, however, unlikely that many readers of this book will be Italians or Spaniards seeking information on how they can get to Switzerland and work there. Broadly speaking it must be said that the great opportunity is now over, and that Latin emigration from Switzerland will exceed immigration into that country from now on for a considerable time.

To obtain the actual work permit that is necessary any immigrant will have to prove that he brings an essential skill, particularly modern technological, unless he is willing to accept brief, seasonal employment with periodical returns home. In this case he should foremostly be a skilled hotel or catering worker or a person willing to labor at the most degrading and arduous of manual work; in return for which he will receive higher wages than many a native Swiss worker with a white collar, and, if provident, should eventually be able to return to his impoverished native land with the accumulated proceeds and live in relative affluence for the rest of his life.

As regards the other type of modern immigration, it was originally British, then increasingly German, American, Dutch and French. The British came first for health and social reasons. Wealthy people could prolong their lives by climbing the mountains and living out their old age in the sun, while they found in Swiss enclaves such as the Vaud, the Ticino and Lucerne a pleasant, cultured, old-fashioned, bridge-playing society of their drawing-room peers.

The attractions of health and society became increasingly overtaken by that of the tax haven. While Britain, carefully emulating the Roman Empire in its path downwards, effectively destroyed its ruling class with the weapons of income taxation and what were nicely described as death duties on estates, so the more enterprising among the true aristocrats of that land removed what remained of their wealth while they could; and Switzerland for a long time provided one of the principal depositories.

Such people went particularly to the Vaud, where income taxes were practically nonexistent by British standards, and to parts of the Ticino where the greatest attraction was that they could leave their money almost completely intact to their heirs.

The result was that certain pleasant towns, such as the outstanding example, Montreux, became scarcely distinguishable from a Cheltenham or Harrogate in their gracious, outmoded ways. Here were the retired colonels and the great, fallen ladies, the long drinks and the clubs and the libraries, the tweeds, brogue shoes and the mutually-destructive cliques with all the intrigues and affairs so vividly reminiscent of what Kipling once wrote about Anglo-Indian society and Maugham wrote about the farther East.

This had its lasting, maybe its permanent, effect on Switzerland itself, which to this day has a curiously British flavor in certain important respects. The British undoubtedly left in this land a legacy of

A characteristic view of Lake Thun.

social politeness and a kind of superficial kindness towards the more unfortunate victims of society and dogs. Their restrained and sensible styles of clothing were responsible for the good taste of the ordinary Swiss in this respect. The sports of skiing, swimming, tennis, football and many indoor games are often legacies of the once pukka sahibs who came—and died.

The neat cemeteries are filled with them. It is possible to wander for reminiscent hours among the headstones and to sentimentalize about the familiar and hyphenated names.

At the time of writing there are only a few of these antediluvians left and even those will soon be gone forever.

The bridge clubs still operate but are now largely sustained by lesser breeds without the law, even by a majority of strangely-bidding French in some cases. (The loud cry "I have two arses" was heard quite recently in one of these places.)

More or less monied and socially pretentious British would have continued to come to Switzerland for health and tax purposes, if in increasingly lesser numbers, had it not been for a change in British exchange control regulations that made it impossible over a considerable period for fortunes to be taken out of the country save at a penal discount, in the region of thirty to forty percent.

Meanwhile the place of the British and their money had been usefully filled for the Swiss by the Germans particularly. Having so fortunately lost what we may all hope could be their final war they were at once constrained by the traumatic experience to work harder than ever before in their hard-working lives—and were immensely sustained financially by dollar aid. They came to Switzerland not so much to settle there and create a society-within-a-society in their old age like the British, as to buy land and build property and so preserve their parvenu fortunes safely. In some parts, such as the Ticino and around the lake of Lucerne and between Montreux and Geneva they created whole estates of expensive, wide-windowed and white-walled modern millionaire houses, estates that often became known locally as "Little Germany." They were so characteristically thorough in this almost military operation that, as in the case of the Italian and Spanish workers, the quiet Swiss were moved to sudden and Draconian measures. The outstanding among these was a law forbidding foreigners to acquire property without the possession of a residence permit. And this was not enough. For some time not even established foreign residents in Switzerland were allowed to buy land or build houses on it. For a while the indomitable invaders got round this by establishing shell Swiss companies and buying property through native Swiss nominees. But they gradually found that this was not only extremely expensive but also so fraught with worrying difficulties as to be scarcely bearable. The indomitable spirit of William Tell had once again prevailed.

The German invasion primarily had the effect of immensely enlarging property values, particularly those of private houses, and of introducing into Switzerland many new, fine and highly expensive techniques of private house building.

The contemporaneous American invasion was less understandable and more influential socially. Undoubtedly a large number of wealthy Americans came to Switzerland in the 1950s and 1960s without properly doing their homework and under the mistaken impression that it would save them tax. They did not, as always, reckon with the almost

The perfect but fearsome road through the Grimsel Pass.

fiendish efficiency of their own internal revenue system. The expatriates found that they must either pay both Swiss and American taxes or else lose their passports.

The American penetration soon became more a matter of business than tax-dodging retirement. The great surge of American overseas investment found Switzerland to be an excellent European base.

Enormous sums of money came over, as well as whole industries and their nominal head offices. The Americans settling in Switzerland were thus second only to the Italian and Spanish workers in age. The British and the Germans had always been old, but hundreds of young families of Americans developed Swiss homes so that they might work, not on behalf of Switzerland but on behalf of themselves and their country. Americans for a long time seemed to obtain work permits without difficulty, because they brought not just money with them but also new skills, methods and factories.

The Americanization of Switzerland that occurred as a result of this immigration was largely in the industrial field, although the young families of the managerial immigrants did undoubtedly have some perceptible influence upon the social customs of the natives, an influence that was more marked in styles of clothing, haircuts and night life than anything else. Problems of youth could often be traced to customs of sexual promiscuity and drug-taking that had been imported in that way.

But the Americans hugely benefitted Switzerland with a fertilization of money and ideas, as they had similarly helped so much of the world at that time; and the social effect of their arrival was really of little importance. Unlike the British they did not impose their everyday way of life firmly upon the alien scene. They were even worse at languages than the British and more nervous about eating strange food and drinking local water. They kept to themselves, and developed their own schools and other institutions. It was always obvious that they were in the country for only a short time and that they would do their best not to die there. They were quite different from the British who came usually to settle, grow old, and die, and like the Germans whose primary object was the acquisition of property which they could use for holidays and in an emergency across a convenient mountain border.

The Dutch and the French monied arrivals were never sufficient to establish a pattern of influence, save perhaps in Suisse Romande, where the increasing arrival of wealthy French duing the financial agonies of their once-great country had the effect during the 1960s of subtly augmenting the Gallic flavor of Geneva and the Vaud.

Meanwhile, throughout the ages indeed, Switzerland had always been a place where the famous of the world had tended to keep a second, third or fourth holiday home. A brief review of the outstanding immigrants of this kind might reveal whether or not the phenomenon was at all influential.

The famous visitors of classical times are too remote now for their sojourns to be noteworthy, although it is always worth mentioning that one of them, Julius Caesar, laid down the law definitively when he wrote "the Helvetii are braver than the rest of the Celts; they are in almost daily conflict with the Germans across the Rhine, with whom they are continually at war."

It was not until the 18th century that Switzerland again became favored as a playground-cum-object-for-conquest, but we should perhaps consider what the French poet Du Bellay said in 1557 after regarding the Grisons particularly (in the excellent free translation of that outstanding writer upon Switzerland, Gavin de Beer):

> Its earth is fertile, the houses ample,
> The stoves gay-coloured, rooms panelled in wood,
> Immutable the laws and constitution,
> The people enemies of wrong and vice.
> They drink night and day like Bretons and Swiss,
> Thick-set and fat, they eat more than for three;
> Such are the friends and the scourges of kings
> Whom good Rabelais once labelled sausages.
> Their habits and customs never have changed,
> Like dogs they howl their barbarous songs,
> They tell their own tale and boast of all.
> They have many fine lakes, and plentiful springs,
> Many fields, many woods. But, truth to tell,
> I forget, so much had I to drink.

Dr. Beer also usefully translates another 16th century poet, de Magny, as follows:

> Rather would I spend ten nights on hard earth . . .
> Rather would I see myself in the dark dungeon
> Of some Spanish Dago, chained fifteen days . . .
> Than cross the Grisons, Aprica and Bernina passes,
> The bridge of Camogasc and the pont Arrasine,
> With their infamous stoves and inhabitants.

Until the second half of the 18th century Switzerland was indeed a place that had to be traversed arduously on the way to and from the high civilization (by comparison) of Italy. But the age of reason and its aftermaths, the French Revolution and the so-called Victorian age, brought mighty personages not only to pause on the way across but also to stay. Thus Voltaire established himself at Ferney, not actually in Switzerland, but just over the border so that he could escape into Geneva whenever it was politic for him to do so; and there is no doubt that his favorite doctrine of cultivating one's garden to the exclusion of less noble occupations that involved interference with others came directly from his contact with the not-so-simple Swiss peasants and their pervading rusticism.

Then Rousseau's romantic writing about girls in the bushes at Clarens undoubtedly whetted some elderly famous appetites to rest awhile thereabouts. Edward Gibbon heard the summons and came to Lausanne and laid fruitless siege to the flirtatious but basically prim young ladies of society there. That he conceived the idea of writing the immortal *Decline and Fall* was his revenge, but alas, from his personal point of view, a Pyrrhic victory.

Meanwhile Mme. de Staël had established a Versailles-type salon at Coppet; and it became fashionable to travel thence from London, Paris, Berlin, Rome, both for conversation and for the possibility of a titillating intrigue.

The love-hate relationship of Lord Byron with Switzerland could be analyzed for hours not unproductively. He gained much from brief sojourns at various places in the Vaud particularly, not least the inspiration for that most historically misleading of so-called poems, *The Prisoner of Chillon*. The Swiss in due course gained even more. Byron himself wrote, most unfairly, that "Switzerland is a curst selfish, swinish country of brutes, placed in the most romantic region of the world. I never could bear the inhabitants." But in public and "poetically" he expressed only the most generous sentiments, that swiftly gave the wise Swiss their first tourist literature. Hotels and restaurants and streets were named after this great seducer of his sister. The very boat he had brought to Switzerland and a few times somewhat grandiloquently used was to become a legend. (Thanks to his boatman Maurice, a typically Vaudois man of commercial sense and sensibility. The Countess of Blessington and others recorded after visits to Switzerland how Maurice had romanticized his brief work for Byron.)

And it could be said that Rousseau and Byron between them left the Montreux-Vevey district with a tradition that was forever to make the lake and the mountains and the pastures and flowers there just a little larger than life.

The remarkable links between the famous of Britain and Switzerland is well exemplified by a curious anecdote. The writer of the present book has a Swiss friend who belongs to the modern Huguenin family. One of the sources for information about Byron's stay in the Vaud was a retired geologist named Roderick Murchison. He lived in the first quarter of the 18th century at Vevey. Murchison's wife had been a Miss Hugonin, niece of that Francis Hugonin of Hampshire who is frequently mentioned in the correspondence of Edward Gibbon. And this English family of Hugonins was connected with that Jean-François

Hugonin, who, as her nephew, was the heir of Mme. de Warens, the young, errant wife of the seigneur of Tour-de-Peilz. That was Rousseau's Mme. de Warens.

During those great days Byron was accompanied by the poet Shelley, the poet and critic Robert Southey, and Shelley's wife Mary Wollstone-craft Godwin, daughter of Godwin the radical philosopher and Mary Wollstonecraft who wrote *A Vindication of the Rights of Women*. At Chamonix the poet described himself in a hotel register as "Percy Bysshe Shelley, Atheist," a gesture that wisely assured him the fame of execration among the scholars for a long time to come. And Mary Godwin quietly asserted herself eventually among these peacock males of the era with her pioneer among horror fictions called *Frankenstein*. This was traditionally conceived in a boat on the lake, and its Gothic trappings were all those of Habsburg Switzerland.

Goethe came frequently to Switzerland. Wordsworth was one of the first great publicists for the Rigi near Lucerne. Among his writings are the flatulent sentences:

> Ten thousand times in the course of this tour I have regretted the inability of my memory to retain a more strong impression of the beautiful forms before me; again and again, in quitting a fortunate station, have I returned to it with the most eager avidity, in the hope of bearing away a more lively picture. At this moment, when many of these landscapes are floating before my mind, I feel a high enjoyment in reflecting that perhaps scarcely a day of my life will pass in which I shall not derive some happiness from these images.

It is only fair to add that meanwhile his sister was writing in her journal mainly about the alleged overcharging and uncomfortable conditions at inns and on stagecoaches, which continually afflicted her illustrious brother.

Richard Wagner spent about sixteen years in Switzerland. He wrote to his wife from Lucerne in 1859: "The last Act [of *Tristan*] promises famously; I drew profit for it even from my excursion to the Rigi. At four in the morning we were aroused by the alphorn—I jumped up, saw it was raining, and returned to bed to go to sleep again; but the droll tune went droning round my head, and out of it rose a very lusty melody which the herdsman now blows offstage to signal Isolde's ship, making a surprisingly merry and naive effect."

Thus the grandeur of the Swiss Alps rather than that of Berchtes-gaden is the making of the essential Wagner, as it had similarly inspired Weber and then Liszt and Mendelssohn. *La Vallée d'Ober-mann* was composed by Liszt after reading the novel *Obermann* at

Bex with his doxy of the moment, la Comtesse Marie d'Agoult. Mendelssohn worked at both his Italian symphony and his Hebrides overture during an extensive visit he made to Switzerland in 1831.

It should be noted that the Rigi alphorn air brought by Wagner into *Tristan* is very similar to the prelude to the fourth movement of Beethoven's *Pastoral Symphony*. A Swiss who knew Beethoven well wrote that the composer always loved to hear anecdotes about "the Falls of the Rhine, the Rigi, Pilatus, and the whole region of Lake Lucerne with its historic associations."

Then Brahms inserted a similar alphorn motif into his *C minor Symphony* after staying with his father in the Oberland, where the peasants sing the same tune to this day.

A long time later—as has been noted by the excellent Dr. de Beer —Stravinsky travelled down the steep funicular from Glion to Territet, a funicular which was outside the window of "Sapper" at the time he was writing the "Bulldog Drummond" stories, and was accompanied by two drunken gentlemen who constantly hiccoughed almost in perfect accord with the clanking of the mechanism; and later Stravinsky remembered the merry noise when composing the feast scene of *Les Noces.*

Ravel and Paderewsky similarly worked in Switzerland, as indeed did such a various bag as Hans Andersen, William Hazlitt, Charles Dickens, Balzac, Strindberg, Dostoyevsky, Thackeray and Captain Marryat.

Rainer Maria Rilke wrote in the Valais at Sierre and Matthew Arnold characteristically platitudinized the scene from and the place-names around the Vaudois Alps. Samuel Butler wrote the very best book about the Swiss mountains in *Alps and Sanctuaries,* and when he made his inhabitants of *Erewhon* regard illness as a crime he was undoubtedly remembering the stoicism of the true Swiss.

The great actor Kemble came to Switzerland to die, as did Humphry Davy the pioneer modern scientist and Krüger the Boer and Mannerheim the extraordinary leader of Finland's winter war. Even a Mrs. Gaskell had to write portions of *Wives and Daughters* at Pontresina. As for Davos and the other awful recipients of 19th- and early 20th-century consumptives the annals of the sanatoria and discreetly-hidden but neighboring graveyards are like a rollcall of modern literary fame especially. One thinks of such as James Elroy Flecker and Katherine Mansfield and John Addington Symonds and D. H. Lawrence and Somerset Maugham and Llewellyn Powys and always of that most inspired of tender observers, Thomas Mann.

Switzerland was a hope for the dying and always a refuge for those self-consigned to the living death of political intrigue. Vevey, of all places, received and sheltered in the 17th century that Ludlow who had helped to murder his king in distant England. Louis Philippe— believe it or not—was for a while a schoolmaster in Switzerland; and the gallant Kosciusko, after his warlike activities in both Poland and the young America, found ultimate sanctuary among the pasturelands of Solothurn. As for the Italians, they were forever hopping over the border: Garibaldi, Mazzini, right up to Mussolini. After the fall of the Paris Commune the little town of Tour-de-Peilz got the painter Courbet; and such timebombs as the anarchist Kropotkin and the revolutionaries Lenin and Trotsky bided their time usefully in what had become Europe's freest, most complacent land.

It was extraordinary how they came—and what a strong influence they had on the fortunes of this little country. For instance, only as recently as 1862 an Englishman came to Zermatt in the heart of winter and wrote: "The villages presented a scene of almost utter desolation. . . . Not a person was in the streets, hardly a light in the houses, and the two inns were barred up and forsaken." One hundred years later, thanks to the arrival of that Englishman and what he and others told others, Zermatt became at the same season of the year a thronged town of international sport and society, sometimes so gay and noisy as to repel the descendants of those who originally sought it out for its beautiful peace and quiet.

Mark Twain made fun of the world, but not of Switzerland, a place that evidently suited his temperament, or he would not have written: "Time and again it has seemed to me that I must drop everything and flee to Switzerland once more. It is a longing, a deep, strong, tug- ging longing—that is the word." In that he would have agreed with the contemporary Dickens who said: "My hat shall ever be ready to be thrown up, and my glove ever ready to be thrown down for Switzerland."

All the same there were many of that era who did not approve. The poet Tennyson said after a prolonged stay: "I was satisfied with the size of crags, but mountains, great mountains, disappointed me." Herbert Spencer found the Alps, if only color-wise, to be "far inferior to Scotland"; and Bret Harte, who in 1879 was living in the hills above the lake of Zurich, considered that California was a far better place.

Even Rilke the poet wrote: "These Swiss mountains? They are something of a stumbling-block to me, they are so terribly numerous.

Their shapes pile up on one another. . . ." And typically Slav was the complaint of Dostoyevsky in 1868: "You know the panorama of the lake; at Vevey it is distinctly better than at Montreux or Chillon close by. But apart from this panorama (and for a few places, the objects of mountain walks which we missed at Geneva), everything else is really too dreadful, and we fear that we are paying too high a price for the panorama alone." Maybe he had reason for his specific feelings at that moment, but the future mental instability of the novelist was assuredly shown by that completely unjust comparison between the views of the lake from Vevey and Montreux–Chillon.

Gogol: "What can I say to you of Switzerland? Beautiful views; always more views. . . . I begin to be sick of them, and if I could now see one of our Russian landscapes, miserable and flat with its grey sky, I would relish it like something new." *Dead Souls* indeed!

It seems that great men either love or hate Switzerland according to their temperaments (and perhaps according to whether or not they could pompously consider themselves to be overcharged or somehow slighted during their stay). Thus it can only be imagined what had occurred that morning at Victor Hugo's hotel before he was constrained to write: "On summits like the Rigi-Kulm one must look, but not paint any more. Is it beautiful or is it horrible? I really do not know. It is at once both horrible and beautiful. It is no longer landscapes we see, but monstrous views. The horizon is incredible, the perspective is impossible. It is a chaos of absurd exaggerations and dreadful diminutions."

Contrariwise those who really got into the true Switzerland were those like John Addington Symonds whose famous sentence is still so valid: "Very much of the charm of Switzerland belongs to simple things—to greetings from the herdsmen, the *Guten Morgen,* and *Guten Abend,* that are invariably given and taken upon mountain paths; to the tame creatures with their large dark eyes, who raise their heads one moment from the pasture while you pass; and to the plants that grow beneath your feet." And it was the same English critic and literary authority on the Renaissance who said with such truth: "Neither Rome nor the Riviera wins our hearts like Switzerland. We do not lie awake in London thinking of them; we do not long so intensely, as the year comes round, to revisit them. Our affection is less a passion than that which we cherish for Switzerland. Why, then, is this?"

Leslie Stephen more or less said the same thing (in the dark ages before air travel) when he wrote to America: "You poor Yankees are to be pitied for many things, but for nothing so much as your distance from Switzerland."

And Wagner was quite specific: "Let me yet create works conceived in the serene magnificence of Switzerland as I was gazing across at the sublime, golden-crowned mountains; they are wondrous works, and nowhere else could I have conceived them."

In this second half of the 20th century the sententious Victorians are forgotten and scarcely anyone bothers to write down literary impressions anymore. What the film stars and pop singers and thriller writers and exiled kings think of Switzerland today is not being recorded as it used to be. But they are all over Switzerland, these distinguished exiles still, and, if anything, they increasingly give the country not only much of their money but also a little of their hard-won experience of life and its affairs.

If a country looks after its scenery and keeps its roads and domestic offices up-to-date and then, by wise laws and tax systems, attracts those who would otherwise spend their money elsewhere, it must eventually become not just a little, nationalistic land but in a sense the true capital of the human world, a place at the hub of affairs where the great congregate and there is, among all the pettifogging regulations, a kind of ultimate freedom: where the artist can paint, the musician can compose, the author can write and the philosopher can eventually find the best way out of the human predicament.

And all this perhaps ultimately derives from the discipline imposed by high mountains.

11

ALPS

FORMERLY A GREAT SEA COVERED WHAT ARE NOW CALLED THE
Swiss Alps (even though the true meaning of "alp" is a mountain
meadow and not a peak). Creatures in that sea died and their shell-
bodies formed a sediment that became chalk when soft and dolomite
limestone when harder. The sediment was deposited on the original
seabed that consisted of a very hard crystalline rock called granite,
once molten when the world was very young.

After aeons of years the world suddenly convulsed, the last great
push of the boiling inferno at its core; and the seabed was pushed high
above the water to make three great folds like the backs of emerging
whales. One fold, running more or less east and west, became the
central line of the Alps. Another fold, with a great valley in between,
became the Bernese Oberland to the north, and another in the south
became the Julian and other Italian Alps.

Thence ensued a lengthy period during which the great sea splashed
against the naked new mountains, and the snow, rain and chemical
products of the atmosphere beat down upon them. In the highest places
the chalk or limestone was in its softness eaten away, leaving the
granite peaks, so reliable for experienced climbers, of such as Monte
Rosa, the Bernina, the Gross Venediger and the Gross Glockner.

Where the emerged folds were not so high, as in the northern and
southern chains, the limestone remained intact, and to this day may be
recognized in the principal skin of the Tyrol, the Dolomites, the Julian
Alps, and parts of the Oberland. The 13,000-foot Eiger is itself sedi-

mentary in crust, and Alpine geologists give that height as roughly the limit of limestone, after which the granite is exposed.

The creation of the Alps was not a moment's work. The great upheaval continued to grumble over a period that was short enough in the history of the universe but maybe longer than all human history. Subsidiary folds were created and the present shapes formed.

Many people hold that the great valleys of Switzerland are glacial and were formed by the passage of ice at remote periods. But it has been more or less established in our time that the convulsed shape of the country was firstly the work of the original subterranean upheaval that has been described. Secondly it was the work of water chiefly. Glaciers as such are far less potent as landscape gardeners than was once thought. They polish the sides of high valleys and they leave piles of detritus. The real carver out of the modern land, on the basis of the shape created by the upheaval, is not ice but water, the water from melting snow and ice, yes, but liquid all the same.

The greatest inundations undoubtedly occurred after the collapse of the so-called ice ages, when Europe was temporarily frozen stiff like the polar regions today. Were these low-temperature periods due to an actual shift of the world's axis-angle, and could another such shift again occur and destroy our little civilization more effectively than any atomic war? Continental drift is another theory to explain what we are talking about.

Anyway, water for millions of years ran down the mountains and wore away the basic hard rock to gouge out the deep valleys that everywhere pattern the Alps today like the bone system of a fish.

It can be seen in Switzerland after every storm how great parts of the hills and mountains are washed down and how whole stretches of riverbed and valley floor are changed. The movement has naturally been downwards from the high peaks to the lowlands and eventually, indeed, to the Mediterranean and North Seas, whose shallow beds today are composed of what came from the Alpine regions ages ago but still yesterday.

How deeply the water has through the centuries gouged away the floors of the valleys is shown by the composition of the 6000-foot top of the Rigi near Lucerne. It is a former seabed mass of pebbles and was obviously once a delta where some great river entered an ocean-lake. Since that ancient time the water running downwards has carried away almost an entire canton of rock and soil, leaving only Lake Lucerne so far below as a puddle-witness to its former gigantic mass.

Thus it is believed now that the most characteristic Alpine valley of all, that called the Valais, which runs roughly from Brigue to Geneva, including Lake Léman (although the Léman part, of course, does not belong to the political Valais) was not gouged out by a mighty glacier but was slowly and pertinaciously cut away and shaped by water that might at first have been the melting of an ice age but that afterwards was a huge running river or moving lake, following which the rains continually came and progressively finished off the job—if it can ever be finished—so that at the present time there is the great Rhône in the middle with its tributary streams and the mass of the land slowly being denuded still.

The Alpine glaciers as such are very interesting but no longer to be regarded as in any sense the makers of this land, the superficial surface of which was fashioned by water responding to the law of gravity. Actually it is the other way round and it could be said that where the temperature is low enough, as in the region of a glacier, there the land remains comparatively unaltered because the destructive

The true Alps as the geologist sees them, granite-covered with eternal snow on the top, then time-eroded limestone, and finally the soft, rolling foothills of green.

element of running water is frozen.

Within their narrow spheres of influence the very slowly moving glaciers do leave certain scars, notably the grooves known as striation marks, cut by stones and large rocks imbedded in the ice. Also they convey heaps of rubbish gradually forward and downward, heaps that are afterwards left in the very high valley and get covered later with a lovely carpet of grass and flowers and were often chosen for the site of a characteristic sharp-spired church.

During an ice age the Rhône glacier stretched from the central backbone of the Alps right down to the Jura. But it was after the melting of the glacier that the real work of carving out the present landscape was done. Principal remains of the former great tongue of compressed snow and ice are extraordinary boulders poised and balancing on tips here and there, and grooves in the valley sides, and piles of rubble on which villages and castles were built.

It is not generally realized, save by mountaineers and by Swiss villagers of the upper parts, that the high Alps have even less knowledge of real rain than the Arizona drylands. This is because rain freezes to snow above 8000 feet.

Snow at such an altitude freezes harder in the night after falling, and then may melt a little in the sun of the next day, after which it is covered by another fall and this time begins to freeze deeply, becoming what is known as *nèvé* or *firn*, which eventually, sliding downwards from the highest flat snowfield, is the father of a glacier.

The sluggish glacier contracts in the summer and moves away from its enclosing walls of rock, leaving formidable chasms indeed, the *Bergschrund*.

A frequent feature of glaciers is the moraine at the lowest end, above which can be a kind of grill of ice for filtering of the stones that continually fall: the moraine eventually becoming a dirty, pushed pile of those stones and other rubble. But like all else in the universe, a glacier never conforms perfectly to rules; and most of the famous specimens differ widely from each other in various respects. The Bossons Glacier that descends into the Chamonix valley ends in a clean tongue of white. The Miage Glacier that descends on the other side of the divide into Italy ends in what seems to be a stony river, until a foot slides and the stones part to reveal the nasty ice below.

Another glacier will specialize in *séracs,* those vertical slabs, even towers of ice and compressed snow that are caused by the narrow and precipitous character of the terrain. But where the glacier bed is wide the opposite occurs: longitudinal crevasses and the famous *mers de glace.*

Strangely enough the glaciers of the Bernese Oberland are the largest, including the magnificent Great Aletsch, some sixteen miles of compressed, frozen water that made it the champion of all the Alps. It might be thought that the main divide should produce bigger specimens than the lower Oberland, but weather conditions are all and more snow falls to the north, a consideration of which fact leads to an explanation of the variation in length of the Alpine glaciers throughout the ages.

Old wives have always been pessimistic about the glaciers of Switzerland. Either the glaciers have been advancing disastrously and betokening a new ice age and the end of the upper farmlands, or they have been receding disastrously and signifying a warm change of the climate that could ruin the tourist industry. A few years ago the glaciers in places were indeed visibly retreating. The good native residents of Grindelwald, notably, became very worried. Their two great glaciers had badly let them down; and visitors had complained about paying money to enter a gorge eventually to view a glacier tongue which was no longer there.

But the historian knows that throughout the ages the glaciers have advanced and receded continually according to often quite freakish variations in weather conditions over a period. Way back in the Middle Ages the glaciers were far less extensive than they are today. The recent diminution of the glaciers was the product of a very rapid melting that occurred in the years 1850–1878, during which the ice flows were temporarily starved of sustaining upper snow by special weather conditions. Since then the diminution has gradually slowed down, and, according to the laws of weather averages, should be reversed eventually—when new troubles will begin for the daring high villages, hotels, ski-lifts and hydroelectric schemes.

The avalanche is another matter. It has two forms, that driven down dryly by the winter winds, the powder avalanche, and that caused so dangerously in spring by the sudden melting of overhanging snowfields when hard, compact masses hurtle down to destroy the works of man, cut swathes through forests, and, with a strange noise like sharp thunder or artillery fire, temporarily kill all life in their path. The Swiss know how to deal with these, and construct various barriers, even thick concrete roofs over railways and roads, but are often taken fatally unawares for all their careful experience.

The snow is all in the Alps, its coming and its going. In former times the peasants understood it perfectly and made their dispositions accordingly, and on the whole retreated downwards when the winter

Snowscape with Pitz Palu in the background.

advanced. For hundreds of years the Alpine cattle have been brought down noisily each autumn to safe byres in the valleys. But, as mentioned in the previous chapter, the development of the modern tourist industry has altered all that. The cattle may have continued, wisely, to come down, but at the same time the hoteliers and restaurateurs and their servants have mounted upwards, to serve the ever-advancing hordes of winter holidaymakers. And matters of the snowline and high weather conditions have become extremely important.

If a tourist agency in New York, London, Paris, Amsterdam or Hamburg should be approached on the subject of a Swiss winter holiday now the clerk invariably inquires: "What altitude do you prefer?" And will explain, if his customer does not know how to answer that question, the varying conditions that normally exist in the resorts at different levels of the Alps according to weather prospects and the exact time of the visit.

It can be said that from about the middle of January till the middle of March there will usually be good snow in the Swiss Alps above 3000 feet, and that this expectation is increasingly likely towards the east of the ranges always. Above 8000 feet there should be perpetual snow, so that the most reliable tourist resorts are those like St. Moritz and Zermatt which are situated very high and have ski-lifts that mount actually to the ever-white regions. As they are the oldest and the highest they are still the best.

It is curious that what for centuries were the least attractive heights of the Alps are now the most popular, although some wise men

Telecabins take skiers up from Crans to a 7546 feet jump-off.

Hochstukli, Central Switzerland.

Anniviers Valley, Valais.

Boys' parade.

(and women and children) would still prefer perhaps those intermediate regions where the snow might not be reliable but the visitor can always depend on sunshine and an early quickening of green grass and such a carpet of flowers as does not exist elsewhere outside of regimented Dutch market gardens.

The tourist future of the Alps is quite certain. It will be an extension of the "trade" eventually with the perfection of personal flying by helicopter and machines not yet invented to the very highest snowfields, far above the existing resorts and ski-lifts. And this development will completely change property values all over the mountains. Nothing will be inaccessible; and chalets and hotels will be built where formerly only the most expert mountaineer trod. Those who own peaks and high ridges will make their fortunes, while those who acquired property on lower levels may lose a lot of money. They will, however, be considerably quieter and will be able increasingly to enjoy their lovely surroundings in peace.

That extraordinary flora of the Alps represents the hardiest of all species (save perhaps man himself) in that it can endure days of sun that raise the temperature to over 100 degrees Fahrenheit, and succeeding nights in which all is frozen stiff. These Alpines vary from the spring crocuses that transform desolate landscapes into a bulb garden, to the white-leathery edelweiss itself, a plant that Switzerland has had to protect by law (one more law which was made to be broken).

Then the varying heights of the resorts, and the different climatic conditions—such an enormous variety—cause the same kind of flowers to bloom at different times in various places. Gentians are blue at 3000 feet in April, but, at 6000 feet, do not flower until July, when they will suddenly duplicate the azure sky among the lichened rocks and the terrible scree. The small rhododendron, which is nicely named alpenrose, will be out on the lower slopes in June but does not bloom among the fastnesses of the Grimsel till September.

The best summer flowerings in the Alps tend to occur after late snow and bad weather in the spring. These blooms are not only children of the sustaining, protecting snow, but their display also depends in many regions on the grass-cutting habits of the local farmers. When the peasant is prevented by bad weather from cutting his pastures early then the flowers have their real chance. This applies particularly to that coy beauty the sulphur anemone, child of the high granite regions, not of the lower limestone mountains. The Alpinist knows that where the sulphur anemone grows there will be good rock for climbing, although usually the man who finds these lovely flowers cannot go far that day. They have been encouraged to appear by the very weather conditions that keep him away from the high places.

There are indeed few parts of the world that, in such a comparatively short distance, provide such an enormous variety of vegetation. In a day's march it is possible to see grapes, almonds and peaches (up to 2000 feet in the Ticino), then sweet chestnuts (up to 3200 feet), after which the climbing woods consist mainly of spruce, larch and cembra pine, until, at about 5900 feet, the true Alps or mountain pastures begin, the little patches of grazing land beloved of the flowers. Before the higher snow line come the alders and dwarf pines sometimes, and the short-stemmed hardier plants that flower so surprisingly in the very late spring and summer. Then with the snowline at between some 7800 and 9200 feet there will still be the remarkable glacier cocksfoot (up to 10,000 feet) and, of course, the indomitable lichens that paint entrancing pictures upon the very highest, naked rocks.

So there is flora in the Alps ranging from subtropical to arctic tundra; and all tastes can be indulged here. Perhaps nothing is so satisfying as those high spots of color which literally peep from the melting snow at what seem impossible altitudes, but, on the other hand, the most glorious floral displays are those sheets of color that are suddenly spilt by a natural painter's hand across the tree-girt pastures of the lower, limestone ranges. The ranunculus glacialis or gentian is a miracle of the rocks. Lower down, along the limestone ways, are so many wild flowers that children of all ages can gather for hours, without doing any harm, such mighty nosegays as seem to contain all the blooms and colors of a poet's madness. Lower down still are such unique phenomena as the narcissi of Les Avants above Montreux. In spring the slopes where the beginners formerly skied are starred like a milky way fallen upon the surprised land—until the cars arrive and everyone is paying one franc for the privilege of gathering as many as can be reasonably taken away, gatherings that, in these days, are sent all over the world by air.

This is an innocent pleasure. It does no harm, even provides the local farmers with some pocket money.

But it is certainly noteworthy that whenever man finds beauty he wants to fall upon it and break it off and take it home. He loves it so much that he must destroy it.

Once upon a time nearly all kinds of wild animals inhabited the Alps. Not so long ago the bear was sufficiently common for a price to be put upon his head and for his image to be the proud insignia of the ruling class of Switzerland in that foremost canton named after him, Berne. There is to this day a pit at Berne where a few of his descendants are preserved, alive. And it was in the Swiss Alps, according to legend, that the last of the true dragons survived. The realist would say this animal, in prehistoric times, was no more than one of the giant lizards that were overcome by climatic changes. But popular belief in the Swiss dragon did not finally die out until the 18th century, and even now the peasantry will sometimes prate of *draconita* or dragon's stones as preserved in their homes, churches or museums. The more daring of their ancestors had procured these stones by stupefying a dragon with herbs and cutting the trophy from his head!

Undoubtedly the most fantastic animals once ranged here, from the sabre-toothed tiger to the great aurochs. Their true bones have been found. But alas, for a long time now the Swiss indigenous fauna have been confined to small, agile and hardy creatures capable of secluding themselves in comparatively inaccessible places, and to similarly elusive birds and fish. Only the other day a shabby dog fox was seen loping across the main street of a little Swiss town by Lake Léman, but usually it is necessary to mount a minor expedition in order to catch a glimpse of real wild life, the chamois and marmots, the beavers and otters and wild boars, the capercailzie, herons, storks and supreme eagles. Just a few red deer survive; and the Engadine National Park has been reestablished with ibex, that solid wild goat with the large, recurved horns.

The native chamois is actually a species of antelope, very difficult to see on the mountainside because of its nicely-designed protective coloring; and it is carefully preserved today by a law that restricts shooting to a single fortnight in September (although in many places it may not be shot at all).

The marmot is perhaps the Swiss animal most likely to survive eternally, because it is very sensible. Shaped like a snug brown rabbit but with only small ears, it is unlike the cony in that it can utter a shrill whistle of warning when dangerous humans come near. It inhabits burrows amid bouldered ground at great heights such as 7000 feet, and when the winter comes it closes its burrow with a thick wad of dry grass and goes nicely and safely to sleep until the enormous thickness of snow above it has melted in spring.

There used to be bearded vultures in the Alps, but the last one was poisoned in 1887, twenty-five years after her mate had been shot; and the royal eagle is now the chief survivor of the great birds. Fortunately they keep very much to themselves on the heights, where their eyries are inaccessible; and their inordinately graceful flights are confined to illimitable distances between precipices that the car-hordes cannot scale. Unlike the foolish extinct lammergeiers or vultures, they do not descend into human places and make away with cats and babies in their hooked beaks, and so they remain as the unchallenged kings of regions that no other creatures desire. (Until those helicopter or personal flying machines eventually come.)

Ptarmigan, all speckled dark and white, grunt in the high Alps; and even over the heads of the holiday crowds at Lucerne and Montreux the dark hawks hover before plunging from a great height into the lake after trout, roach, pike, char, perch.

The brightly dressed heron is an even more impressive fisherman when seen; but it is most difficult of all to catch a glimpse of the very common but naturally nocturnal eagle-owl, elusive like the native bats and the disappearing mountain hares. The nice red squirrels, as elsewhere, are being beaten to it by the American greys; and the hedgehogs and dormice survive only by the fortunate stealth of their methods.

Switzerland is good but not perfect for birds. Too many of them are almost ritualistically slaughtered on the Italian side; and several species find the land less suitable for breeding than the countries like Britain in the north to which they annually migrate from the deep south in spring. Sometimes the migrations pause here curiously, but mostly they pass overhead; and perhaps the most interesting small birds that remain are such as the brilliantly black and white snow finches—who dart about the snowline in flashes of wonder—and that fantastic climber called the wall creeper, who with red wings half folded will ascend sheer rock faces without visible means of support save a tentative toe here and there.

On the whole there is less morning birdsong in Switzerland than in the center of London's West End.

Conversely there are many more strange butterflies, moths and rare insects in this country than in most other parts of Europe; and when the cicadas sing in summer it is as if the heat of the dry land has composed its own characteristic symphony: a real but benign heat that also brings out the companionable lizard from cool crevasses in the warm rocks to bask and then suddenly flick away under a tolerant sun.

Perhaps the true indigenous creatures of the Alps today are the human climbers, heirs of those solitary English dons and aristocrats who first arrived not much more than one hundred years ago. Today in all seasons they doggedly scramble up and down the highest of the mountains, only seeming to disdain the lower, limestone peaks which are relatively free from the attack still. And they act only

The true mountaineers.

as the advance guard of the thousands of visitors *and* Swiss whose pleasure is to be pulled up slopes by various kind of mechanical apparatus and then slide down again on prepared pistes with the help of, originally, proper skis, but increasingly ski-bobs like wheel-less bicycles, and finally the new short ski which is not very adventurous but at least permits the elderly to have their turn.

The Eastern Alps are most favored by the modern school of climbers, originally based in Germany, who achieve the humanly impossible largely by mechanical means; and elsewhere such difficulties as the north face of the Eiger and the Grandes Jorasses have been frequently overcome by daring young men with nylon ropes and various metallic contrivances (almost like scaffolding) although just sufficient of them have fallen from great heights to make the sport continuously worthwhile.

It is worth noting all the same that if the large-scale conquest of the mountains was largely achieved by British climbers in the first place, and the final humiliation of the most difficult precipices was the work of at first German and then American mechanical ingenuity, yet the native Swiss really led the way. They from the beginning were the guides, a race of men self-effacing but apart, and averse to publicity that might spoil the smoking-room stories of their affluent clients. It was as if the real Swiss of the mountains preferred the credit to be given to rich customers who might thus be encouraged to come back again. Thus eighteen guides made possible the pioneer ascent of Mont Blanc by Saussure and his valet; and the Meyer family mastered the Jungfrau and the Finsteraarhorn as long ago as 1811 and 1812. Three Swiss guides led Whymper's party to the first ascent of the Matterhorn in 1865, and probably four of that triumphant party would not have been lost through the breaking of a primitive rope if local advice had been properly followed.

Throughout the ages the Swiss did not bother to scale their peaks because all their time was devoted to making a poor living from the precipitous land and to keeping marauders at bay. But of course when they found that foreigners were willing to pay good money in order to enjoy the pains and hazards of high climbing they at once did their best to cater for the craze: and there were sufficient of good, local Swiss boys about who had always braved the slopes in their spare time and could now sell their expertise dearly.

The Swiss Alps contain 115 important summits and there are many, many more of lesser importance, but nearly all have been effectively climbed many times. The remaining attraction of the whole

Lake in the lovely Gruyère region of the Fribourg Alps.

area is surely its capacity for relieving a spoiled modern man of his various mental afflictions; and this is best achieved by sensible climbing according to certain golden rules, the first of which is that climbing is best done in expert company, and the second of which is that maps and equipment should be carefully chosen. Then the facilities offered by the famous Swiss Alpine Club should not be ignored. A large number of club huts, often little, austere hotels, are dotted over the region. They are still very cheap, and available to non-members at a charge.

As it is possible to walk about two and a half miles an hour up the gentle slopes, so it is usual to climb about one thousand feet an hour by normal methods. Once again the wise man employs moderation as his principal guide and gets most pleasure from his Alps by proceeding deliberately and slowly, not as quickly as possible. He observes the uphill gait of the Swiss peasant, which involves almost a perceptible pause between each step. And if he sensibly prefers long-distance ski touring to the trivial up-and-down prepared pistes of the resorts then he will seek the companionship of experts and be sure that his equipment is adequate. There is no more satisfying

Thus the tourists ascend the high mountains today—this one being Pilatus above Lucerne in the giddy distance down.

sport; and journeys can be arranged, especially in the Pennines or central Alps of the Valais, which traverse miles of magnificent mountains along their ridges. But informed local people are required in the party if the outstanding hazard is to be avoided, the hazard of the avalanche. Passing under or indeed over a snow-covered slope after a heavy snowfall or during föhn weather is the danger. Travellers of this kind are thus advised to carry both a shovel to dig themselves out if necessary and a trailing red avalanche rope so that rescuers can in an emergency try to pull them out from the high white tomb in which they have been immured by their folly.

Everywhere in the Alps today the traveller is aided by various kinds

Black and white silhouettes in the snow as the people ascend to their playgrounds impudently.

of lift, ranging from old-fashioned but wonderfully engineered rack railways to the simple sledge lifts as originally developed by the peasants for taking supplies up to their eyries from the valleys. There are true funiculars, with cars on rails pulled up by steel cables; there are chair lifts, seemingly precarious to the innocent when hoisting him suddenly over steep canyons, many kinds of modern ski lift, and, most daringly, the newest téléfériques, beautiful scarlet cars like scarab beetles that start from businesslike stations surrounded by restaurants and car-parks and then are pulled under wires across broad valleys, higher and higher, till eventually they ascend precipices into the clouds that swirl around peaks such as those of Les Diablerets.

Indeed no people in the world have such good heads for heights as the Swiss. Anyone who lives in a Swiss town will be amazed to observe his neighbors, how when repairs are required they just walk up and down high, sloping roofs as if upon the ground a hundred feet below. If Hitchcock had made his film *Vertigo* in Switzerland it would have had absolutely no point. Thus age-old familiarity with their mountains has led the Swiss to develop a certain contempt of them: and hence the new chalets that are built on high cliff edges, the hotels that are cheekily perched on peaks, and these aerial rope-ways that convey thousands of vertiginous tourists annually up to horrific heights across abysses that are sometimes many kilometres across and even more deep. It is especially noteworthy, this pheno-menon, in that it shows everywhere how man can impudently master the most dangerous aspects of his environment provided that he concentrates his energies and his spirit on that job and does not fritter them away on the foolishnesses that enervate the cities of the plain.

There is even a language of the Alps, which has since become the jargon of mountaineers the world over. In alphabetical order this can be briefly explanatory of much that is important in Swiss life, from the *aiguille* or needle-sharp peak to the *alpenglow* or rosiness shed on the snow mountains by the low-angle sun, from the *arête* or sharp ridge to the *bergschrund* or gulf between a glacier and its containing rock walls. The *bise* is the thermodynamic cool wind that comes down from the peaks to the valley, especially at the end of a northeaster day, and fountains or springs are *brunnen*. A *cabane* is a refuge, and, please, please, not a refuse hut, and a *chimney* has nothing to do with that hut but is a narrow and precipitous gully. A *col* is the culminating point of a pass and a *couloir* is one more gully.

Crap is not what it might be but Romansch for rock. *Furka* comes

A famous ski-run and aerial ropeway near Verbier.

from the Latin through the German and means a pass, but a *gendarme* is a rock pinnacle on a ridge. The term *ice-fall* in the Alps stands specifically for the huge crack that occurs in a glacier when the level of its bed suddenly changes; and *joch* is German for yoke or a pass. A *matte* is a pasture; and the very ancient Romansch language gives

One of Switzerland's 800 ski-lifts through beauty.

us the strange *mortèl* for a stony waste and *ova* for water. A cliff wall in the Alps is known as a *paroi* and a slope as a *pente*. *Piz* is Romansch for a peak and *pun* for a bridge (also for one of our most ancient forms of humor, a bridge linking dissimilar words amusingly or the contrary).

Sass is the ancient, local word for stone or rock. *Séracs* are the needles and towers of ice on a glacier, while narrow, steep paths are described as *steigs*.

After the individual words what about the literature itself? Every writer knows that his choice of theme is all-important to the fineness of his style. Not even the greatest artists with words can produce their best when given an uninspiring theme. Conversely there are subjects with which even very poor authors cannot go wrong, and one of them is the Swiss Alps. Around those mountains has developed a literature that has been evoked by no other range in the whole world: indeed by no other single geographical feature. This literature has in its time been overpraised. For all the donnish prattling about Mummerys and Whympers there is not a single book about the Alps as yet that can be regarded as among the greatest books of man. But the Alpine books on the other hand have a uniformly high standard and are all quite lyrical in places, as if the subject has made even the most naturally dull writers sing. When authors come to the Alps they are like undistinguished young women who are momentarily transfigured by their first loves.

This Alpine library was nearly all written in the hundred years between 1850 and 1950. Prior to 1850 there was Addison's *Remarks on Several Parts of Switzerland* (1705); and it must be agreed that Rousseau was at his very best as an evocative writer when he was describing either his natural surroundings in Savoy and the Vaud or his unnatural vices everywhere.

Peaks, Passes and Glaciers, the first series of which was published in 1859, contained contributions by many loving hands and is still the first great source book on the Alps. Few of the writers who contributed were aught but well-educated amateur mountaineers, but their subject frequently enabled them to rise far above themselves as literary artists, witness one description of the dawn by Sir Claud Schuster:

> On the glacier, the light of a day still to be born put out our candles. . . . We halted to watch the procession of the sun. He came out of the uttermost parts of the earth, very slowly, lighting peak after peak in the long southward array, dwelling for a moment and then passing on. Opposite, and first to catch the glow, were the great mountains of the Saasgrat and the Weisshorn. But more beautiful, like the loom of some white-sailed ship far out at sea, each unnamed and unnumbered peak of the east took and reflected the radiance of the morning.

That is better in its way than all the effusions of professionals like Byron, Shelley and Ruskin. It is genuine emotion recollected in tranquillity by an ordinary man who had been momentarily transformed by the magic of the Alps into a real poet.

John Tyndall published in 1860 and 1871 two books, *The Glaciers of the Alps* and *Hours of Exercise in the Alps,* which are little more than their dull titles promise, but still contain passages among the chapters of scientific description that can be given to school children as examples of the finest kind of English prose.

And when we come (in 1871 also) to the outstanding Alpine classic, Edward Whymper's *Scrambles among the Alps,* we know at once that these mountains are unique in the way they produce their men. This in parts is a poor, even a boring book. But in other parts it is supremely fine. Whymper had come to Zermatt as a typical scholastic Englishman of his generation and had returned again and again as a human being dedicated to the conquest not of a mountain, the Matterhorn, but of himself. His book shows in its brilliantly outstanding passages how he achieved his aim. But at what fearful cost! *Scrambles* is thus not just an Alpine book. It is also—but in parts—the record of how the Swiss mountains can inspire human beings not only literally to rise above themselves.

This is so in spite of the fact that Whymper's essential honesty, the first requisite of a good writer, forces him to interlard his bald and then inspired descriptions with accounts of such squalid side issues as his anger against rivals and those who afterwards accused him of negligence—and of that moment when, going down the mountain after the tragedy, old Taugwalder, the guide who might really have been responsible, could talk only of who might pay him now that his master Lord Francis Douglas had died.

Also in that great year 1871 was published Leslie Stephen's *The Playground of Europe.* This was written by another outstanding, indeed archetypal man of his age. Stephen was a don whose brand of muscular Christianity seemed at the time perfectly to express the Latin adage *mens sana in corpore sano,* although very soon his students were doing their utmost with mockery to destroy what he had labored for and represented. His work for the *Dictionary of National Biography* must all the same endure and his writings about Swiss mountaineering very frequently ignite with the enthusiasm of true art and have given spiritual motive-power to several generations of human mountain goats. Also he was the father of Virginia Woolf.

A. F. Mummery was the fourth Alpine writer of occasional startling insight. His important book was *My Climbs in the Alps and Caucasus,* published in 1895.

Then there were the lesser men such as D. W. Freshfield (*Italian Alps,* 1876), Martin Conway (*The Alps from End to End,* 1895, and

The Alps, 1904), C. E. Mathews (*The Annals of Mont Blanc,* 1898), Frederic Harrison (*My Alpine Jubilee,* 1908) and Walter Larden (*Recollections of an Old Mountaineer,* 1910). They and many late Victorian and Edwardian contributors to *The Alpine Journal* and *The Cornhill* such as A. D. Godley, Geoffrey Winthrop Young, F. W. Bourdillon and R. L. A. Irving really brought this remarkable effusion to a pre-1914 end. It had been a unique era.

Since then many fine writers have been stirred to some of their best moments by the Swiss Alps. Arnold Lunn not only wrote good books and compiled useful anthologies. He became one of the great organizers of mountaineering; and Switzerland should award him a statue for his fine propaganda work. Right up to this present time of writing there have been occasional writers about the Alps in the

The Matterhorn as the mountaineer sees it from the rear.

The silver thistle of the Alps.

classic tradition still, such as that splendid climber, modest poet and epitome of the old English public school spirit Wilfrid Noyce (who fell eventually to his death on a very foreign mountain after writing a book on courage).

C. E. Montague was a still underestimated writer of the 1920s, some of whose Alpine passages have no equals elsewhere; and Samuel Butler wrote in *Alps and Sanctuaries* a work that may well survive many others. Guido Rey will always be remembered by Alpinists for his study of the Matterhorn.

Thus the writers came and, ignoring nearly all else that was Switzerland, found their principal inspiration in the challenge to climbers presented by the central mountains. It is a phenomenon in the history of literature, but also one more sociological indication of what makes the idea of Switzerland tick. Always back to the mountains. There, undoubtedly, is the Promethean fire that made and still makes this land. It even made temporary poets out of a dull bunch of English schoolmasters.

What it could make of a really important writer is shown in Thomas Mann's *Magic Mountain,* not only the very best book inspired by a Swiss theme but also one of the finest novels ever written and the obituary of our age.

12

THE CONTRIBUTION

THE PURPOSE OF THIS BOOK HAS BEEN TO ANALYZE WHAT SWITZER-
land has, or has had, which a sick world could copy or study as a
basis for self-improvement. The analysis has now been made, but
should perhaps be summarized—after a brief survey of direct contributions made by Swiss who actually left their beloved country in order
to help.

Possible improvements in civilization have been imposed by many
countries on others by conquest and mass emigration: what is now
known pejoratively as colonization. The Swiss have never been good
colonists. In fact they have not been colonists at all save in the one
instance of that district called "New Switzerland" in Ohio, where
emigrants from the Vaud under Jean-Jacques Dufour in 1803 con-
sciously tried to establish viticulture in North America. Many of
America's modern vineyards descend from those Vaudois grapes,
which also sired a large proportion of the important vines in France
and Switzerland and Germany today, being reimported into Europe
as basic stock to replace what was destroyed by the great vine disease.

Within ten years 66 Swiss immigrants were at work on 37,000
acres and Dufour wrote *The American Vinedresser's Guide, and the
Process of Winemaking, Adapted to the Soil and Climate of the
United States.*

Not even the most ardent enemies of colonialism could complain
too much about introducing the art of wine-making into such a rough

Horse-drawn sledges in the Engadine.

young country as the United States then was; and apart from that the Swiss never attempted to settle other lands on a large scale.

Sometimes Helvetians of strong personality, like Christophe de Graffenried, named an infant town of the New World after the European place from which they came: New Bern in North Carolina;

Engelberg in Kentucky; New Glaris in Canada; New Freiburg in Brazil. That, and the good wine, was the colonial all.

Meanwhile individual Swiss in considerable numbers visited and occasionally settled in various parts of the world—and mostly left their mark as engineers. They had this one special skill that all nations wanted, particularly in the 19th century, a skill based on experience with high mountains and an extreme thoroughness of nature. Only Scottish engineers were better at that period.

In many ways a Swiss called Jean-Rodolphe Perronet was responsible for the basic structure or urban system of Paris. His father had been born in Chateau-d'Oex and had become an officer of the Swiss Guard at Versailles. The son became a civil engineer and constructed many of the roads that run in and out of Paris, also the main canals, and such bridges as the Pont de la Concorde and that of Neuilly-sur-la-Seine.

A savant of Geneva, Dr. Paul-Emil Schazmann, has specially investigated this subject, and in his valuable books on the Swiss abroad has described, for example, how Franz Mayor de Montricher built that enormous viaduct that carries drinking water to the city of Marseilles. He started the work in 1839, and he was a Vaudois who had been educated in Bienne. Later he was given the job of attempting to drain Lake Fucino in the Abruzzi. Malaria from swamps here had helped the Roman Empire to fall, and all the attempts of civil engineers in the ancient days, and right up to Montricher, had been unable to master this unsavory region—which the good Swiss promptly transformed into a prosperous and healthy area of fertile farmlands.

Perhaps the most daring feat of 19th-century engineering was the Trans-Andean Railway from Buenos Aires to Valparaiso—as constructed, sometimes at an altitude of 19,700 feet, 4000 feet higher than Mont Blanc, by an engineer trained at Zurich named Schatzmann and another from Geneva named Dominicé.

Guglielminetti was a Valaisan civil engineer whose techniques in road construction with asphalt spread like liquorice across the world, and Chevrolet was a Bernese from La Chaux-de-Fonds, the home of the great watchmakers, who went to America and constructed an automobile that founded the fortune of the world's greatest corporation, General Motors (who to this day assemble their Swiss cars at Bienne not far from Chevrolet's birthplace).

The greatest watchmaker in the world was the 18th-century Breguet. He and other Swiss more or less christened the Quai de l'Horloge in Paris; and he was born in little Boudry near Neuchâtel. Jean Petitot,

Astronomical clock of 1530 in old Berne.

another Swiss, was enameller to Louis XIV; and Louis-David Duval, as goldsmith to the czars at St. Petersburg, established the art that eventually gave Carl Fabergé a more certain fame. Similar work was done by Hedlinger of Schwyz in Sweden.

When the great 18th-century porcelain factories of Germany wanted a supreme modeller of figures they employed a Swiss, Bustelli from the Ticino; and many of the best sculptures at Paris in the Luxembourg and Tuileries gardens, in the Invalides and on the Arc de Triomphe, were executed by Pradier (from Geneva). It has been described elsewhere in this book how Swiss architects contributed to the building of Italy, and how Le Corbusier transformed world architecture in recent times.

The Swiss have particularly contributed to international culture as editors and publishers, from Vieusseux in Florence with his Literary Cabinet to Peter Mark Roget of Geneva with his English classic *Thesaurus of English Words and Phrases*. Julliard and Payot in Paris were originally Swiss, as was Elrico Hoepli (of Amriswil) in Milan. And the true creator of the London magazine *Punch* was Sir Francis Burnand, from the Vaud.

The pattern of the skis.

Angelica Kauffmann, that delicious 18th-century lady painter (particularly of table-tops and trays) came from Coire, and Madame Tussaud of the Waxworks from Berne, and Madame Marcet, whose book *Talks on Chemistry* exhausted sixteen editions in under fifty years, was the daughter of a Swiss banker from Yverdon.

Little Boudry near Neuchâtel has been mentioned as the birthplace of that maker of lovely watches, Breguet. It also knew the first days of Jean-Paul Marat, whose sinister reign of terror during the French Revolution was suitably ended in his bath by Charlotte Corday.

Marat, like Rousseau, was a Swiss whose desire to improve the conditions of the human race somehow went wrong. The most effective improvers who came from this little land at once to help humanity and themselves were medical and other scientists, such as that Théodore Tronchin who widely introduced in Europe (although of course he did not originate it) the idea of vaccination against smallpox. And a medical scientist from Aubonne on the foothills of the Jura near Geneva was the first to isolate the bubonic plague bacillus. He was Alexandre Yersin.

The Morat man Louis Agassiz became one of the greatest of natural scientists, particularly noted for his marine research, and a pioneer of Harvard methods (founder of the Museum at Cambridge, Mass.).

How Swiss children begin to know no fear.

He opposed the theory of evolution and may one day be regarded as a pioneer in that respect also. Jean-Jacques de Tschudi was a Swiss who wrote the definitive works on the fauna and antiquities of Peru, while much valuable excavation was done by the Swiss archaeologists Edouard Naville and Gustave Jéquier in Egypt and Paul Schazmann in the eastern Mediterranean.

Probably more Swiss brought their skills to Britain in the 18th and 19th centuries than to any other country; and many famous families owe names such as Cazenove, Mallet, Marcet, Rieu and Romilly to this origin. But in Britain the Swiss did not succeed so much as craftsmen and scientists and engineers (although Jean de Labélie of Vevey built Westminster Bridge). They seemed primarily to become official administrators, often Governors of the Bank of England and Secretaries of the Royal Society (J. G. Scheuchzer of Zurich and Joseph Planta of Zuoz). A Swiss from Geneva and a Swiss from Yverdon both became Governors-General of Canada. Ceylon was brought into the British Empire by Colonel Charles Daniel de Meuron of Neuchâtel. Clive of India profitably followed the advice given to him by his Swiss military instructors, the Captains Paradis and de Gingins.

A Peter Clias of Berne introduced gymnastics into the Royal Navy and British Army. And meanwhile the Popes in Rome sheltered not just behind their faith but also behind their sturdy Swiss Guard.

It might seem, therefore, that the first requisite for relative success as an organized body of kindred men is geographical centralness. Followed by another physical attribute, that of altitude. Switzerland has hitherto been situated at main European crossroads, and, as Europe itself becomes a junction in our time between East and West, so Switzerland may expect to remain almost at the exact center of world affairs.

Throughout history the successful powers have been those in the right place at the right time: Rome at the exact hub of the old Mediterranean culture; the empire of Charlemagne centered on the Rhine that was the principal artery of dark Europe after the balance had shifted away from Rome; the empire of the Habsburgs similarly owed much if not all to the central position of Austria then—as the Spanish and Portuguese strength partly came from the convenient status of the Iberian Peninsula as a jumping-off platform on the edge of the old world for the exploration of the new. The hegemony of Venice was the product of geographical position partly; and Napoleon failed just because France had insuperable barriers, for that time, between herself and the necessary conquests of Britain and Russia. The British in the 18th and 19th centuries were, however, most excellently situated in the geographical sense for the development of a new world hegemony based on sea power and colonization.

But Switzerland has been at the hub from the beginning and is

Murren under the dreaded Eiger, the Monch and the Jungfrau.

more surely there today than ever before. Even if her people were wholly bad they would still have to be very successful.

That they are far from bad may be due to racial composition but it seems more likely to be the product of altitude.

There is no doubt that people who live in mountains are different or become different from those who live on the flat. Their lives are relatively harder and this makes them more resourceful, more thorough, more independent, more courageous, more cruel perhaps but also at the same time in other ways kinder and more helpful to each other. When avalanches fall there have to be rules about digging each other out.

Then living at an altitude heightens the senses, sharpens the mental as well as the physical vision, enlarges the vital spirit. The thinner, clearer air makes human beings more precise in thought; and the great landscapes and perspectives from the heights encourage little men to think big.

The average height of even Switzerland's main cities (which seem to be on the flat) is about 1600 feet above sea-level. The lowest place in the geographical sense is Locarno, and even that is 600 feet above London. (When the Americans started to build skyscrapers was it a subconscious effort to add altitude to their other extraordinary assets?)

Anyway Switzerland is principally different in the physical sense from other countries in that she consists of mountains at the cross-roads between France, Germany, Austria and Italy; and with this she has always been and remains *small*. There is no doubt that the most important contributions in human history have been made not by the giant but by the little, compact conglomerates of peoples: Greece, the early Rome, what we now call Israel, Britain. These have made the contributions that most count, those of the human spirit. The giants—and many small countries have indeed wrecked themselves by becoming such monsters through war and colonization —have given humanity some important techniques and pages of history, but not the fructifying ideas. All India has left behind a tithe of what the diminutive Jewish people have almost carelessly flung off. And great China will always lag behind the much smaller Japan in the kind of progress that eventually counts the most.

It might, however, not be the smallness as such that prevails, but the national mentality that eschews wide territorial expansion. The peoples that do their best to remain small might just have the mentality requisite for the kind of success in living that is the object of this investigation. And Switzerland has so often resolutely turned away from the schemes of conquest that have wrecked so many others. With her superb military abilities she could long ago have mastered Europe. Indeed, she could have gone farther and briefly enjoyed her own world empire. But she did not; and as a result her energies have not been dissipated in tropic sands or the steaming jungles of remote delusion. They have remained at home and have fortified the gradual development of a way of life that has given the Swiss freedom from so much that has plagued her always rampaging neighbors.

Utopia should thus be laid out in a central position, for the purposes of trade and influence, and among high mountains for health of body and mind, and it should be kept firmly within quite narrow bounds so that men may know each other and not be corrupted by indulgence of power over others.

Let us next consider the way that the Swiss live, and note at once that it is still essentially a peasant way of life. Four-fifths of the people still live outside the big cities. They still deeply love the primitive habits of the countryside. Their happiest days are spent on the mountains or among the farms and flowers, and their happiest evenings not in the slick surroundings of cosmopolitan man—although they can provide these for tourists and rich strangers—but in hostelries and brasseries that, decoratively speaking, have remained unaltered for hundreds of years. A great part of their money and strength has been devoted to the building of communications that enable them quickly to get away from the enervating influences of modern life to the primitive places and the crude habits of their forefathers.

In this, however, they have not completely despised the techniques of industrial society. Far from it. Theirs has been an effort to keep right to the forefront in such techniques. The economy is constantly reformed so that it does not fall behind. Farming is rigidly confined to the possibilities of a poor, rocky land. It is largely a milk-producing agriculture with that universal food, cheese, as a principal end-product. Similarly the various manufacturing industries are almost rigidly shaped to suit the capabilities of the Swiss and the world situation. This means constant modernization—but only so that the people gain the money and time to return to nature as frequently as possible. A dentist will labor with the most advanced equipment in Lausanne all the week so that he can live the life of a primitive lake-dweller or nasty, brutish and short mountaineer on the weekend—the increasingly long weekend.

The great cities of Switzerland are accordingly dormitories of modernity with a tidy but over-restored medieval background. There is no single city of the land today that is truly urban or urbane in the same way as Aventicum must once have been. The peasant people of the locality shunned the site of that great Roman center of civilization after it had been destroyed, and they never wished to build it up again. Instead they grumbled about the extension of a conqueror's castle into the administrative village that Berne has been ever since; and they saw but did not altogether approve of the growth of a Zurich into a center of bankers and other gnomes; and they permitted Basle to develop similarly but never as part of the *real* Switzerland. Erasmus and Paracelsus might have shaken the

Excursionists set out on a lovely old lake steamer from Lucerne.

world there with big ideas, but the true Swiss remained prouder of small places such as Schwyz and Appenzell. Geneva became for them not the flower of the Reformation and the birthplace of eventual revolt against that same puritanism, but a largely alien agglomeration, not in the least *sympathique* by comparison with some small mountain village such as Evolène. Lausanne has its charm of doctors and femininity but most Swiss would agree that its principal product of importance was Favre, the supreme builder of Alpine tunnels.

It has been suggested that this peculiar nation is largely the product of geography. But the origins of the people must be important also, the origins or their myths (since what we want to believe true is almost just as potent as the actual truth).

The Swiss throughout the ages have thus been basically Celts, whatever that means, as distinct from Teutons or Latins or Slavs. They have shared with other so-called Celtic peoples the long heads, scrolled art forms, high-mindedness, sad-song-singing and enduring quality of the kind. There is still more affinity between the Swiss and the Cornish or Welsh or Scottish people today than between the

Swiss and the Italians or the Prussians. But then the Romans came, and the Germans, and the Burgundians, and the Savoyards and the original blood was diluted and even changed. The Celtic basis remained but the subsequent infusions had the same effect on the Swiss as they did on the old English. If the fault of the Celtic type is hot-headedness it was mastered in the Swiss by what the invaders brought.

But the fiery spirit remained underneath and, according to the favorite legends of the people, erupted terribly at the crucial moments in their story. The Perpetual Pact of 1291 brought the peasants of the original forest cantons together for the first time legally, but the actual physical routing of an Austrian bailiff and his men by the hill farmers under the leadership of a great folk hero was the influential memory that inspired the Swiss for hundreds of years as the Scots were inspired by the story of Robert the Bruce and the English by the legends of Arthur and Robin Hood. The historian coldly notes that the feudal nobility were smashed in Switzerland at the battle of Sempach in 1386, but the school-child still thinks primarily of Arnold von Winkelried and the way he flung himself upon the outstretched spears.

So their history to the Swiss is a record of struggling heroically and successfully against oppressors. The routing of Charles the Bold in 1476 is significant but, of course, the defeat of their ancestors by the Italians at Marignano in 1515 is scarcely remembered at all—because it was so supremely important.

Marignano was in actual fact the chief turning-point in Swiss history. Thereafter the people often stood and fought. Often they had to. They remained proud of their military tradition and continued to think, right up to this time of writing, that if necessary they were unbeatable and would always die to the last man if invaded. That was the myth, and like all myths it has been most fruitful and stimulating. Peoples like people must think well of themselves or they die. The most successful peoples are those with the most self-gratifying myths.

But in fact the Swiss after Marignano seemed to have learned the vital lesson that it does not pay to leave one's nice country and attempt the conquest of others. Never again did they indulge in a war of aggression. The world was safe from them and should consequently like them more than any other people.

If the Swiss are not truly loved then it is because of their success, not only as businessmen but as one of the few peoples ever to resist the temptation to hit out in all directions at others. We naturally like most those whom we can despise and patronize. Prostitutes and petty criminals have always been more popular than great ladies and men of affairs. Man has reserved his worst enmity for the few saints among him, and the most approved of the parables is the story of the prodigal son. Who has ever spared a tear for the good boy?

Observe, then, that the Swiss learned much earlier than the rest of the world not only how to get together in village councils and organize successful cooperative stands against aggressors, but also how to be content with their existing territories and resist the temptation to make evil use of the strength they had developed in a good cause. At the same time they were fortunate to be rid of their aristocracy earlier than other nations and it was never necessary for them to dissipate energies in class wars and revolutions.

They did not, of course, remain spotless. They remained internally as quarrelsome a people as any. Since most other stimuli to contention had been perhaps chancefully removed they reacted chiefly to parochial and sectarian differences. At this time of writing there are no industrial disputes in Switzerland, nor are there any involvements in foreign wars. But young men of the Jura region occasionally march about the streets and demand that their district be accorded cantonal status and independence from hated Berne. Throughout Swiss history it has been so, but especially after the comparatively little lesson of Marignano turned the fighting instincts of the people inwards. Protestants and Catholics continually found cause to struggle with each other and eventually organized themselves into two warring blocs of cantons.

Switzerland and its internal politics can best be understood by those who know village life anywhere in the world. Villagers stick together because they have to. Very rarely are feuds taken to the extreme of mutual ostracism for the simple reason that people must meet each other every day. Switzerland might thus be described as the apotheosis of the village mentality. There are scandals and quarrels but there is also a mutual feeling that this village is better than others and in the long run the people stand by each other and their communal idea.

Unfortunately, however, this kind of village life tends eventually to enervate if not to debase the inhabitants. When Napoleon came to Switzerland he found it easy to subdue.

This was partly because popular opinion in Switzerland at the time approved of what Napoleon, at that juncture, represented. He was the young and supremely modern man who was fighting on behalf of an essential European revolution, and his schemes for the reorganization of Europe seemed infinitely preferable to a continuation of the old, decadent regimes. But Napoleon occupied Switzerland easily because this had become no longer a military nation. It had literally gone soft, and was helpless against well-organized marching soldiers as any village is an easy prey to strong forces from a neighboring town.

The essential wisdom of the Swiss people was revealed in the 19th century after their tyrant occupier had been defeated by the British, a similar freedom-loving people but one that had a real fighting force. The country and its constitution were so reorganized that the former weakness due to internal strife and lack of an army was eliminated. The work done by the legislators during the 19th century was well done and demands the attention of anyone who has the future good of humanity at heart. The Federal Constitution with its built-in system of checks was so designed that several troubles were eliminated from the body politic, troubles that have ruined many other countries since.

This Constitution provided for a President at the top who was neither a figurehead nor a monster. He wielded power for a brief period only, like the chairman of a rotary club, but he was chosen from the small committee of leading politicians who, on the basis of ability and popularity, had worked themselves to membership of the Confederation's executive council. That council itself was turned over frequently so that no small group could dominate for long. The National Council was balanced by a Council of States elected by the cantons. Legislation could be possible only by agreement between these bodies.

The process of getting a law passed in Switzerland accordingly became at once more difficult than elsewhere and more sure. Several years might be required to obtain the necessary majority agreement, but when that agreement was obtained it could be said that the country had got what it really wanted.

The system was designed also to prevent any one group from obtaining lengthy and undisturbed power. Under it the state could not be dominated for a whole generation by one of two political parties, as in the United States and elsewhere. On the other hand firm government was provided for by the system, which was so designed that minority factions could not defeat the desires of the majority.

Those minority factions were in turn catered to by sections of the Constitution that permitted referenda on the direct initiative of groups of people. This development of the ancient Roman device known as the plebiscite could very definitely be studied with profit by peoples who find that their old democratic systems of government entirely through representatives elected for long periods are no longer viable systems under large-scale modern conditions. The private development of the Gallup and other opinion polls may surely be a symptom in ailing democracies of what is needed; and the Swiss have for a hundred years now most effectively developed the answer. There can be no sense of injustice when citizens have the ultimate right, at any time (provided there are sufficient of them in agreement) to demand a change in the laws.

Switzerland, like many other nations, was originally several nations, each with its own pride and institutions. The stresses and strains caused by joining together separate parts of this kind were largely countered here by very wise and ingenious provisions in the written constitution for dividing responsibilities between the central government and the constituent states. The cantons retained control of all local affairs and the executive and legislature in Berne were assigned the responsibility for foreign policy, defense, and national services like the railways and post office. Thus the cantons continue to develop as separate entities and cannot, as in America, be bullied by the central government into accepting ways of life that are alien to their local needs.

Then the 19th-century creators of the viability that is modern Switzerland turned to that matter of national defense that had been exposed by the predations of Napoleon, and they constructed the citizen army that is still one of the strongest in Europe, judged by readiness for mobilization. This was, and is, based on a system of military service that, in its severity, has no equal elsewhere. There is very little escape from it and all men must go to camp until late middle age. Weapons and other equipment are kept at home. The seemingly peaceful country is actually organized in a constant state of siege, with iron rations in the basement and bullets in the tool shed. A small but exceedingly active general staff regularly changes its war plans to accord with conditions; and the great mountains are honey-combed with gun emplacements and ammunition stores and constitute a veritable redoubt of defiance in the heart of Europe.

Those legislators determined that Switzerland should not be caught napping again, and they planned so well that in neither of the world wars was their country attacked.

This has always looked good on paper, a perfect Utopian scheme of laws and checks and defenses, but of course they would not be any good if the individual Swiss man and woman did not approve or collaborate. The spirit must be there, no matter the excellence of the constitution or the modernity of the guns. Imagine how that system of cantonal independence in most internal affairs would have worked out in a country where the populace allowed, let alone encouraged gangsters to proliferate!

The Swiss devised in the 19th century an excellent legal system for their country in all aspects of life, but Switzerland's freedom from wars and strikes and class conflict since could not have been assured by the system alone. The people had to want it that way and be willing to observe the laws and assist their enforcement. And the Swiss people had undoubtedly so developed that they were thus willing.

Yet other countries have men of goodwill and perhaps lack the system that would give their better sentiments a chance to operate.

The Swiss could not, of course, have developed their pocket Utopia with wise laws and a law-abiding populace alone. They had to have the money also, and this they acquired, particularly in the present century, by keeping up-to-date in commercial and industrial techniques, by developing a sensible taxation system that at once attracted capital from abroad and enabled the Swiss themselves to build up resources—and by working hard.

As the last is the most important so it should be considered rather carefully. Work is to so many people a four-letter and a dirty word always that it is necessary to ask why certain folk continue to labor hard and lengthily while others do not.

It is, of course, primarily a matter of sentiment and social custom and habit. If all the houses in a village have neat gardens it is very difficult to avoid working in your own. The snowball principle applies: as soon as a majority of people get up early the others tend to follow —indeed they have to, because it is impossible to sleep while the early workers round about are making a noise.

And so the stranger who settles in Switzerland even to this day will find that he soon rises earlier and does more with his twenty-four hours than he had been doing at home. Also he throws down his cigarette cartons and chocolate papers at first but finds himself picking them up and stuffing them in his pocket—under the social weight of so many accusing eyes.

Italians who stand about in town squares at home, picking their noses all day and leering at women's legs, utterly incapable of turning to and making an Eden again out of their time-shattered land, will work in Switzerland from dawn till dusk with continual energy and determination—because the rhythm of life in Switzerland demands it, and must be obeyed (failing which working permits will be withdrawn immediately and the immigrant be sent back to his native slum, unable anymore to send home bundles of crisp Swiss notes each month).

Undoubtedly the world trend towards less work and more play is being followed here, but still at a safe distance. Zurich puts in more financial hours than Wall Street and will always do so. Executives might now arrive at 8:30 in the morning instead of the 7:30 that was the custom of their fathers, but they are still far ahead of the lordly Londoners who are not at their desks until 10 o'clock.

Those Londoners boast about it. "My husband has sold his business and taken a job with a big corporation," said a young wife recently. "Now, like the others, he will be able to sleep in each morning and catch the 9 o'clock train. Why should we be worse off than them?"

Americans are not quite like that, yet, but most people are in Britain and also in France, Belgium, Italy and countries of British origin overseas such as New Zealand.

Many of the modern Swiss like to come in late but would never be proud of doing so. On the contrary they would be ashamed and would try to cover up the habit. This is because the Swiss are a nation composed largely of the descendants of peasants of German racial origin. In a village of peasants from the cold, stimulating northeast of Europe it will always be seen how the smallholders vie with each other in their strength and activity. The best man is the earliest out in the fields and the deepest digger of the soil. Whereas, of course, the best man in England, France, Italy has always been a lord. The highest ambition in an aristocratic society is to get up late and the outstanding value to a peasant is quick money for a good crop of beans. That is the difference, and that is the reason why Switzerland and Germany at this time of writing are outstandingly successful economically by comparison with Britain and France and Italy.

Does hard work make for happiness? The answer to that probably is that nothing as such makes for happiness, which is not the result of any course of behavior but an absolute: a quality within the individual man, woman and child. Some lazy people will be happy and some hard workers. Switzerland has never been a happier country than others, and it is no use reforming constitutions and introducing social reforms as an effort to increase the sum total of pleasure in a human community.

But it does remain that Switzerland thanks to working so hard for long hours within a clever framework of laws suffers less from social troubles than most other countries and, per head of its population, has probably the highest material standard of living in the modern world. If other countries want to be free from the fears of wars and strikes and insurrections that ruin their contemporary lives, if they want lower taxes and prices for goods in the shops accompanied by higher wages, if they want to be certain that a dollar or pound of today will be worth as much tomorrow, if even they want to be proud of themselves and their countries again, then they could at least try Swiss methods for a change: methods that are exactly contrary to those of their own philosophies.

The alternative must certainly be disaster: either world economic depression, far deeper than that of the 1930s, or world war.

This book would never have been written if an over-intellectual friend had not said: "The Swiss? A worthy people, but absolutely lacking in real achievement. Can you point to a single important name?"

The names are dotted throughout this book and make a feverish work of its index. Even the moderns have cult-names of quite recent Swiss origin, such as Le Corbusier, Carl Jung, Paul Klee, Giacometti; and they can scarcely write a would-be erudite book nowadays without mentioning Paracelsus, even though they forget how both Erasmus and Holbein were complete intellectual products of Basle.

It has, however, been learnt primarily in the writing of this book that the world could be indebted most in the artistic and cultural senses not to the Switzerland of those names so much as the Switzerland of the peasant arts and crafts, the superb architecture of farmhouses and barns and country inns and burgher houses in town streets that spring directly from the fields. The stained glass heraldry of humble windows and the awful masks of the Grisons, the primitive landscape painting of such as Witz, and the color prints of people in local costumes, of landscapes and town views and soldiers, by such unknown masters as Biedermann, Lory, Aberli, König and Wocher, the genre aquatints of such as the Greuze-taught Freudenberger: they teach an over-sophisticated, essentially decadent age that the purpose of art is to apotheosize the everyday, nothing more, nothing less; and that when art departs from that simple purpose it is doomed.

And how plain-spoken and excellent the everyday in Switzerland can be! What is to be done in life but to endure it as quietly as possible and along the way, perhaps, improve conditions a little for future generations—in intervals of eating, drinking, making love, and reading good books? And in Switzerland all that is very possible and visibly catered to. All the books are there, mint new and widely understood. The women are not so much uninhibited as perfectly natural and of great character, qualities encouraged by their legal suppression for so long until recently. Relieved of the awful responsibilities assumed by the more modern women of other countries they have been able to develop their true natures. They have become strong, uncomplicated, chic, and the powers behind all thrones.

Follow the Swiss way with wine and enjoy it again as the Romans must have done. Here is no pseudo-philosophy of the wine-cult people who sniff and mouth and bite, no anthropomorphism of the common-rooms and restaurants where they talk of the personality of a vintage and the sensibility of a *cru*. Nor are the actual wine-producers almost forced, as they are in those posturing places, to doctor the stuff with chemicals and then charge high prices for the disgusting privilege. The wines of Switzerland are an everyday drink like beer and tea and milk elsewhere. Everyone, save foolish strangers, calls for a carafe of the local and drinks it down without thought or theatrical byplay. Strong laws enforce purity, and the mind and bowels alike are irrigated and cleared by a natural medicine.

The food is like the wine, forced to be unadulterated not only by law but also by custom. Whereas a poor American or British housewife will buy only the whitest of bread and the most highly-colored of other comestibles, the Swiss in all walks of life naturally prefer untreated loaves—better bread than even that of France today—and they are increasingly a nation of vegetarians who believe that much meat is bad for the mind as well as the body. They have elevated the eating of cheese dishes into a way of life, and they know that there are few pleasures equal to that of the simple table, which they adorn with appointments of spotless cleanliness and pots of primitive beauty in the great ceramic tradition. They will motor, mainly in functional white or grey German, French or Italian cars, with the whole family on a Sunday morning—some of them still after church—to inns of the country where the midday meal is lengthily discussed in an ambience of mock-old beams and bucolic bygones; and around these tables, with the carafe of white in the center, much of the real business of the nation is decided (and decided quite wisely with such gently-stimulating fumes in the head). No foreign drugs

A short distance up in the sky from Lucerne.

are required by such a people, whose anodynes are all wholesome and homemade, even to much of the tobacco, that, on a late summer's day, can be seen in acres of crisp brown rows, hanging up to dry, in the lower reaches of the great Valais.

Other nations could also wisely copy the immigration policy of the Swiss. Tax concessions that attract the retired and their savings, also foreign corporations with their expertise and capital, have enabled modern Switzerland safely to import more than is exported, also to brighten their towns with cosmopolitanism and their industries with modernity. The strict application of the temporary work permit system has meanwhile provided the country with hand labor that cannot disproportionately blackmail the community at large. This labor at the same time improves the ingrowing blood of the people with outcross-

Old timbers and young blossom: a Swiss scene if ever there was one.

ing; and if Switzerland is a little more Latin tomorrow it will not necessarily be for the worse. The Latin element in western man is also the central core of his civilization (and when the sociologists once sought a completely carefree and also cancer-free community in the United States it turned out to be an isolated town of the mountains almost wholly populated by simple Italians).

It is not a perfect country, even though this book might seem to make it so. But then the purpose of the book has been to study the best of Switzerland and what it can offer a world that sorely needs that kind of help. If the book's object had been to assist the Swiss in the improvement of their country then it would have contained some violent criticism indeed. For improvement it is necessary to know first what is wrong and to have it underlined by a wise teacher.

But if Switzerland naturally has its faults—and some of these have at least been hinted at—then its modern virtues so far outweigh those that men of goodwill everywhere will prefer to forget about the one while closely studying the other. A deputation sent to Switzerland to find out why it has such a high standard of living with such poor natural resources, and why it is relatively free from the political and social troubles that ruin other countries today, would of course concentrate on Swiss achievements rather than failures. That is what this book has tried, no matter how unsuccessfully, to do.

The writer can himself see what should be copied from Switzerland, the heart country of modern western civilization. Primarily there is the way of life of the people, based on the primitive virtues and often accompanied by primitive habits in modern clothing: diligent work and open-air play, a belief in manliness as against the perversities of over-civilization, a love of country that is not flag-waving patriotism but a deep, influential emotion that actually controls the warlike impulses. Why march into other lands for unpleasant fighting when it is so good at home?

Then the various devices for living in Switzerland are so sensible, from the gadgets of the workmen to the laws of the communes, cantons, confederation and the great Constitution. Each one of those laws, as so often discussed in this book, could be adopted helpfully in other countries whose constitutions and precepts have proved recently to be so out-of-date and unsuited to the needs of a dynamic age. Why do fools blunder on when wiser men elsewhere have clearly shown them a far better way? Surely they can see at last that tomorrow there will be only the one choice, between reformation and utter disaster?

INDEX